# Microsoft® SQL Server 2000
# Weekend Crash Course

# Microsoft® SQL Server 2000 Weekend Crash Course™

## Alex Kriegel

## Hungry Minds™

Best-Selling Books • Digital Downloads • e-Books • Answer Networks
e-Newsletters • Branded Web Sites • e-Learning

New York, NY • Cleveland, OH • Indianapolis, IN

**Microsoft® SQL Server 2000 Weekend Crash Course™**
Published by
**Hungry Minds, Inc.**
909 Third Avenue
New York, NY 10022
www.hungryminds.com

Library of Congress Control 2001089349

ISBN: 0-7645-4840-9

Printed in the United States of America

10 9 8 7 6 5 4 3 2 1

1B/RW/QZ/QR/IN

Distributed in the United States by Hungry Minds, Inc.

Distributed by CDG Books Canada Inc. for Canada; by Transworld Publishers Limited in the United Kingdom; by IDG Norge Books for Norway; by IDG Sweden Books for Sweden; by IDG Books Australia Publishing Corporation Pty. Ltd. for Australia and New Zealand; by TransQuest Publishers Pte Ltd. for Singapore, Malaysia, Thailand, Indonesia, and Hong Kong; by Gotop Information Inc. for Taiwan; by ICG Muse, Inc. for Japan; by Intersoft for South Africa; by Eyrolles for France; by International Thomson Publishing for Germany, Austria, and Switzerland; by Distribuidora Cuspide for Argentina; by LR International for Brazil; by Galileo Libros for Chile; by Ediciones ZETA S.C.R. Ltda. for Peru; by WS Computer Publishing Corporation, Inc., for the Philippines; by Contemporanea de Ediciones for Venezuela; by Express Computer Distributors for the Caribbean and West Indies; by Micronesia Media Distributor, Inc. for Micronesia; by Chips Computadoras S.A. de C.V. for Mexico; by Editorial Norma de Panama S.A. for Panama; by American Bookshops for Finland.

For general information on Hungry Minds' products and services please contact our Customer Care department within the U.S. at 800-762-2974, outside the U.S. at 317-572-3993 or fax 317-572-4002.

For sales inquiries and reseller information, including discounts, premium and bulk quantity sales, and foreign-language translations, please contact our Customer Care department at 800-434-3422, fax 317-572-4002 or write to Hungry Minds, Inc., Attn: Customer Care Department, 10475 Crosspoint Boulevard, Indianapolis, IN 46256.

For information on licensing foreign or domestic rights, please contact our Sub-Rights Customer Care department at 212-884-5000.

For information on using Hungry Minds' products and services in the classroom or for ordering examination copies, please contact our Educational Sales department at 800-434-2086 or fax 317-572-4005.

For press review copies, author interviews, or other publicity information, please contact our Public Relations department at 317-572-3168 or fax 317-572-4168.

For authorization to photocopy items for corporate, personal, or educational use, please contact Copyright Clearance Center, 222 Rosewood Drive, Danvers, MA 01923, or fax 978-750-4470.

# Credits

**Acquisitions Editor**
Terri Varveris

**Project Editor**
Valerie Perry

**Technical Editors**
Allen Wyatt and Trevor Dwyer

**Copy Editor**
S.B. Kleinman

**Project Coordinator**
Dale White

**Graphics and Production Specialists**
Joyce Haughey
Adam Mancilla
Betty Schulte
Brian Torwelle

**Quality Control Technicians**
Laura Albert
Susan Moritz
Angel Perez
Charles Spencer

**Permissions Editor**
Laura Moss

**Media Development Specialist**
Travis Silvers

**Media Development Coordinator**
Marisa Pearman

**Proofreading and Indexing**
TECHBOOKS Production Services

# About the Author

**Alex Kriegel, MCSD**, has worked for Psion Teklogix International Inc., Integration Services Group for the past three years. Their main product is TekRF Integration Components for SAP R/3. Alex participated in designing and implementing it from the very beginning back in 1997. In addition to programming, he is also responsible for troubleshooting SQL Server installations, optimizing performance, and devising SQL stored procedures and such. For the past two years Alex has taught a course on SQL/SQL Server for a group of SAP analysts.

*I dedicate this book to my teacher in a previous life, Dr. Isaac I. Garbar, for everything I did not have time to accomplish in the physics of wear and friction of metals while I was taking my time to explore Zen teachings.*

# *Preface*

SQL Server 2000 is a major milestone for Microsoft, which is trying to position itself as a significant player in the database market. The demand for database-driven sites on the Internet is exploding (some major sites are running SQL Server 2000 as their back end, Microsoft included), creating a demand for qualified people who understand the product — from technical support people to analysts to programmers without database experience.

With so many SQL Server books on the market you may wonder why there is any need for another one. There is more than one way to tell a story, and I like to think that this book offers a special angle from which to approach the rather complex topic of Relational Database Management Systems in general and SQL Server 2000 in particular.

I intend for this book to provide a no-nonsense, hands-on introduction to SQL Server for the widest audience possible: technical-support people whose company product includes SQL Server as part of its solution, small companies' "jacks of all trades" doing in-house maintenance, beginning and intermediate programmers breaking into the field or switching careers or upgrading from some other database system, managers who would like to know what SQL Server can do for them without getting involved in a "holy war" of database vendors — and so on.

## Who Should Read this Book

This crash course is comprised of a set of short lessons that you can grasp quickly — in one weekend. While writing this book I kept two kinds of people in mind:

> Those who need to learn SQL Server 2000 fast and do not know where to start. These people have just the right mix of basic technical knowledge and curiosity, and need to feel comfortable using SQL Server.

> Those who worked with previous versions of SQL Server and would like a brief, hands-on introduction to SQL Server 2000 — one basic enough for beginners, but deep enough for intermediate users.

## What You Need to Have

In order to make the most of this book, you'll need the following:

- A computer (Pentium 166 or higher) running Windows NT 4.0 Server or Windows 2000 Server.
- Microsoft SQL Server 2000 Standard Edition installation.
- Lots of patience and the desire to find out what SQL Server 2000 is all about.

You can get by with most of the material in this book using Windows 98 and the Personal Edition of SQL Server 2000, though this could not be considered "making the most of it."

## What Results Can You Expect?

Can you become a SQL Server database administrator in a weekend? As much as I would like to say the opposite, the answer is no. It takes much more than just three days of studying to become a database administrator. Can you become a competent user of SQL Server, and gain an understanding of some of the finer points of SQL Server 2000 features, in a weekend? Absolutely.

This is not a reference book and it does not pretend to cover each and every aspect of SQL Server in depth. It will help you to get up and runningand, at the same time, show you where to look for further information.

You can expect to learn how to set up SQL Server 2000 with most standard features (and troubleshoot the installation if anything goes wrong). I will provide a thorough introduction to the most important SQL Server features and objects — SQL Server administration, creating and destroying database objects, optimizing performance, publishing information on the Internet, and much more — and to using them for your own purposes.

## Layout and Features

This book follows the standard Weekend Crash Course layout and includes the standard features of the series so that you can be assured of mastering basic SQL Server 2000 skills within a weekend — 30 hours, to be precise. The book contains 30 sessions, each about one hour long, to be read over the course of three and a half days. At the end of each session you'll find "Quiz Yourself" questions, and at the end of each part you'll find Part Review questions. These questions enable you to test your knowledge and exercise your newly acquired skills. (The answers to the part-review questions are in Appendix A.)

## Layout

This Weekend Crash Course contains 30 one-hour sessions organized into six parts. Each part corresponds to a time during the weekend, as outlined in the following sections.

## Part I: Friday evening

This is the "get started" part. You will go through the complete process of setting up SQL Server 2000, starting from hardware and software considerations to selecting installation options to having an up-and-running instance of SQL Server. You will go through the process of installing and configuring your server and will also get a glimpse of what lies ahead.

## Part II: Saturday morning

In this part you will get into the fundamental concepts of relational databases, both examining SQL Server system databases and getting an introduction to creating and using user databases. You also will get an introduction to Structured Query Language (SQL), the language of relational databases.

## Part III: Saturday afternoon

In these sessions you will take your SQL Server 2000 programming skills to a new level: You will be introduced to stored procedures, triggers, and cursors. The session on indices will give you a thorough understanding of this important concept. This part also includes in-depth discussions of locking, transactions, and the integrity mechanisms of SQL Server 2000.

## Part IV: Saturday evening

This part will introduce you to some advanced features of SQL Server such as Data Transformation Services, backing up and restoring, and replication. It also will cover the basics of user management in the context of SQL Server 2000.

## Part V: Sunday morning

Here you will be introduced to database-management issues. You will learn about distributed transactions, obtaining system information, and automating administrative tasks with SQL Server Agent. The sections in this part will show you how to configure SQL Server to send and receive e-mail. You will also learn how to optimize and tune the performance of SQL Server.

## Part VI: Sunday afternoon

In this part you will learn about disaster recovery and receive a comprehensive introduction to SQL Server 2000 security. The sessions in this part will also address connectivity issues and give an overview of the most advanced features in SQL Server 2000.

## Features

As you go through each session, look for the following icons that let you know how much progress you've made in the session:

Remember, these are just suggestions: You may need more or less time to finish the section. The book also contains other icons that call your attention to special points of interest:

**These alert you to important pieces of information that you should file away in your head for later.**

**These give you helpful advice about the best ways to do things, or tell you about a tricky technique that can make your HTML programming go more smoothly.**

**These tell you where you can find related material in other sessions.**

## Accompanying CD-ROM

You will find a CD-ROM at the back of this book. It contains a skills-assessment test, a PDF version of the book, and as many useful tools and as much information as it is possible to fit there. For a complete description of each item on the CD-ROM, see Appendix B.

## Reach Out

I know this book could have been better given enough time and space (uh . . . about five more years to write and 5,000 pages to hold the information). Neither you nor I have this luxury. Any feedback that will help to make revised editions of this book better and more comprehensive will be appreciated. Send your comments about the content of this book to:

    alexkriegel@hotmail.com

As the saying goes, all you know today is obsolete. With this cheerful thought, you are ready to plunge into the relational database world — through the SQL Server 2000 entrance.

# Acknowledgments

My gratitude goes to Grace M. Buechlein, who introduced me to the world of book-writing and convinced me that I could do it. Thank you very much, Grace!

I thank with all my heart my Development/Project Editor Valerie Perry, who taught me how to be eloquent without sacrificing technical details along the way, and who helped me with every step — all in spite of power shortages in California. I really appreciate your help.

I am very grateful to my acquisitions editor, Terri Varveris, who pressed me hard to meet deadlines, and who encouraged me and guided me with extreme patience through all the intricacies of writing a technical book. Thank you, Terri!

I am very grateful to my copy editor, S. B. Kleinman, for all the work she did to make the original text better, a lot better.

I would like to express my gratitude to my technical editor, Allen Wyatt, for actually reading through these pages, picking out inconsistencies, bloopers, and outright errors, and making valuable suggestions about how to improve the content of the book, chapter by chapter. My thanks also go to Trevor Dwyer, my other technical editor who helped edit the first several chapters of this book.

This book would have been impossible without the meticulous work of the Hungry Minds team that helped me to get everything in shape: Kyle Looper, Laura Moss, Marissa Pearman, Nancy Maragioglio and Dale White. Thank you.

My thanks also go to Bradley Ruste, my colleague, for helping me to write the chapter on SQL Server 2000 backup, as well as the general discussions of the SQL Server topics we're having from time to time.

I thank my parents, Lazar and Raisa Kriegel, for their lifelong understanding and support, sometimes even against their best judgment.

My deepest gratitude goes to my wife, Liana, for her support when I needed it most, and to my two sons, Phillip and Michael, for giving me endless hours of fun as I explained to them the finer points of relational-database systems, and being there for me when I needed them. Thank you.

# Contents at a Glance

# Contents

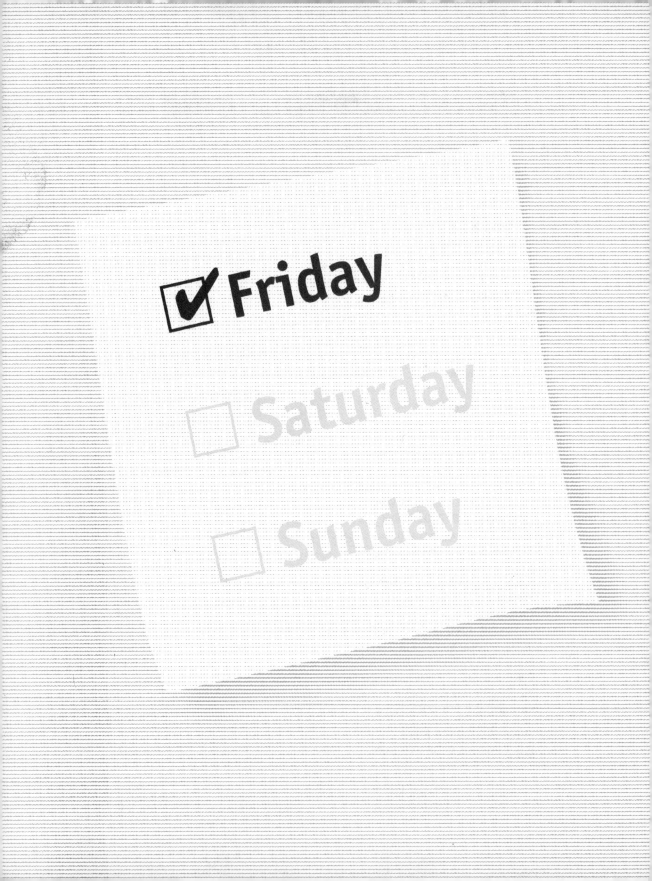

## Part I — Friday Evening

**Session 1**
*Getting Started*

**Session 2**
*Go Configure*

**Session 3**
*First Look at Enterprise Manager Console*

**Session 4**
*Second Look at Enterprise Manager Console*

# PART

# I

## Friday
## Evening

# *Getting Started*

## *Session Checklist*

✔ Understanding Microsoft SQL Server

✔ Installing SQL Server 2000

**30 Min.
To Go**

T his session will introduce you to SQL Server and guide you through the installation process step-by-step. It explains hardware and software requirements and the reasons for making necessary choices along the way. The final sidebar comparing SQL Server to other major players on the database market lists the costs and benefits of various database-system implementations.

## *Understanding Microsoft SQL Server*

Microsoft SQL Server is a scalable database system whose primary purpose is to serve as a back-end database for a client program, such as your Web browser, an accounting program, or a human resources application — anything that makes use of the data. In the most common usage scenario, a client program connects to SQL Server and requests some information, whereupon SQL Server processes the request and returns results. The client must then interpret and display these results (for example, a custom human-resources application displaying a list of employees in alphabetical order).

Unlike text editors or games, which do not require any additional components in order to be useful, MS SQL Server does not make much sense as a stand-alone program or as a program that runs on a stand-alone computer. Although it is possible to have both a client and SQL Server running on the same computer, it is not very useful. It would be something like hammering nails with a microscope, as SQL Server is meant to be part of a network (local, wide, Internet — you name it) and to serve more than one user.

SQL Server can store structured information in a variety of formats, and it enables you to manipulate this information. For example, you can instantly search through millions of records and view the results of the search in many different formats; you can combine different data into one set; you can transform some formats into others; you can set security rules to be enforced by SQL Server; and so on.

Advanced features of MS SQL Server 2000 include On-Line Analytical Processing (OLAP) and Data Mining, which enable you to analyze huge amounts of data to discover hidden trends. Whatever business you're in and however many users you have, SQL Server will provide support for all your data needs and seamlessly integrate into your enterprise.

You cannot expect SQL Server to think for you. To be even marginally useful, it has to be told exactly what to do. SQL Server is very flexible, but it won't prevent you from shooting yourself in the leg.

**20 Min.
To Go**

## Installing SQL Server 2000

Installing SQL Server 2000 is a snap — that is, if you stick to the default settings. I recommend that you postpone trying your hand at mission-critical installations until you actually understand the options and their ramifications.

All SQL Server 2000 installations require a Pentium 166 or higher computer that's equipped with a VGA monitor and at least 95MB of free disk space (the typical installation uses about 250MB). Unless you're planning on installing from a network, a CD-ROM drive is also required.

**Microsoft warns against installing the product on older Cyrix processor-equipped computers. They might not support the full set of instructions that SQL Server requires.**

## System requirements

Table 1-1 lists the operating system and RAM requirements as well as an overview of the most important features.

**Table 1-1**
*Overview of SQL Server 2000 Editions*

| Edition | Features | Hardware Requirements | Notes |
|---------|----------|----------------------|-------|
| Enterprise Edition | Maximum database size: 1,048,516 TB Maximum SMP CPU: 32 (on Win2000 Datacenter Server) | RAM: 64MB minimum; 128MB recommended OS: Windows NT Server or Windows 2000 Server | Supports all features available in SQL Server 2000 |
| Standard Edition | Maximum database size: 1,048,516 TB Maximum SMP CPU: 8 (on Windows NT 4 Server, Enterprise) | RAM: 64MB minimum; 128MB recommended OS: Windows NT Server or Windows 2000 Server | Designed as a database server for a workgroup or department; supports the majority of SQLS Server 2000 features |
| Personal Edition | Maximum database size: 2 GB Maximum SMP CPU: 2 (supports only 1 on Windows 98) | RAM: 64MB minimum; 128MB recommended OS: Windows NT Server Windows 2000 Windows 98 | Used mostly by mobile users running applications requiring SQL Server support on a client computer |
| Developer Edition | Maximum database size: 1,048,516 TB Maximum SMP CPU: 32 (on Win2000 Datacenter Server) | RAM: 64MB minimum; 128MB recommended OS: Windows NT Server or Windows 2000 Server | Supports all features available in SQL Server 2000 but is licensed only for development and testing |

*Continued*

**Table 1-1** *Continued*

| Edition | Features | Hardware Requirements | Notes |
|---------|----------|----------------------|-------|
| Desktop Engine | Varies according to the application it ships with | Varies according to the application it ships with | A re-distributable version that can be packaged with an independent vendor's application |
| Windows CE Edition | Bound by Windows CE limitations | OS: Windows CE 3.0 | A SQL Server version for Windows CE devices; can be synchronized with a enterprise database |

After you figure out your system requirements, you can start the installation.

**Before you start your installation, make sure that all nonessential services are stopped, especially all members of the Microsoft BackOffice family: Close your e-mail program, anti-virus program, and so on. You also need to be logged onto your computer with full administrative privileges (thus having a full access to Windows registry on that machine).**

## Before you begin the installation

I have chosen Standard Edition for my examples, as it is the edition most suitable for a workgroup or small department. For the purposes of this book I will assume that you are running it on a Microsoft Windows NT 4.0/ 2000 Server. (I assume that you're installing MS SQL Server 2000 on a machine on which no previous versions of the product have been installed; if you are upgrading from any previous MS SQL versions please refer to Appendix C.) If you've followed me this far, you are ready to install SQL Server 2000 Components.

If you are running MS Windows 95, you must first install SQL Server 2000 Prerequisites (Common Controls Library Update). Keep in mind that Windows 95 supports only the client connectivity option, which allows applications to access instances of SQL Server 2000 on other computers — that is, you will need a server to connect to; you also may need to upgrade to Microsoft Internet Explorer 5.0 and HTML Help 1.3. You can update Internet Explorer and HTML Help by downloading the latest versions from `http://www.microsoft.com`. The HTML Help update file is named Hhupd.exe. SQL Server 2000 was not designed to run on Win95, and if you're serious about learning SQL Server, it's time to upgrade.

### Stepping through the installation

Follow these steps to perform the installation:

1. Insert the Microsoft SQL Server 2000 Standard Edition CD into your CD-ROM drive. If your computer supports the autorun feature, the installation will start automatically; otherwise, find your CD-ROM from Windows Explorer and start autorun.exe.

2. From the very first installation screen, select SQL Server 2000 Components. The next screen gives you the following options:
   - Install Database Server
   - Install Analysis Services
   - Install English Query

   You may want to consider installing Analysis Services and/or English Query — some other time. These are advanced options that deserve a separate book, and I recommend mastering the basics before moving on.

3. Click Install Database Server. The Installation Wizard comes to life. It guides you through the whole installation process. (You can go back and change your choices until you click Finish.)

   You can install SQL Server 2000 either locally or on a remote machine, as shown in Figure 1-1. You need to specify your computer (server) name if you are installing on a remote machine. Virtual Server is an advanced option for enterprise-level database systems.

   The installation program detects any previous instances of SQL Server running on your machine and gives you appropriate install and/or upgrade options. Depending on what is already installed on your computer, you might have slightly different installation options enabled or disabled.

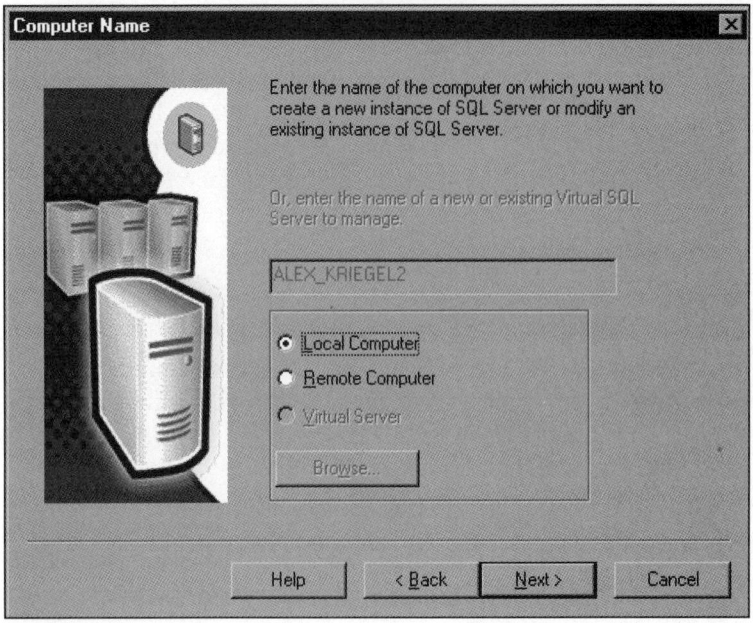

Computer Name

Enter the name of the computer on which you want to
create a new instance of SQL Server or modify an
existing instance of SQL Server.

Or, enter the name of a new or existing Virtual SQL
Server to manage.

ALEX_KRIEGEL2

○ Local Computer
○ Remote Computer
○ Virtual Server

Browse...

Help    < Back    Next >    Cancel

**Figure 1-1**
*This screen enables you to specify the computer on which you're going to install SQL Server 2000.*

**New Instance means that you can install and run several copies of SQL Server 2000 on the same computer at the same time. All instances will be administered from a single management console, but each instance is absolutely independent of the others.**

Because you're creating a new instance of SQL Server, the default option shown in Figure 1-2 is the one you want. After you install SQL Server, you can always change configuration settings and upgrade, remove, or add components. Click Next to continue.

**Advanced options are — as the name implies — for advanced users; after you finish this book, you may want to explore them on your own.**

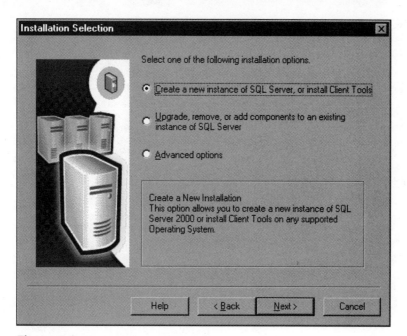

**Figure 1-2**
*Choose an installation type on the Selection screen.*

4. Enter your name and the name of your company in the spaces provided. Click Next to continue to the License Agreement screen.

5. Before you can proceed, you need to agree to the terms of the license agreement that comes with your copy of SQL Server 2000. Later in the installation process, you will be prompted to select a licensing mode; therefore, make sure that you select the proper licensing options.

6. Specify installation options, as shown in Figure 1-3. Choose Server and Client tools and click Next. (The two other options are for users working from remote servers.)

7. In order to install an instance of SQL Server, you need to specify a name (I specified MYVERYOWNSQL, as shown in Figure 1-4); every subsequent installation will have to have a different unique name. Only one instance will be designated as the default (the grayed-out check box on this screen indicates that I already have a default instance of SQL Server running). Click Next.

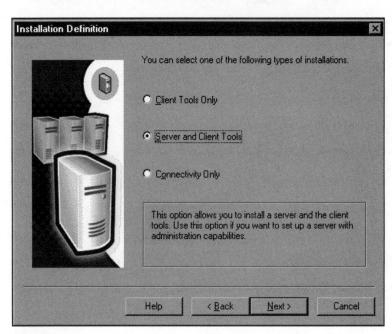

*Figure 1-3*
*Select what you're going to install.*

**Keep instance names to less than 15 characters; it makes them easier to read.**

**8.** Select the type of setup you wish to perform. I recommend sticking with the Typical setup type until you have more SQL Server experience. Click Next.

You also may want to change the physical location of the program and database files by clicking Browse. Generally, it is not a very good idea to keep program and data files in the same directory, as this can cause costly mistakes when you are maintaining your databases or installing service packs and upgrades.

**I strongly advise against installing the minimum required options, because if you do, you will not have most of the features I am going to talk about in this book.**

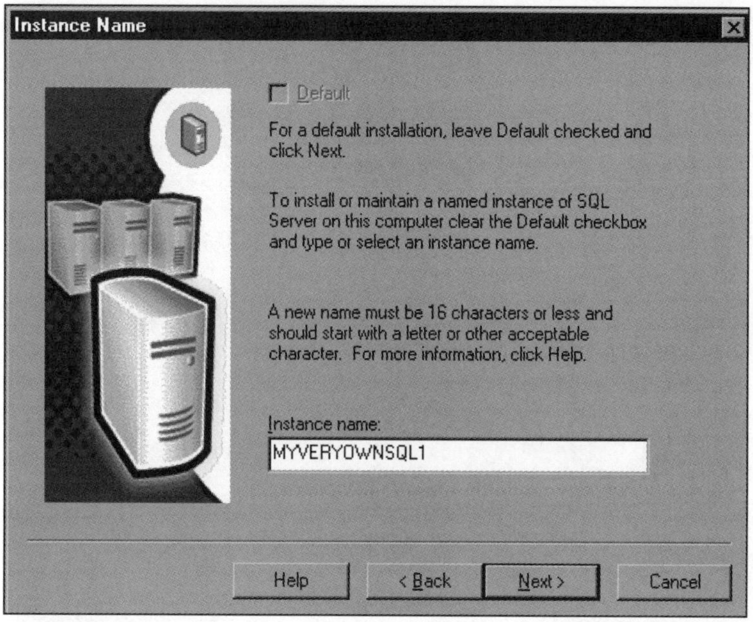

**Instance Name**                                                         ☒

☐ Default

For a default installation, leave Default checked and click Next.

To install or maintain a named instance of SQL Server on this computer clear the Default checkbox and type or select an instance name.

A new name must be 16 characters or less and should start with a letter or other acceptable character. For more information, click Help.

Instance name:

MYVERYOWNSQL1

| Help | < Back | Next > | Cancel |

**Figure 1-4**
*Name your SQL server or use the default name.*

9. Choose your SQL Server collation order, default language, and so on, as shown in Figure 1-5. *Collation* defines how your data will be compared and sorted. For English and any language using Latin characters, the choice is easy; for Asian characters, it might not be so obvious. The collation order specified here determines the default code page and sort order for all non-UNICODE characters and is the UNICODE collation order for all SQL Server system databases. The sort order determines whether operations on your data will be case-sensitive or not. Click Next.

> **You can always reconfigure your server for a different collation/sort order later. There is a high price to pay — you have to rebuild all your databases and possibly lose some data. It is better to use the correct order from the beginning.**

10. Unless you have a valid reason (for example, if you need direct access to your server from the Internet or from a client running on an Apple computer), I recommend leaving the Network Libraries screen with its default values, which are Named Pipes and TCP/IP. Click Next.

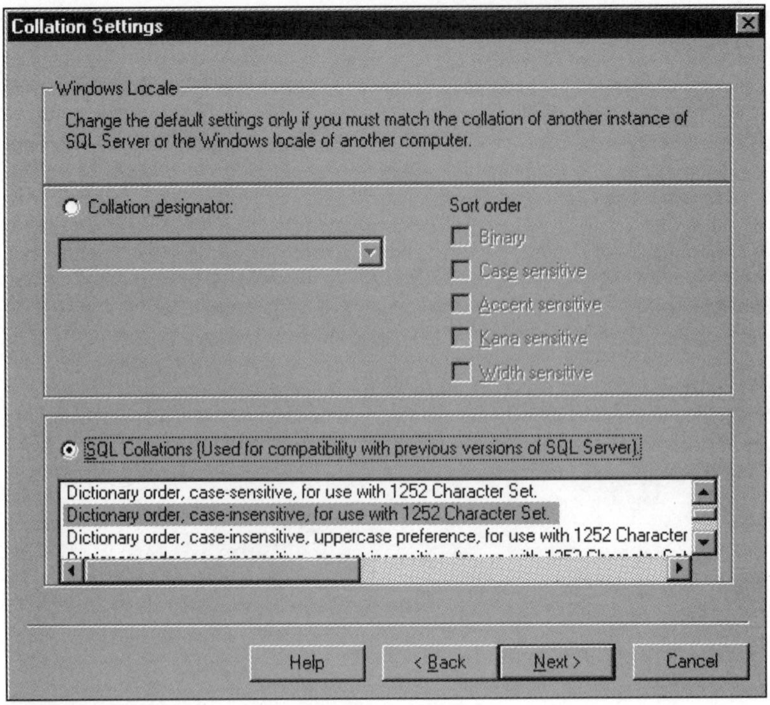

**Collation Settings**

**Windows Locale**

Change the default settings only if you must match the collation of another instance of SQL Server or the Windows locale of another computer.

○ Collation designator:

Sort order

☐ Binary
☐ Case sensitive
☐ Accent sensitive
☐ Kana sensitive
☐ Width sensitive

⊙ SQL Collations (Used for compatibility with previous versions of SQL Server):

Dictionary order, case-sensitive, for use with 1252 Character Set.
Dictionary order, case-insensitive, for use with 1252 Character Set.
Dictionary order, case-insensitive, uppercase preference, for use with 1252 Character

| Help | < Back | Next > | Cancel |

**Figure 1-5**
*Select the options for collation order.*

11. Define Services Accounts (see Figure 1-6). You can start each service on a different account, thus fine-tuning access privileges. I recommend selecting the same account for each service and auto-start for SQL Server. That way, the SQL Server and SQL Server Agent services will be started each time you log on to you machine account and won't require special authorization. Click Next.

**If your computer is part of a network, you should install SQL Server on a domain user's account, which does not need all the privileges of your administrator's account.**

12. Specify the authentication mode to be used to start up SQL Server. SQL Server 2000 has built-in security to protect data from unauthorized access. If you choose Windows Authentication Mode your SQL Server databases will be accessible as soon as you log onto your account with your Windows NT/2000 login; Mixed Mode requires a user ID and password in order to connect to SQL Server after you log on. Click Next.

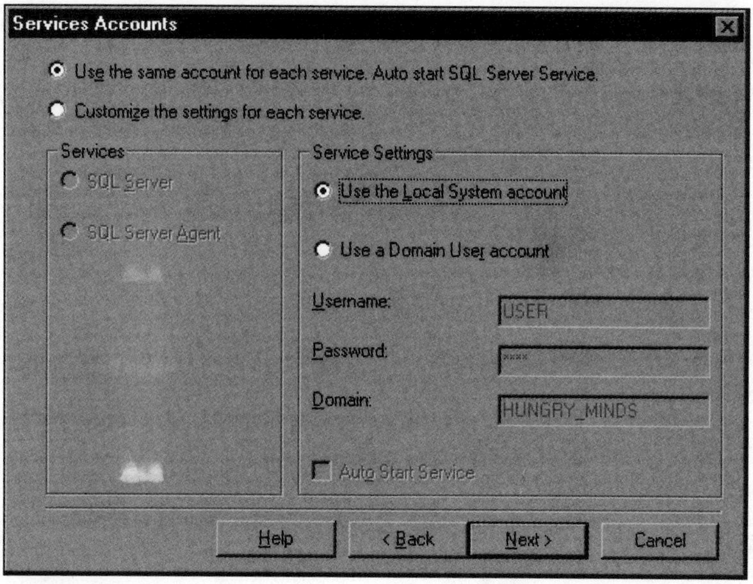

**Figure 1-6**
*Set up your Services Accounts.*

> **Note**
>
> **If your computer is a part of a network and you have access rights to this network, you will normally use your domain user account if your machine is part of the domain. A *domain* is a group of computers defined by an administrator; it has a unique name and its own set of security policies that apply to all the computers that comprise it.**

13. The setup process informs you that it has collected enough information to start the installation. This is your last chance to change your settings before the install. (Once you've got SQL Server up and running you'll always be able to change it through SQL Server itself, using the SQL Server Enterprise Manager interface or built-in commands.) Click Next.

    Unless you are installing evaluation software you see one more screen, which prompts you to choose your licensing mode. For the purposes of this book I select Licensing Per Seat — meaning that only one connection to my installation of SQL Server will be allowed at any one time.

## How Does SQL Server 2000 Compare to the Other Guys?

Microsoft SQL Server has come a long way from obscurity in 1988 to being one of the major databases employed around the world today. Some estimates indicate that more than half of the Web servers running on Windows NT/2000 use SQL Server as a back end. It is reasonably priced, robust, relatively easy to set up and administer, and very well integrated with Windows and the rest of the Microsoft products. It enjoys tremendous popularity, which means that you do not have to pay an arm and a leg for database expertise.

In a recent survey of five database vendors, Microsoft SQL Server came first in terms of pricing, value, and programming expertise. SQL Server gets less stellar marks in terms of customer referrals, service, responsiveness, features, innovation, reliability, availability and so on. IBM's DB2 came in first in these areas, followed by ORACLE, Sybase Adaptive Server, and Informix.

Keep in mind that Microsoft fights for market share against entrenched rivals with well-established customer bases that are heavily invested in the ORACLE or DB2 products. Some companies believe that "serious" applications require UNIX, on which SQL Server does not run; others believe that the "cool" applications run on Linux... You get the idea.

Consult the license agreement that comes with your installation package. The Per Seat licensing mode requires a Client Access License for each device that will access SQL Server 2000. Per Seat is often the most economical choice for networks in which clients connect to more than one server. With Processor licensing you need a license for each processor installed on the computer running SQL Server. The Processor license allows any number of devices to access the server, whether over an intranet or the Internet.

**10 Min.
To Go**

### Completing the installation and rebooting your computer

Depending on your computer resources the whole installation process should take between 15 minutes and an hour. Depending on the operating system you are running, the last screen you see may or may not prompt you to reboot. It is always a good idea to reboot your computer after installation, even if the install program doesn't suggest it.

If you have followed the preceding steps, after restarting your computer and logging on you should see a small icon (a computer tower and a small encircled green triangle or encircled red square) in your system tray (usually in the lower right-hand corner, with the clock). This icon provides you with quick access to your SQL Server Service Manager. Make sure that the icon displays a small green triangle: This means that SQL Server is up and running. You can bring up the SQL Server Service Manager console by right-clicking the icon and then check the status of installed services: MSDTC, SQL Server and SQL Server Agent. You also can stop, start, or pause any of these services from this console. Depending on your installation you may or may not see some additional services, but these three should always be there.

**Done!**

---
## REVIEW
---

- I described the different editions of SQL Server 2000 and their major features.
- I discussed the hardware and software requirements for SQL Server 2000 installation.
- You performed a complete installation of the Microsoft SQL Server 2000 Standard Edition.

---
## QUIZ YOURSELF
---

1. What is SQL Server?
2. Can you run more than one instance of SQL Server 2000 on the same machine?
3. On which operating systems does SQL Server 2000 run?
4. What authentication modes are available for SQL Server 2000?
5. What licensing modes are available for SQL Server 2000?

## Session Checklist

✔ Fixing a faulty installation

✔ Running SQL Server Service Manager

✔ Managing configuration tasks

✔ Locating SQL Server files

✔ Adding components

✔ Uninstalling SQL Server

**30 Min.
To Go**

I f you followed all the steps in Session 1, you should not have any problems with your installation. If for some reason your SQL Server installation was unsuccessful, however, there is still hope. This session begins by showing you how to fix a faulty installation. If you don't need to do this, skip to the explanations of how to run SQL Server Service Manager, manage configuration tasks, add components, and uninstall SQL Server.

## Fixing a Faulty Installation

Start by examining the error-log files that SQL Server installation process has created for sqlstp.log (located in the Windows directory) and errorlog (with no extension). It can also be helpful to examine the event log on your machine.

The first file — sqlstp.log — contains detailed information about all the errors (and events) that occurred during setup. Although most of the messages may seem incomprehensible, they can still help you determine the cause of your problem — or help you explain the problem to an experienced database administrator (DBA).

The errorlog file is created during the configuration portion of the setup. At this stage, all program files are already transferred, and setup tries to start SQL Server and connect to it. Any errors that occur during this process are recorded in errorlog (some are also recorded in sqlstp.log).

If you find some clues to what might have happened, you might be able to fix the problem right away; read Books Online or on the Net for more information. Setup problems are usually caused by inadequate administration privileges, software incompatibility problems, currently running programs, corrupted OS installation, previous SQL Server installations, or hardware problems.

**The Web sites listed on the accompanying CD might help you solve the problem. Make sure that you know the error description, error number, your computer configuration, and so forth because it all might be useful.**

## Running SQL Server Service Manager

Figure 2-1 shows the top-level options that Microsoft SQL Server Standard Edition has installed on your computer. Select Start ➪ Programs ➪ Microsoft SQL Server to access these options. In this session, I address the Service Manager option only.

You can start SQL Server 2000 as a service (which is its normal operational mode) or from the command line as a standard Windows program. You can also start SQL Server in single-user mode in order to perform advanced administration procedures and troubleshooting.

NT Service is a special type of executable. It gets special treatment from the Windows operating system and is not allowed to have any kind of user interface. Start the Service Manager from the system tray taskbar or from Start (Start ➪ Program Files ➪ Microsoft SQL Server ➪ Service Manager). You will see the dialog box shown in Figure 2-2.

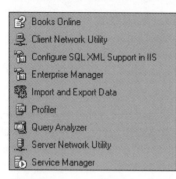

**Figure 2-1**
*Microsoft SQL Server 2000 offers these top-level menu options.*

**Figure 2-2**
*Microsoft SQL Server 2000 Service Manager.*

The Server drop-down list box contains a list of SQL Servers accessible from your machine: If you have sufficient privileges, you can start and stop the services of any of these. The Services drop-down list box contains all the following services pertaining to the SQL Server that you have selected from the Server list:

- **SQL Server** — SQL Server can run in two modes: as a command-line program or as a service. Normally you use it as a service, resorting to command-line mode only to troubleshoot your server or change some advanced configuration options.

- **SQL Server Agent** — You can use the SQL Server Agent for jobs, alerts, or tasks automation. I cover it in greater detail in Session 24.

- **Microsoft Distributed Transaction Coordinator (MSDTC)** — The Distributed Transaction Coordinator is a transaction manager that allows any client application to work with disparate sources of data within one transaction (the application should not care whether the data it requested is local or somewhere across the network).

You can start, pause, or stop any of these services using either the SQL Server Service Manager utility or the command-line utility. SQL Server Service is usually marked for auto-start when OS starts by default, and if you decide to use the SQL Server Agent, you'll probably want it to auto-start as well.

## Managing Configuration Tasks

**20 Min. To Go**

Let's look into the most common configuration tasks that you may need to do. If you selected automatic startup of the SQL Server Service during installation, your service will be up and running after you log on to your machine; if you opted for a manual startup, you need to start up your SQL Server Service before you can proceed. You can do this from the SQL Server Service Manager utility, as I described earlier in this session.

After you install your SQL Server, you will be able to connect to it with the user ID and password that you specified during installation. No matter what interface you use to connect to SQL Server (Query Analyzer, Enterprise Manager, a third-party application), you will be prompted for a user ID and password. Unless you have selected integrated security (wherein your OS login will be your SQL Server login), at this point, you should change your password and ID so that you can remember them. It is good practice to change your login entries after installation.

**It is all too common for users to leave the default options for login and password (sa and a blank password). Doing so compromises the security of your system. Change your login and password as soon as possible.**

In the next two sections, I'll show you how to change the login account information for Windows NT and Windows 2000, respectively.

### Windows NT

Follow these steps to change SQL Server Services login account information for Windows NT:

1. From the Control Panel, double-click the Services group. The Services dialog box presents the full list of services running on your machine.

2. Double-click the service for which you want to change account information. In the Services dialog box, under Log on as, select This account and enter your information.

   You now need to change the user-account information in SQL Server Enterprise Manager (I cover this in Session 3).

## Windows 2000

Follow these steps to change SQL Server Services login account information for Windows 2000:

1. Select Start ⇨ Programs/Administrative Tools.
2. Select Services.
3. Right-click the MSSQLServer service.
4. Select Properties.
5. Click the Log On tab and change your password.

You must set up each service individually. You can set distinct IDs and passwords for each service. These changes take effect after the service is restarted. You must have administrator privileges to change security entries.

**I'll cover issuing SQL Server commands in Sessions 7, 8, and 9.**

## Locating SQL Server Files

SQL Server 2000 installs many files and alters some Registry settings. Table 2-1 shows files shared for all instances of SQL Server running on your machine.

**The dBinn, Data, HTML, and 1033 directories are sacred. Never delete or modify these files; you will need to reinstall SQL Server if you do.**

**Table 2-1**
*Locations of SQL Server 2000 Files*

| Location | Description |
| --- | --- |
| \Program Files\Microsoft SQL Server \80\Com | Dynamic-link libraries (DLLs) for Component Object Model (COM) objects. |
| \Program Files\Microsoft SQL Server \80\Com\Binn\Resources\1033 | Resource files (RLLs) used by the DLLs in this COM directory. (Note: 1033 is for U.S. English; localized versions use different directory numbers.) |
| \Program Files\Microsoft SQL Server \80\Tools\Binn | Tools for use with SQL Server — resource executables, command-line utilities, and so on. |
| \Program Files\Microsoft SQL Server \80\Tools\Binn\Resources\1033 | Resource files used by the executables in the Tools\Binn directory. |
| \Program Files\Microsoft SQL Server \80\Tools\Books | SQL Server Books Online files. |
| Program Files\Microsoft SQL Server \80\Tools\DevTools\ | Files for use by developers creating SQL Server client applications. |
| Program Files\Microsoft SQL Server \80\Tools\Html | HTML files containing the graphical interface to SQL Server used by Microsoft Management Console (MMC) and SQL Server. Opening these files in your Web browser is not recommended. |
| Program Files\Microsoft SQL Server \80\Tools\Templates | Template files containing SQL scripts for creating database objects. |

Some of the advanced features of SQL Server will actually require you to look into the Tools\Binn directory. Some executable files in this directory (such as bcp.exe) can be invoked from the command line; others (such as the DTS Wizard executable) have a visual interface. Normally, the path to these utilities is automatically added to the environment when you install SQL Server, though some programs you may install on the machine at a later time can change this convention.

## Adding Components

Whenever you need to add a component for SQL Server, you need to rerun the installation. Follow the steps described in Session 1 until you reach the screen presented in Figure1-2; then follow this procedure:

1. Instead of creating a new instance of SQL Server, choose the Upgrading, Adding, or Removing components option from this screen and click Next.

2. If you want to modify the default instance of SQL Server, click Next. Otherwise, uncheck the default check box and select the name of the SQL Server you wish to add components to.

The SQL Server installation detects installed components and in the Select Components dialog box presents you with a list of those available for installation. All components are grouped in a hierarchy, and you can select a top level and everything beneath it or select subcomponents individually. When you select an item a brief description appears in the Description box in the Select Components dialog box.

**If you need to change your character set sort order or UNICODE collation order, you must rebuild your master database (which I show you how to do in Session 6); all custom databases will be tossed (with all the data), and you will need to rebuild them from scratch. It is not as scary as it sounds, but it requires careful planning. You should have a very good reason for even considering it.**

Unselecting a component does not remove it from the installation; you have to remove SQL Server completely to do so. Selected components will be added (or reinstalled, if they existed before) after you click Next on the Start Copying Files dialog screen.

## Uninstalling SQL Server

If you plan to uninstall SQL Server 2000 you have two options:

**10 Min.
To Go**

- Rerun the setup program and select Uninstall.
- Select the Add/Remove Programs utility from the Control Panel.

To uninstall SQL Server Installation from the setup program (the first option) follow these steps:

1. Start SQL Server Installation (from CD-ROM or the network).
2. Select SQL Server 2000 components and then select Install Database Server.
3. Select the name of the computer (local or remote).
4. Select Upgrade, Remove, or Add Components.
5. Select the instance name from the presented dialog box. Leave the default selected if you want to uninstall the default instance of SQL Server.
6. Select Uninstall your existing installation.
7. Click Finish on the final dialog box to complete the uninstallation.

**Quit all applications before uninstalling SQL Server, as some of them may interfere with the process. Removing SQL Server from the standard Control Panel option is no different from removing any other program. To remove SQL Server from the Control Panel, double-click the Add/Remove Programs icon and select the instance you wish to remove. Each named instance must be removed separately.**

When SQL Server 2000 is uninstalled, some files may remain on your computer. You may have to manually delete remaining directories and files whose physical locations are specified in Table 2-1.

**Done!**

## REVIEW

- Examining error-log files is the first step in fixing a faulty installation.
- SQL Server, SQL Server Agent, and MSDTC are the three essential SQL Server 2000 services.
- It's good practice to change login entries after installation.
- You must rerun your installation before adding components.

## Quiz Yourself

1. Where do you look for clues if an installation fails?
2. How do you reinstall a SQL Server component?
3. What are two options for uninstalling SQL Server 2000?
4. Why do you need to change your login properties?
5. What is a service?
6. What services are accessible from the SQL Server Service Manager?

# *First Look at Enterprise Manager Console*

## Session Checklist

✔ Starting up Enterprise Manager

✔ Creating server groups and registering servers

✔ Inspecting SQL Server nodes

✔ Considering your options

✔ Accessing SQL Server Books Online

**30 Min.
To Go**

**I**n this session, you learn about Enterprise Management console — what it is and how to find your way around it. You go through the complete process of registering SQL Server and organizing your SQL Servers into groups. I also explain SQL Server 2000 nodes and their use, as well as the most useful options on the SQL Server toolbar and menus.

## Starting the Enterprise Manager

Fire up the SQL Server Enterprise Manager (Start ⇨ Programs ⇨ Microsoft SQL Server ⇨ Enterprise Manager). For the time being, it is your main means of communicating with SQL Server (it isn't the only means of interacting with SQL Server, but it is the most convenient). Some other means of connecting to and administering SQL Server 2000, such as command-line utilities and system stored procedures, are covered in later sessions. The Enterprise Manager, however, provides access to virtually every feature of SQL Server you may need or want to use.

**From the Enterprise Manager console, you can also administer different versions of SQL Server, namely 7.0 and 2000. You can view Version 6.5 from the same console, but your administrative capabilities are rather limited. The Enterprise Manager uses standard Microsoft Management Console (MMC) for presenting information: a tree view on the left pane of the console and details about the selection on the right (see Figure 3-1).**

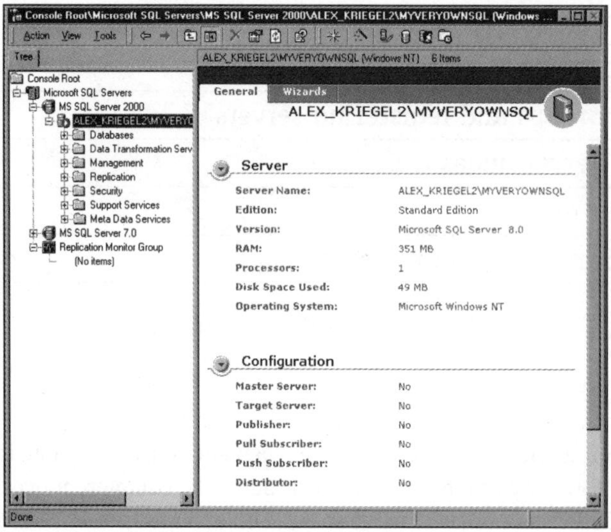

*Figure 3-1*
*The Enterprise Management console for SQL Server administration.*

**MMC serves as an integrated management console container hosting a variety of administration snap-ins that can either come from Microsoft (as in the case of SQL Server or the Internet Information Server) or be custom-developed. You can also organize them into groups to create a custom administration console.**

The choices presented by the Enterprise Manager, which enable or disable various features, can be a bit overwhelming at first glance, but these choices provide you with a great deal of power and flexibility. You can access most of the options from the toolbar menu as well as from the right-click menu.

## Creating Server Groups and Registering Servers

The tree pane lists all the registered SQL servers. In order to administer SQL Server installation through the Enterprise Manager console, you must register a server. By default you have one registered server — the one you've just installed. You can add any available SQL Server to the console, provided that it is accessible to your network. These servers will appear as valid choices in the wizard's list box. You can also remove all the servers from the console and have none (which pretty much defeats the purpose). Microsoft enables you to organize all registered servers into SQL Server groups. Just specify the group under which you want the server to be registered (or create a new group altogether).

**Your left pane may look different from the pane in Figure 3-1 unless you have selected the Taskpad option from the View menu. (I will cover the Taskpad option later in this session.)**

By default you have SQL Server Group node that you can rename to reflect your particular needs by using the right-click menu. The group nodes shown in Figure 3-1 might be top-level nodes or sub-nodes of any of the existing groups that enable you to create a structure of SQL Servers nodes.

Follow these steps to register a SQL Server under a particular group:

1. Select the group and right-click it. Choose New SQL Server Registration from the pop-up menu.

2. The very first wizard screen, shown in Figure 3-2, outlines the three tasks you must perform in order to register a new SQL Server. Click Next to continue.

**Figure 3-2**
*Using the Register SQL Server 2000 Wizard.*

3.  The screen that appears asks you to select the SQL Server you want to register. The Available Servers list box presents you with a list of all servers currently active on your network. Make your choice and click Next.

4.  Select an authentication mode. If you are connecting to the SQL Server installed on your machine, you can use Windows authentication (meaning that you will use your Windows ID/password to connect to the server). Click Next to continue.

5.  The last screen asks you to confirm your selection: This is your last chance to go back before registering the server. If you selected SQL Server authentication during the installation, you should enter the same login name and password that you specified before. If the server you wish to register is across the network, then you need to supply a valid login/password combination.

**According to your network speed, it might take a long time for the program to retrieve the list of available SQL Servers. If you know the name of the server you can just type it in.**

After you're proficient in the use of SQL Server, you might want to skip the wizard altogether by selecting this option on the wizard's start-up screen. Instead of going through all the selection steps, you will have access to a unified interface (see Figure 3-3) that contains some additional configuration options that are selected by default.

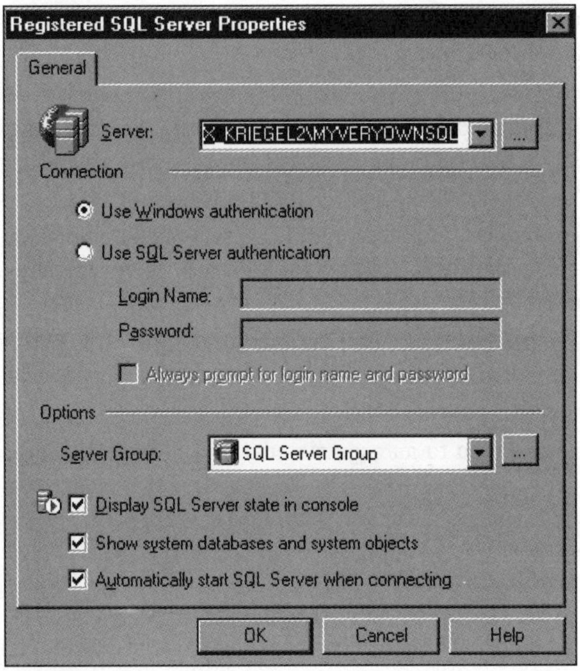

**Figure 3-3**
*Changing properties through the Registered SQL Server Properties screen.*

## Down Under: Inspecting Registered SQL Server Nodes

**20 Min. To Go**

The following nodes under the registered server node provide an interface you can use to view and manipulate all SQL Server 2000 objects (see Figure 3-1):

- **Databases** will contain all SQL Server system databases (covered in Session 6) and database objects (tables, views, stored procedures, and so on).

- **Data Transformation Services (DTS)** provide you with a means of consolidating data from a variety of sources and of transforming data from or into a number of different formats. It also has a programmable interface that enables you to create custom data-transformation packages as part of your custom solution. DTS is covered in Session 17.

- **Management** and its sub-nodes enable you to perform database-maintenance tasks, view current activity and server logs, and administer SQL Server Agent (used for automating most of these tasks and discussed in Session 21).

- **Replication** (covered in more detail in Session 15) enables you to distribute data and database objects from one database and to synchronize them. Typically, replication is used between physically distributed servers.

- **Security** (covered in more detail in Session 28), as its name implies, handles all security-related activities and states for your SQL Server installation as well as for linked and remote servers.

- **Support Services** includes the Distributed Transaction Coordinator (DTC, covered in Session 22), full-text search, and SQL Mail, which enables you to receive e-mail messages from SQL Server.

- **Metadata Services** enables you to manage metadata, or data about data.

## *Considering Your Options*

*10 Min. To Go*

The left pane of the SQL Server toolbar contains the three following menu choices, which are shown in Figure 3-4:

- **Action** provides access to most administrative tasks, such as starting, stopping, and pausing a server, registering a server, and editing registration properties, as well as to more advanced Data Transformation Services options. The menu structure is identical to the one you get by right-clicking the top levels of the tree pane.

- **View** enables you to customize your console, much as you would in Windows Explorer: You can choose details, the size of the icons, and similar preferences. I recommend that you select the Taskpad option — it provides you with a very convenient interface to common SQL Server configuration settings as well as to a list of wizards (add-on programs that guide you through a variety of tasks).

- **Tools** gives you access to every task you may need or want to perform in your budding DBA career. Though most of the options presented under this menu choice will be explained later in this book, some are rather complex and require an understanding of the SQL Server world that goes beyond the scope of this book.

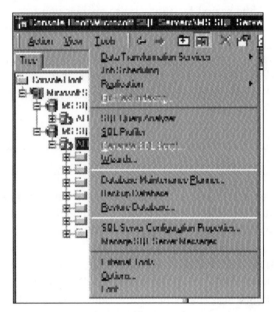

**Figure 3-4**
*Accessing advanced options.*

- **External Tools** enables you to launch any Windows NT/2000 application directly from the SQL Server Management console. In order to do this you must add the desired application (and specify its command-line parameters, if any).
- **Options** is an advanced menu choice that provides you with an interface to such configuration options as servers status polling, login/query timeout, and some start-up options.

You should refrain from changing settings that you do not fully understand. Though incredibly stable and intelligent, SQL Server requires expertise to administer. Changing a setting option without understanding the ramifications can result in an unusable installation.

## Accessing SQL Server Books Online

SQL Books Online is a great source of information. It installs with every SQL Server installation (Standard and Enterprise). Greatly improved from the previous versions in content as well as in format, it provides a wealth of information on all SQL Server 2000 issues. Its interface is based on that of Internet Explorer, and it provides a table of contents, index, and search features. It also enables you to group your most visited topics in the Favorites category. You can access SQL Server 2000 Books Online via the Help menu or from the Start menu (Start ⇨ Programs ⇨ Microsoft SQL Server ⇨ Books Online). The standard F1 hot key invokes SQL Server Books Online in the context of the object currently selected in the Enterprise Manager console. You can go through a table of contents, access a topic by index, or perform a search for a specific keyword, error code, and so on.

**Done!**

## REVIEW

- The SQL Server 2000 Enterprise Management console is your main means of accessing the SQL Server functionality. It's based on the standard MMC interface for SQL Server registration, and the organization of registered servers into groups.

- Understanding the SQL Server administrative console structure (nodes representing objects in SQL Server 2000) helps you to navigate SQL Server.

- SQL Server Books Online is your best source of information. It has a table of contents, an index, and powerful search capabilities.

## QUIZ YOURSELF

1. Is Enterprise Manager the only means of communicating with SQL Server?
2. Why do you need to register SQL Server?
3. What are registered SQL Server nodes and what are they used for?
4. What functionality do external tools provide?
5. How do you invoke Books Online?

# Second Look at Enterprise Manager Console

## Session Checklist

✔ Meeting the wizards

✔ Running command-line utilities

✔ Understanding Data Transformation Services

✔ Accessing SQL Server Agent

**30 Min.
To Go**

**T**his session introduces wizards and command-line utilities — a number of small programs supplied with SQL Server 2000 to help you with database administration chores. You'll also learn how to use SQL Server Agent to automate those utilities.

## Meeting the Wizards

The easiest way to make SQL Server do something useful is to use a wizard, a program that provides step-by-step guidance to help you accomplish a given task. Microsoft provides a number of different wizards with its SQL Server 2000 installation, and some of these wizards are actually useful. If you look at the Taskpad pane on the right side in your SQL Server Enterprise Manager console, you should see something very similar to what is shown in Figure 4-1. Alternatively, you can access these wizards from the SQL Server Tools menu (see Figure 4-2).

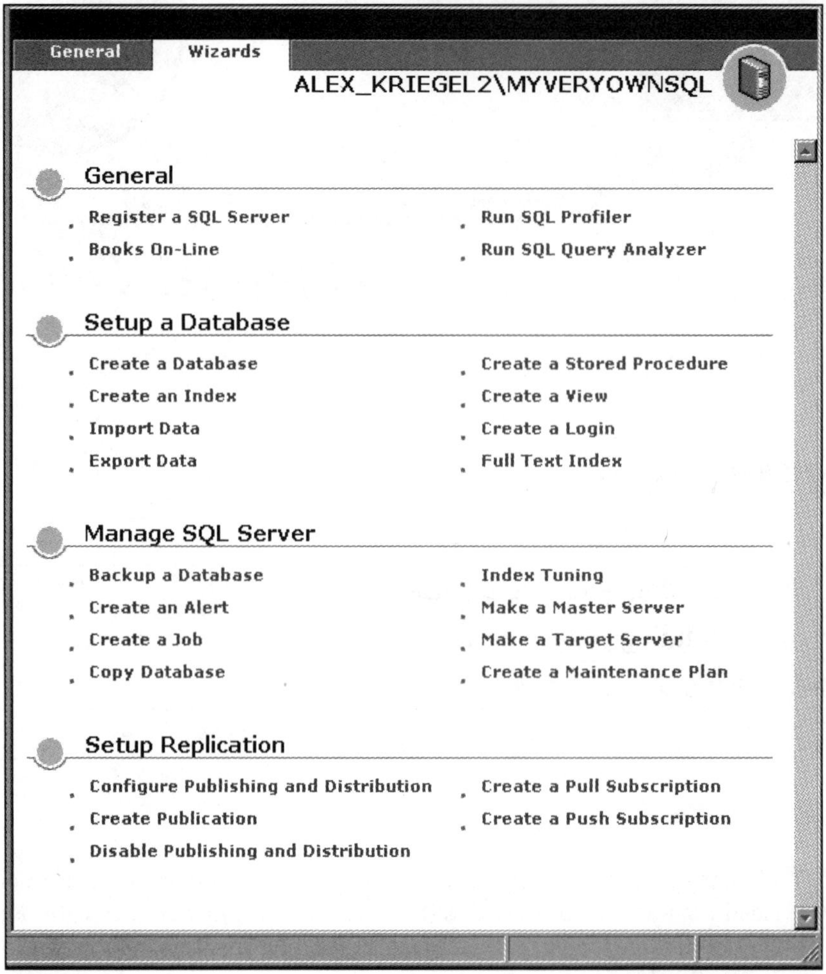

General     Wizards

**ALEX_KRIEGEL2\MYVERYOWNSQL**

**General**

. Register a SQL Server     . Run SQL Profiler
. Books On-Line     . Run SQL Query Analyzer

**Setup a Database**

. Create a Database     . Create a Stored Procedure
. Create an Index     . Create a View
. Import Data     . Create a Login
. Export Data     . Full Text Index

**Manage SQL Server**

. Backup a Database     . Index Tuning
. Create an Alert     . Make a Master Server
. Create a Job     . Make a Target Server
. Copy Database     . Create a Maintenance Plan

**Setup Replication**

. Configure Publishing and Distribution     . Create a Pull Subscription
. Create Publication     . Create a Push Subscription
. Disable Publishing and Distribution

**Figure 4-1**
*A complete set of wizards in the Taskpad view assists you with database chores.*

**Almost every task in SQL Server can be performed through a wizard. Although it might not be the only choice and is not always the best choice, it's a good idea to use these wizards until you gain more experience.**

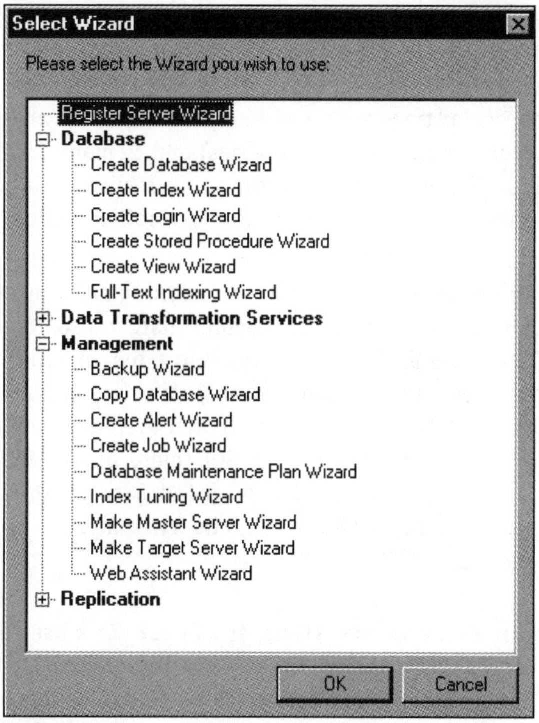

**Figure 4-2**
*Try this alternative interface to access wizards' functionality.*

I'll discuss these wizards in more detail in later sessions. For now, let's take a whirlwind tour of some wizards to gain a better understanding of what you can use right now and of what to expect later.

## Database administration wizards

As a database administrator you will often have to create, maintain, and query objects in your SQL Server system. Under the General tab of the Taskpad view (shown in Figure 4-1) are four wizards to help you:

- **Register a SQL Server** — Before you can manage a SQL Server from the Enterprise Manager console, you must register it here. (See Session 3 for details on registering SQL Server.)

- **Books Online** — This is the most up-to-date source of information on SQL Server 2000, except for the official Microsoft SQL Server Web site. See Session 3 for more information.

- **SQL Profiler** — This tool, supplied by Microsoft, enables you to take a closer look at SQL Server events. It is used primarily to find problems and fine-tune SQL Server by monitoring a specific part of the SQL Server programs. All events for a particular trace are saved in a file and can be analyzed later for problems (such as slow-running queries) and to monitor SQL Server performance. SQL Profiler also supports auditing for security-related actions (such as unauthorized connection attempts). SQL Profiler will be covered in Session 26.

- **SQL Query Analyzer** — This is your primary tool for designing and executing queries dynamically. But its usefulness goes beyond that: It also enables you to execute Transact-SQL statements stored in a file, directly execute stored procedures (covered in Session 11), analyze query performance, modify data (insert, update, and delete rows), and even add your favorite commands to the Tools menu. You can run SQL Query Analyzer from the Start menu (Start ⇨ Program Files ⇨ Microsoft SQL Server ⇨ Query Analyzer), from the Enterprise Manager (Tools ⇨ SQL Query Analyzer), or with the command-line isqlw.exe utility.

**When SQL Query Analyzer first starts, it will ask for a user ID and password as well as for a target server name in order to connect. Leaving the server name blank or specifying (local) — the parentheses are important — connects you to the default SQL Server running on your computer.**

## Database wizards

The next group of wizards is the database wizards, which you will find under the General tab of the Taskpad view. These wizards enable you to perform tasks such as creating a database, an index, a view, or a stored procedure; importing or exporting data; and creating logins or a full-text indexing catalog for your database.

**Importing and exporting data will be explained briefly later in this session and more thoroughly in Session 17.**

SQL Server Managing wizards comprise the next group in the General section. Most common server-management chores are addressed here: backing up a database, creating jobs and alerts, setting up master/target servers (for multi-server environments), fine-tuning your database performance, and creating a database-maintenance plan.

## The Replication Wizard

Replication is one of the technologies that enables you to keep virtually identical sets of data across multiple sites. This means that you can keep timely and accurate data accessible. I will discuss the SQL Server 2000 Replication Wizard in Session 19.

**20 Min.
To Go**

## The Web Assistant Wizard

The Web Assistant Wizard enables you to generate HTML (HyperText Markup Language) documents based on the data contained in SQL Server 2000. Figure 4-3 shows sample HTML containing data from two tables of the Pubs database (covered in Session 6) displayed in a Web browser. The Web Assistant is the next best thing after dynamically generated Web pages (such as Active Server Pages or Cold Fusion). The static HTML file is generated and subsequently can be served by a Web server (such as Internet Information Server); moreover, you can use a trigger to schedule automatic updates for the file based on a scheduled job (Session 24) or a change to the data (Session 11).

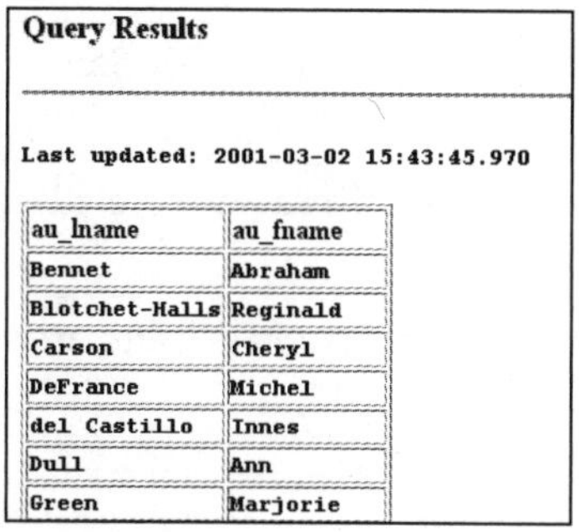

**Query Results**

Last updated: 2001-03-02 15:43:45.970

| au_lname | au_fname |
|---|---|
| Bennet | Abraham |
| Blotchet-Halls | Reginald |
| Carson | Cheryl |
| DeFrance | Michel |
| del Castillo | Innes |
| Dull | Ann |
| Green | Marjorie |

**Figure 4-3**
*The results of a SQL query appear as HTML in a Web browser.*

In response to an ever-increasing demand for database-driven Web sites, Microsoft provides tight integration between IIS and SQL Server 2000. In addition to Web Assistant-generated HTML files, IIS supports dynamic queries run directly from a Web page over HTTP (HyperText Transfer Protocol). These queries generate HTML or XML output, which greatly improves performance, as most of the work and formatting is done by SQL Server.

## Running Command-Line Utilities

In addition to the visual interface of the Enterprise Manager console and all the wizards, SQL Server provides you with a number of command-line utilities that you can run either from the DOS prompt or from Windows Explorer. Table 4-1 shows the full list of command-line utilities (and installation directories) that are automatically installed with Microsoft SQL Server 2000. All of these utilities are located in the Program Files\Microsoft SQL Server\MSSQL\Binn directory, except distrib, logread, replmerg, and snapshot — you'll find these in Program Files\Microsoft SQL Server\80\Com.

**Table 4-1**
*Command-Line Utilities Installed with Microsoft SQL Server 2000*

| Utility | Description |
| --- | --- |
| bcp | Copies bulk data between SQL Server and an external data file |
| isql | Executes Transact-SQL statements from the command line |
| sqlservr | The main SQL Server executable; used to start SQL Server manually |
| vswitch | Enables you to switch among different versions of SQL Server (2000, 7.0, 6.5, or 6.0) |
| dtsrun | Runs DTS (Data Transformation Services) packages (covered in Session 17) |
| dtswiz | The Data Transformation Services Import/Export Wizard; assists in creating DTS packages (covered in Session 17) |
| isqlw | Enables you to start SQL Query Analyzer from the command line |
| itwiz | Enables you to execute the Index Tuning Wizard using a command-prompt utility (covered in Session 26) |
| odbccmpt | Enables or disables the compatibility option (different SQL Server versions) for applications using the ODBC interface |
| osql | Enables you to connect to SQL Server and execute Transact-SQL statements |
| rebuildm | Rebuilds the Master database (covered in Session 27) |

| Utility | Description |
| --- | --- |
| wiztrace | Enables you to execute the Index Tuning Wizard using a command-prompt utility; unlike itwiz, it has a visual interface (covered in Session 26) |
| scm | A command-line interface to the SQL Server Service Manager |
| sqlftwiz | The SQL Server Full-Text Indexing Wizard (covered in Session 30) |
| distrib logread replmerg snapshot | Replication Agent Utilities (covered in Session 19) |

**A well-behaved command-line utility is supposed to display a list of the arguments (switches) it accepts, along with a brief description of each. All you have to do is ask by entering in the utility name followed by a slash and a question mark at the prompt (for example, bcp /? will display a list of arguments for the bulk-copy utility).**

You can run any of these utilities either from a command line in the directory where it is installed or by specifying the full path. For the purposes of this book you will be concerned with only a handful of these utilities:

- **BCP (Bulk Copy Program)** — Copies bulk data between SQL Server and an external data file. This utility dates back to the dawn of Microsoft SQL Server (version 6.0, that is), and is very useful when you need to transfer large amounts of data among different SQL Servers. It sometimes performs the data transfer faster than any other available option, but this speed comes at a price. BCP has an arcane syntax that supports over 30 optional arguments (including one that enables you to set the version-compatibility level) and using it requires an understanding of how SQL Server treats data (for example, that computed columns are ignored with BCP).

- **OSQL** — A command-line utility used to connect to SQL Server and execute Transact-SQL statements (covered in Session 8). The results of the executed commands will be displayed in the DOS console window. OSQL uses the ODBC (Open Database Connectivity) interface to connect to SQL Server.

- **ISQL** — Uses the DB-Library interface to communicate with SQL Server. It is a database-specific interface and is not portable. In addition to this, ISQL does not support many of the new features in Microsoft SQL Server 2000.

- **ISQLW** — Essentially a way to start SQL Query Analyzer from the command line.

> **Open Database Connectivity (ODBC) is an application program-mer's interface (API) that exposes underlying database cap-abilities. An abstract layer (called an ODBC Driver) allows applications to access virtually any relational database manage-ment system without paying much attention to the differences between them (as long as you have an appropriate ODBC driver). In SQL Server 2000, all utilities except isql use the ODBC API and the SQL Server ODBC Driver. To facilitate the use of ODBC by pro-grammers, Microsoft has provided thin wrappers called active data objects (ADO) and data access objects (DAO) around its functions. To take a look at all ODBC drivers installed on your machine, go to Settings ⇨ Control Panel ⇨ Data Sources (ODBC). DB-Library is a proprietary SQL Server programming interface, supported mainly for backward compatibility.**

## *Understanding Data Transformation Services*

**10 Min.
To Go**

The *Data Transformation Services (DTS)* group includes Import and Export Wizards. DTS is a very important part of SQL Server that I explain in detail in Session 17. Just like the bulk-copy utility, DTS is a tool for transferring large amounts of data; unlike the bulk-copy utility, it has a visual interface and allows data transforma-tion and data-objects transfer via views, stored procedures, indexes, and so on.

Data Transformation Services wizards can also create DTS packages — collections of tasks, transformations, and rules and constraints. For now, you may think of a DTS package as a program that is executed according to a schedule and that per-forms some data-transfer or transformation tasks based on particular business logic. You can create these packages either by using DTS Designer or programmati-cally by using Visual Basic or Visual C++ (or any COM-compliant language). Either way you must understand relational-database principles as well as business logic.

## *Accessing SQL Server Agent*

SQL Server Agent will assist you in automating some of your database-management chores. It executes scheduled *jobs*, raises *alerts*, and enables you to specify *opera-*

*tors*. (See Session 24 for more information about SQL Server Agent.) Here are definitions of these terms:

- **Job** — A sequence of operations to be performed once, scheduled for execution, or run when a certain predefined condition occurs. SQL Server Agent maintains a complete job history for every job, recording time of execution, duration, and final result.

- **Alert** — Enables you to take an action in response to an event that has occurred on the system. SQL Server Agent monitors the Event Log of your machine; once it encounters an event for which you as a user created an alert, it responds by taking an action. It can respond by invoking a job, sending a message (via e-mail or to a pager), or (in a multi-server environment) passing these alerts to another SQL Server to process. It is integrated with various performance counters, allowing it to take an action whenever a certain threshold is crossed (such as when memory usage climbs above a preset limit).

- **Operator** — The contact to whom a notification about an alert will be sent. You can specify e-mail, pager, or net send notification.

**The Net Send command, issued from a DOS window, sends a message across the network to a specified computer or user. This method is not supported for computers running the Windows 95/98 operating systems.**

You can access SQL Server Agent through the Create a Job or Create an Alert option on the right pane of the Enterprise Manager Wizards section. These options are also available through an alternative wizards interface shown back in Figure 4-2.

---

## REVIEW

- The SQL Server Management console provides a consistent interface with which you can access all the features of the RDBMS system.

- SQL Server 2000 wizards provide the fastest way to accomplish even complex database tasks.

- SQL Server provides command-line utilities for some administrative tasks that cannot be easily accomplished through the visual interface, as well as for backward compatibility with previous versions of SQL Server. In general, they are for more experienced users.

**Done!**

- Data Transformation Services are used to import, export, and transform large amounts of data between various sources.
- You can use SQL Server Agent to automate database tasks and keep a close watch on the performance of SQL Server.

## QUIZ YOURSELF

1. What is a wizard in SQL Server 2000 and what is it used for?
2. What is DTS and what is a DTS package?
3. What are command-line utilities and how do you install them?
4. What is SQL Server Agent?

# PART

# I

## *Friday Evening*

1. What is SQL Server 2000?
2. On what operating systems can you install SQL Server 2000?
3. Name at least three installation versions of SQL Server 2000. What are the differences between them?
4. What is collation order and how do you choose one?
5. What is a named instance and how does it differ from a default server?
6. What are the two authentication modes supported by SQL Server 2000?
7. What visual tool does Microsoft supply to manage SQL Server?
8. What are SQL Server services and how do you manage them?
9. How do you register a server with the SQL Server Enterprise Manager?
10. How many top-level objects do you see for each registered SQL Server?
11. Can you change your SQL Server configuration options?
12. How do you add or remove SQL Server components after installation?
13. How do you uninstall SQL Server 2000?
14. What are the SQL Server Books Online and where can you find them?
15. What is a wizard in SQL Server 2000 context?
16. What is RDBMS? What does it have to do with SQL Server?
17. What is the purpose of the BCP command-line utility?
18. What are ISQL and OSQL?
19. What are SQL Server Agent jobs and alerts?
20. What is the Web Assistant Wizard?

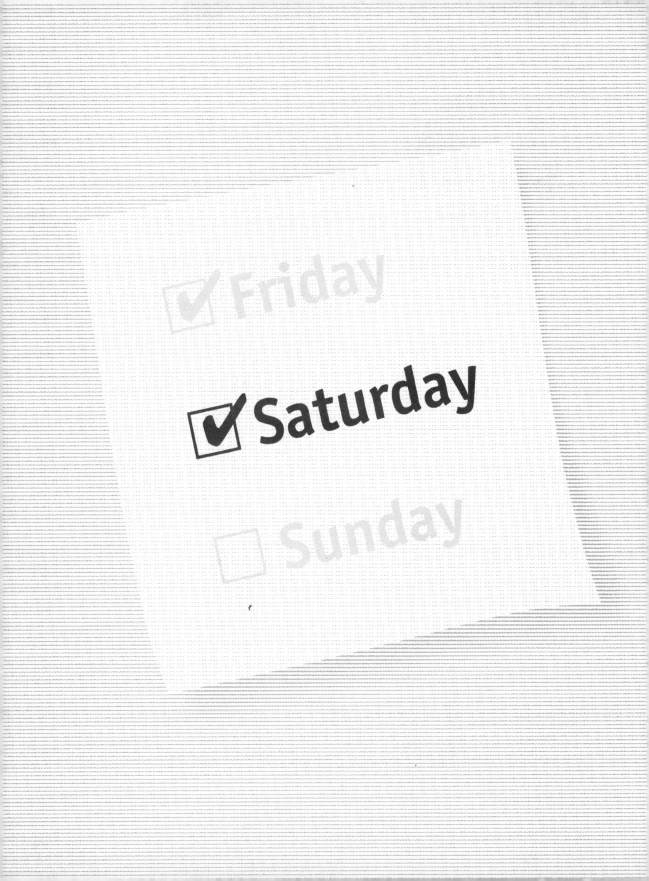

# PART

# II

## *Saturday Morning*

# *Relational Database Concepts*

## *Session Checklist*

✔ Identifying the limitations of spreadsheet programs

✔ Understanding legacy database models

✔ Understanding the relational database model

✔ Exploring relational database–management system implementations

✔ Learning relational-database terminology

**30 Min.
To Go**

This session will give you some background in the evolution of database systems. You will be introduced to three major database models — hierarchical, network, and relational — with more emphasis placed on the last of these.

## *Identifying the Limitations of Spreadsheet Programs*

Tabular representation is one of the most basic ways to organize data in order to extract some useful information. You can get by with a spreadsheet system if you are the only user. Of course, you will have to remember where the information is stored. If the information changes in any way, you will have to go through all the worksheets and manually update data (or write a neat macro to do it for you). Do not forget to maintain (and update) multiple copies just in case the working copy becomes corrupted or lost. If that does not scare you, I dare you to imagine sharing the data with your coworkers by sending them a copy of your file, or loading it from the network, thus effectively blocking everybody else from making any changes to it. If everyone works independently for a while and you need to merge data, how would you know which file was current? You could open both files at the same time, call in your coworkers, and spend a couple of days arguing about which changes to include in the final version. But imagine 200 people working on the same file in addition to doing tons of manual work, handling unstructured inconsistent data, and dealing with awkward search capabilities. It becomes obvious that something is terribly wrong with this approach.

All these problems (and much more) are taken care of automatically in any modern database. Although the solution comes at the price of increased complexity and cost, and the need for a higher degree of technological savvy, the alternative — using a spreadsheet — is not really an option.

## Understanding Legacy Database Models

As promised, this section will discuss the two types of database models:

- Hierarchical
- Network

### Hierarchical databases

The concept of the hierarchical database model is fairly intuitive: as the name implies, the data within the database is stored in a hierarchy of tables. There was nothing wrong with hierarchical databases, to start with. They were fast and efficient, and fit well into the existing tape-storage systems used by mainframe computers in the early 1970s.

 **A *table* is a basic structure wherein data are stored in the database. It is composed of columns and rows, which in database terminology are referred to as fields and records, respectively.**

You can visualize the structure as multiple tree roots flowing from one "root" table. Take a look at Figure 5-1, which shows the hierarchical database structure, also known as an *entity-relationship diagram*, for some fictitious company. At the root level is a Department table. The next level consists of a Projects table and an Employees table, which lead to the Workers and Dependents tables, respectively, on the next level.

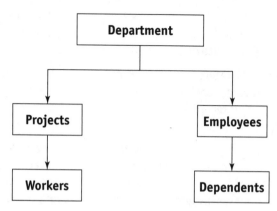

**Figure 5-1**
*A hierarchical database diagram.*

All relationships within a hierarchical database are represented by a parent/child paradigm: a parent table can have many child tables but a child table can be related to one and only one parent. These tables are linked explicitly, meaning that in order to maintain this relationship each table has to store some information (a record) about the parent- or child- related table.

The data access within this model must begin from a root table and work its way down the hierarchy sequentially, table by table. In the sample structure presented in Figure 5-1, you would have to follow these steps in order to find information about an employee assigned to a specific project:

1.  Start with the Department table.
2.  Find out whether this department deals with this particular project.
3.  Use the Workers table to find the ID/SSN of an employee assigned to this project.
4.  Submit a new query through the Department table to retrieve the information about this employee from the Employees table.

This procedure implied an intimate knowledge of the database structure as well as difficulty in changing this organization to accommodate new conditions or business rules. The other drawback was redundancy of data: If performance was to be satisfactory the data had to be duplicated in several places to address *many-to-many relationships*. In other words, in the sample database on Figure 5-1, employee data must be duplicated in the Workers table, especially if an employee has been assigned to several projects. However, there were some advantages to this model: For one thing, data retrieval could be very quick because the user knew the exact location of the data. In addition, the *referential integrity* could not be compromised because it was enforced by the structure itself.

**Referential integrity refers to a state of data in which there are no "orphaned" records; each record in the child table must be linked to an existing record in the parent table.**

Hierarchical databases served their purpose well and human ingenuity devised a number of workarounds to compensate for most of its shortcomings. Nevertheless, the increasing complexity of data and the need to analyze them created a demand for database enhancements. The next evolutionary step was the network database.

## Network databases

Network databases took the hierarchical concept one step further. In a hierarchical database, a child table could have one and only one parent; the network database has replaced the parent/child relationship with the *owner/member* relationship. This means that data access did not have to begin from the root table; instead, one could work through the database structure by starting from any table and going backward or forward through the related sets of tables. Data redundancy was greatly reduced because users could access a member table from more than one owner. Network databases were fast and efficient but they had the same major drawback as hierarchical databases: They required that the user be familiar with the structure of the databases to access any data. This structure could not be easily adapted to include new business logic.

## Introducing the Relational Database Model

In 1970, Dr. E. F. Codd of IBM introduced the relational-database model (though it took almost a decade for the first implementation to show up on the market). Relational databases store data in files that are mapped to tables. Each table is

**20 Min.
To Go**

composed of records and each record is composed of one or several fields. Fields contain some unique value or *key* and maintain their relation information in some other field (a *foreign key*).

This model allows data to be maintained in the table independently of its physical location in the computer. Figure 5-2 represents the same sample database you saw earlier in this session in its relational incarnation (I am assuming that projects cannot be shared between departments and that each employee works for only one department).

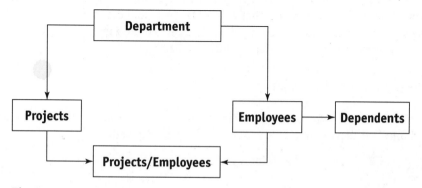

**Figure 5-2**
*A relational-database diagram.*

As in hierarchical and network databases, the tables maintain relations; unlike them, relational databases offer three elegant schemes for any type of relation:

- Many-to-many
- One-to-many
- One-to-one

## Many-to-many relationships

The *many-to-many* relationship is effectively the one that led to data redundancy in legacy databases. This is because the user has to remember a relationship, rather than understand database structure, in order to access data. For example, let's say that you'd like to know a number of dependents of an employee working on a particular project. This is not an easy thing to determine with a legacy database, but it is a snap with the relational database because you can access data by specifying the desired tables and fields within these tables. The relationship is *declarative*: that is, the Employees table is related to the Departments table by the fact that both contain the field DepartmentID. That field is a primary key for Departments and a foreign key for Employees.

## One-to-many relationships

An example of a one-to-many relationship exists in the case where each employee can be assigned to one and only one job, and each job can be assigned to one or more employees. The Projects and Employees tables are examples of a many-to-many relationship. This means that a given project can be assigned to one or more employees. This situation is managed by an intermediate ProjectsEmployees table, which consists of two one-to-many relationships.

## One-to-one relationships

Employees whose information is stored in the Employees table can work for one and only one department: this is a *one-to-many* relationship.

**See Session 6 for a further discussion of relationships.**

# Exploring Relational-Database Management-System Implementations

The hardware of 1970 is clearly not up to the task of running RDBMSes — relational database management systems. As processing capabilities, memory, and data storage improved dramatically in the mid-1980s, it became feasible to run RDBMSes and numerous implementations begun to sprout, first for mainframe monsters (IBM DB2 and Oracle), and then for PC-based systems. Dbase by Ashton-Tate became an almost instantaneous success, and was followed by FoxPro, R:BASE, and Paradox. These database systems were relatively crude by today's standards but they had the advantage of being the first relational PC-based databases. The evolution of database-management systems did not stop there; rather, it was taken to a new height with the advent of *client/server* computing databases in response to the need for data-sharing across the network.

There are many different RDBMSes on the market and they all support various levels of relational databases. All RDBMSes are supporting a subset or *entry level* of SQL in addition to their proprietary extensions; Microsoft SQL Server and Sybase support Transact-SQL, and ORACLE uses its own PL/SQL.

**Two main standards of SQL exist: ANSI/ISO SQL Standard (1992) and the ever-more-popular SQL-99 (also referred to as SQL3). Microsoft SQL Server 2000 fully supports the entry level of SQL-92 and many features of the intermediate and full levels. This is in addition to its own advanced proprietary features, some of which comply with the emerging SQL3 standard.**

The good news is that if you use only the standard entry-level subset of the SQL-92 standard your SQL applications will be highly portable among different database systems; the bad news is that you won't be able to harvest the full power of the RDBMS of your choice.

Recall that the choice of your RDBMS is affected by the operating system you're running, as follows:

- Microsoft SQL Server is a Windows-only application; the client application can run on any platform, but the server requires Windows.

- Oracle Server is available for UNIX (any flavor), Linux, and Windows; Oracle client libraries are available for the Macintosh.

- IBM DB2 is available for Windows, UNIX, Linux and, OS/2 operating systems.

- Sybase Adaptive Server is available for Windows, UNIX, and Linux.

- Hordes of less known RDBMS implementations include Informix (UNIX/Linux/Windows), INGRES (UNIX/Linux /Windows), MySQL (UNIX/Linux/Windows), OCELOT (Windows), and more.

You may want to know how these databases match up in terms of performance, computing power, user-friendliness, and such. There are no obvious criteria because all of these benchmarks are environment-dependent: the hardware, operating system, and load conditions are just a few variables. The independent Transaction Processing Performance Council (TPC) provides such information in the form of standard TPC benchmarks. These benchmarks come in several flavors and are quite complex: See the TPC frequently asked questions (FAQs) at http://www. tpc.org/tpcc/faq.asp for a full explanation. The recent benchmark TPC measures raw data throughout. The benchmark gives Microsoft SQL Server 2000 first place among the top 10 databases, followed by IBM and ORACLE database servers.

**10 Min.
To Go**

## Learning Relational-Database Terminology

Like every profession and trade, the RDBMS world has its own terminology. If you are going to speak with other database professionals you should know the language with which to convey your questions and ideas, and understand the answers. Here is the absolute minimum you need to get by, and I strongly encourage you to learn more:

- **Table** — A basic structure wherein data is stored in the database. Each database has at least one table.

- **Field** — A column within a table. Each table may have one or more fields. The maximum number of fields you can define for a table is 1,024.

- **Record** — A row within a table that can contain one or more fields. No physical limit exists on the number of rows allowed per table, but performance deteriorates as the number of fields increases.

- **Key** — Essentially, a field that has a special meaning within a database table. Keys serve a special purpose: A *primary key* uniquely identifies a record within a table and a *foreign key* establishes a relationship between two tables. Key fields are the basis of referential-data integrity.

- **Data integrity** — Refers to the consistency and accuracy of data in the relational-database model. There are different levels of integrity, all of which I discuss in Session 6.

- **Index** — A dependent structure within a database. It is used to speed up searches, especially in large tables containing thousands of records. An index is created for a table and is used by an RDBMS to locate the requested records. The concept of a database index is almost identical to that of a phone book.

- **Entity** — Think of an entity as an object or a concept that has its own attributes. I will explain entities in detail in Session 6. An entity is usually represented by a table that contains information relevant to that entity.

- **Entity-relationship diagram (ERD)** — A diagram representing a relationship between entities; covered in detail in Session 6.

**Done!**

## REVIEW

- Relational databases enable you to automate spreadsheet functions.
- Hierarchical databases represent relationships using the parent/child paradigm.
- Network databases represent relationships using the owner/member paradigm.
- Relational databases maintain data in a table regardless of its physical location on the computer.

## QUIZ YOURSELF

1. What are the disadvantages of legacy database models?
2. What is an RDBMS?
3. How do you retrieve data from a relational database?
4. What is a record? What is a field?
5. Do all RDBMSes use the same query language?
6. What are the major RDBMS implementations?
7. How long did it take the relational-database model to be implemented after the concept was introduced?

Part II—Saturday Morning
Session 5

# SQL Server Databases

## Session Checklist

✔ Understanding the SQL Server system databases

✔ Exploring the SQL Server sample databases

✔ Learning the basics of relational-database design

**30 Min.
To Go**

E very SQL Server installation comes with several preconfigured system and sample databases. In this session you will learn about them, their purpose, and what you can do with them. I will explain the database-design fundamentals as well as rules of normalization to help you get started with database design.

## Understanding the SQL Server System Databases

Every newborn SQL Server database system initially contains only six databases: Master, TempDB, Model, MSDB, Pubs, and Northwind. The first four of these are databases; Pubs and Northwind are sample databases provided to help you master relational-database concepts. I describe these two in the next section.

**Although it is possible, you should never try to modify any system database directly through the use of Transact-SQL statements, as this may — and often will — render your RDBMS unusable. Consider any system database (especially Master!) a sanctum sanctorum and treat it accordingly.**

## The Master database

The Master database contains information about your whole SQL Server system: login accounts, configuration settings, and a record of every custom database (and its location) that you might have created. It also contains initialization information that SQL Server uses on startup, system stored procedures (precompiled chunks of Transact-SQL programs that perform various administrative tasks), extended stored procedures (external compiled programs callable from within SQL Server), and more.

**System stored procedures are discussed further in Session 11 and Session 23.**

**Always maintain a current backup of your Master database. Create a new backup (as covered in Session 18) every time you change system settings (such as collation order, default language, and so on).**

## The TempDB database

TempDB holds all temporary tables (for intermediate results of sorting, for example), static cursors (covered in Session 13), and temporary stored procedures. It is a global workspace for every SQL Server process, available if any of those processes requires some type of temporary storage. Unlike every other database in SQL Server, TempDB is recreated, not recovered, every time SQL Server is started. This means that SQL Server gets a clean copy of TempDB on startup; consequently, TempDB never contains any information about previous SQL Server sessions.

Operations in TempDB are logged with just enough information that they can be rolled back if necessary (all other databases log information sufficient for recovery).

This behavior is new in SQL Server (starting from version 7) and is intended to increase performance.

Otherwise, TempDB behaves just like any other database in the system: It automatically increases in size as needed (unless restricted to a particular size), is capable of setting access rights, and so on.

**Set a sufficient initial size for TempDB in order to boost your SQL Server performance. Because TempDB is recreated at startup with the Model database as a template, make sure that the size of your Model database is the size you want your TempDB to be.**

## The Model database

The Model database is simply a template for all databases created on a system. A newly created database will inherit all the objects and properties of the Model database: permissions, sizes, tables, rules, datatypes, stored procedures, and so on.

**You can modify the Model database to include certain characteristics you'd like to see in your custom databases and in TempDB; the latter is created with the Model database as a template.**

## The MSDB database

SQL Server Agent (covered in Session 24) uses the MSDB database for scheduling alerts, jobs, backups, and replication tasks.

**You cannot easily delete any system database; it is not even an option in the Enterprise Manager console. You can delete physical files containing system databases in many ways, but there is not a single reason why you would.**

In SQL Server 2000 each database — system databases included — is placed into a separate non-shared file. Each system database consists of at least two files, a data file and a log file. Table 6-1 is modeled after the table from Books Online; it provides the names and default sizes of the system databases. The default size of the database is dependent on the setup type.

**Table 6-1**
*SQL Server 2000 System File Names and Locations*

| Database file | Physical file name | Default size, typical setup |
| --- | --- | --- |
| Master data | Master.mdf | 11.0MB |
| Master log | Mastlog.ldf | 1.25MB |
| TempDB data | TempDB.mdf | 8.0MB |
| TempDB log | Templog.ldf | 0.5MB |
| Model data | Model.mdf | 0.75MB |
| Model log | Modellog.ldf | 0.75MB |
| MSDB data | Msdbdata.mdf | 12.0MB |
| MSDB log | Msdblog.ldf | 2.25MB |

You should make any changes to system databases using the administrative tools provided by SQL Server system.

**Tip**

**Though it is possible, do not code Transact-SQL statements that directly query the system tables unless that is the only way to obtain the information required by the application. In most cases applications should obtain catalogues and system information from INFORMATION_SCHEMA views (see Session 23).**

## Exploring the SQL Server Sample Databases

Each installation of SQL Server 2000, regardless of type, will include two sample databases: Pubs and Northwind. These are databases for two fictitious companies, created by Microsoft to illustrate its database concepts and features. Both databases are referred to extensively throughout SQL Server documentation and Books Online.

### The Pubs database

The Pubs database is intentionally simple. It takes approximately 2MB of your hard-drive space and can be deleted safely. I recommend leaving it, however, as it provides you with a safe environment within which to master your database skills — especially Transact-SQL usage. You can do with the Pubs database and the data it contains as you please, as you can restore this database any time by running a script in the SQL Query Analyzer window. You'll find the file — instpubs.sql — in the \Install sub-directory of your main SQL Server installation directory.

### The Northwind database

The Northwind database was originally developed for MS Access (and is still shipped with it as a sample database) and demonstrates more advanced concepts than Pubs. It takes twice as much space (around 4MB) but can be deleted from your SQL Server system just as safely. Just as with the Pubs database, too, I recommend leaving the Northwind database: Some samples in this book (and in a lot of others) will use it. Feel free to use the database however you like, as you can restore it to its original state by running the script instnwnd.sql.

**10 Min.
To Go**

## Learning the Basics of Relational Database Design

While the sample databases Northwind and Pubs are useful, obviously they were not your main reason for installing SQL Server. At some time or another you will want to store and manage your own data and luckily, that is what a database server does best. At some point you will need to design a database.

A database does not exist in a vacuum; it serves some specific business purpose. A database for a pet store would be much different from a database for an automobile manufacturer, and must be designed (and implemented) differently.

Database design is still more of an art than an exact science. If you design a database from scratch you had better establish and follow the proper procedure for analyzing requirements and collecting and analyzing data. The topic of database design is well beyond the scope of this book — numerous books, some of which are listed in the recommended reading section, are dedicated solely to this art.

Relational database management systems (RDBMSes) are in the business of storing and retrieving data, ideally — any data. Before you can store anything in a relational database you need to tame the chaos by structuring your data in such a way that they can be represented in a table format as a set of rows and columns. The basic building unit of a database is the table.

In database-modeling jargon a table stores data concerning an *entity*, or object. The Pubs database was designed to represent the business model of a small publishing company. If you look at the list of the tables inside Pubs you'll see such tables as Departments, Employees, and Authors. They all represent entities: The Departments table contains information about the different departments in the company, the Employees table contains information about each employee, and the Authors table contains information about the authors the company deals with. Each row in these tables corresponds to one and only one department, employee, or author, respectively.

When you first start analyzing business requirements for your database, you try to identify entities in the specific business model; each entity is a prime candidate for being a table in your database.

Once you've identified the tables, think of their *attributes*. An attribute is something that defines an entity. For the Employee entity you might think of something that identifies an employee, such as Social Security number, name, or age. These attributes become columns in your table. Figure 6-1 shows the relationship between entities and attributes.

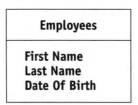

| Employees |
| First Name |
| Last Name |
| Date Of Birth |

*Figure 6-1*
*Defining an entity and attributes.*

**Give meaningful names to your tables: it will simplify development and maintenance, and might provide some insights into your database structure. Usually table names are construed in the plural, which reflects their purpose: Employees rather than Employee, for example.**

Relational databases are all about tables and the relationships among them. Relationships are defined in terms of the parent/child paradigm, are derived from the business model the database is designed for, and are implemented as primary/foreign key pairs. Unlike in the real world, in the world of relational databases it is the responsibility of a child to keep track of its parent. A parent table contains the primary key, which becomes the foreign key in the child table.

Take a look at the Pubs database. Each employee from the Employees table is assigned to do a specific job: these jobs are listed in the Jobs table. In order to keep track of which employee has been assigned to which job, you have the column Job_ID in the Employees table and the Jobs table; this column is the primary key in Jobs and the foreign key in Employees. If you think about it, Job_ID fits naturally into the concept of the Jobs table and is external to the Employees table — tomorrow a new job may be assigned and the Job_ID column may hold a different value.

Should the business model require that many jobs be assigned to one employee, the distribution of foreign/primary keys is different: The Jobs table contains an Employee_ID column in addition to the Job_ID column, and the Employees table does not have a Job_ID column at all. The strange-looking lines and shapes in Figure 6-2 describe a one-to-many relationship.

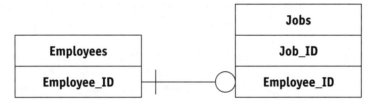

**Figure 6-2**
*Defining a one-to-many relationship.*

Figure 6-2 is a diagram of a system wherein an employee can be assigned to one and only one job (this is an example of a one-to-one relationship, indicated by the notation 1:1), and one job can be assigned to one or more employees (one-to-many, or 1:N). The special case of the many-to-many (N:N) relationship is resolved with an intermediate table: If every employee can be assigned to one or more jobs at the same time and each job can be assigned to one or more employees, then you need to convert one N:N relationship into two 1:N relationships.

Take a look at the diagram in Figure 6-3: the Employees table contains nothing to link it to the Jobs table, and the Jobs table does not contain a foreign key for Employees. Instead there is a third table, Employee_Jobs, which links them through the use of the primary keys of both tables: Employee_ID and Job_ID, respectively.

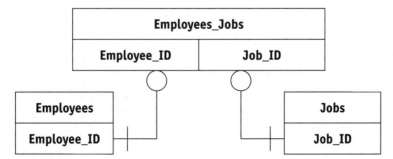

**Figure 6-3**
*Resolving a many-to-many relationship.*

## Get normal

Once you have established relationships in your database it is time for the normalization process. Normalizing a database means disassembling large tables into smaller ones in order to prevent data duplication. Some relationships may disappear and new ones be added as you go through this process.

A *normal form* is a set of rules that you apply to a table to ensure its compliance. At each level of normalization specific problems are addressed and solved.

The five normal forms measure the degree of normalization, but levels beyond the third normal form are of mostly theoretical interest and are rarely applied (if at all).

The first normal form deals with repeating groups. Consider the previous example of the Employees and Jobs tables. You can combine both tables to hold the same information, and the table structure (its fields) would look like what is shown in Figure 6-4.

| Employee_ID | Job_ID |
|---|---|
|  |  |

**Figure 6-4**
*Combining two tables into one.*

Surprisingly, this structure would actually work if it weren't for the fact that several jobs can be assigned to one employee. To amend the table structure to take this fact into account, you have to add more fields to this table to record jobs assigned to an employee, as shown in Figure 6-5.

| Employee_ID | Job_ID1 | Job_ID2 | Job_ID... |
|---|---|---|---|
|  |  |  |  |

**Figure 6-5**
*Assigning several jobs to one employee.*

The inefficiency of this design is obvious: If an employee is assigned fewer jobs than there are fields in the table, some fields remain empty; if an employee is assigned more jobs, you need to change the table's structure.

Job_ID fields comprise a repeating group, and once discovered such a group is a prime candidate for a separate table — Jobs, in this case. The two-table design is efficient and elegant. You need to analyze every table in your database and make sure that none has repeating groups.

The second normal form establishes that there can be no non-key attributes (fields) that depend on a portion of the primary key. Now, what does that really mean? A primary key is a field or a group of fields within the table that uniquely identifies the record; it cannot be repeated in any subsequent row no matter how many rows are added. A group of fields that together serve as a primary key are called the *composite key*, and your second normal form really concerns itself with composite fields. If your table contains fields identifiable only by part of the primary key then those fields really should be put in a table of their own.

Let's take a look at the Employees_Jobs table from the previous example of a many-to-many (N:N) relationship. You could define a composite primary key containing two fields: Employee_ID and Job_ID. Now, if you add some more fields to this table, such as Job_Description (depends on Job_ID only), or Employee_Name (depends on Employee_ID only), this table is in direct violation of the second normal form. Put these fields where they belong — into the Jobs and Employees tables. Your database design becomes clearer as the N:N relationship between the Employees and Jobs tables becomes clearer.

The third normal form declares that there should not be attributes (fields) depending upon other non-key attributes. That means that only relevant information describing an entity has a place in your table. Though it might be tempting to consider, a Job_Description field would be completely out of place in the Employees table; it belongs to the Jobs table. It might take some practice to figure out what is relevant information and what is not.

**Note**

**Most database designs stop at the third normal form, as a higher degree of normalization negatively reflects on the performance of the database. Even the third normal form should be approached with caution, as normalizing increases the number of tables in the database and degrades performance as a result. In some cases denormalization of a database may increase performance considerably as the number of joins needed to collect data decreases.**

### Common pitfalls of database design

If the only tool you have is a hammer, every problem starts to look like a nail. Nothing could be more true with regard to the mistakes people often make while trying their hands at database design. It is previous experience that bogs us down while we're trying to learn new things. Programmers with previous experience in non-relational databases may tend to design databases that resemble flat files or spreadsheets.

### Flat-file design

*Flat-file design* derives its name from the early days when data were stored without structure in computer files, much as you store your records in a file cabinet. If your table is designed this way it will have one or more of the following problems:

- Duplicate fields that present the same evil that the first normal form is supposed to eliminate.
- Calculated fields, wherein the table contains fields whose values can be calculated from the other fields existing in the table — such as an Age field in addition to a Date of Birth field.
- Multipart fields, such as a field called Address containing the street address, ZIP code, and city. Such fields are very inefficient, as in order to find the ZIP (for example) you have to parse the field's value to extract this piece of information.

In addition, you may find that the table is difficult or virtually impossible to index, as there is no single field or group of fields to uniquely identify the record, and that it tends to represent more than one subject.

### Spreadsheet design

Recall that a spreadsheet can't serve as a substitute for a database. It suffers from the same problems as the flat file and adds more of its own — such as an inability to deal with many-to-many relationships.

### Design tied to a particular RDBMS implementation

It can be really tempting to use every single hack a system might offer in order to get better performance. Each system has its own features — documented or otherwise — that you can use to improve performance, but at a price. The feature you are using might not be supported in future releases, your company might migrate to a totally different RDBMS. Your database would need to be amended at best or redesigned from scratch at worst — a sobering thought. There is no substitute for good design principles, which you must apply with a full understanding of what the results will be.

**Done!**

---

## REVIEW

- Every SQL Server 2000 installation comes with predefined system databases containing all the information about your server. This installation also includes two sample databases, Northwind and Pubs, that you can use to study relational-database concepts.

- Once you start building your own database you should follow the rules of relational-database design. Each table in your database should go through the normalization procedure to at least the second normal form.

- Never use non-relational paradigms such as flat files and spreadsheets when designing a relational database.

---

## QUIZ YOURSELF

1. How many system databases are installed with SQL Server 2000?
2. What is the purpose of the Master database?
3. What serves as a template for each database created in SQL Server?
4. How does TempDB differ from every other database in SQL Server — either system or custom?
5. What is a normalization process?
6. What is a normal form?
7. What are some of the problems inherent in flat-file design?

# Creating and Using a Custom Database

## Session Checklist

✔ Creating a new database in SQL Server 2000

✔ Modifying database and transaction-log properties

✔ Deleting a database

**30 Min.
To Go**

N ow that you know your way around the sample databases Northwind and Pubs, you can start storing and managing your own data. This session will teach you how to create, modify, and delete a database with the Create Database Wizard. I'll explain the most common options and some of the considerations involved in selecting them. Successfully creating and manipulating database properties is the foundation of success with SQL Server.

## Creating a New Database in SQL Server 2000

SQL Server 2000 gives you three ways to create your very own custom database:

- **The Database Wizard visual interface** — This is the best method for beginning database users. The Database Wizard provides step-by-step guidance with a short explanation of every step.

- **The Databases node** (right-click menu option New Database) — This is a visual interface for more experienced users that combines all the Database Wizard steps on one screen. It also enables you to make use of the more advanced option settings, such as collation order.

- **Direct Transact SQL commands** — This method is for advanced users and those creating databases through a command-line connection; it will be covered in Session 9, once you've mastered Transact-SQL basics.

**These three methods are essentially the same, as behind the scenes your Database Wizard builds and executes the T-SQL statements that create your database.**

There are at least two major components of each database: the data component (which includes database objects like rules, roles, stored procedures, and so on) and the transaction-log component. As I mentioned before, in SQL Server 2000 a database is physically stored in separate non-shared files — one (or more) for the data (default extension .mdf), and one (or more) for the transaction log (default extension .ldf). The database can span several files; by convention, the extension of the primary file is .mdf and that of each secondary data file is .ndf. These files are exactly the same as any Windows file and are treated as such by the operating system.

**You can give your database file any extension you want, though adhering to conventional standards reduces confusion and makes file management easier.**

Let's create a database using the Database Wizard interface. You can access it from the Enterprise Manager Tools ➪ Wizards menu.

1. Select Create Database Wizard and click OK. The first screen explains the steps you're going to take to create your database. Click OK.

2. The second screen prompts you to specify a name for your database as well as a location for the files for your primary database file and transaction log. Click Next to continue.

**If you leave the default Unrestricted file growth option selected, SQL Server will enlarge your database file as necessary automatically. It's a good idea to stick with the default values until you have a little more experience in creating databases, but keep in mind that unrestricted file growth can affect your system's performance.**

**3.** The next screen prompts you to name your database file. By default SQL Server will name your database file *<your database name>*_Data.mdf and will name your transaction-log file *<your database name>*_Log.ldf. You can change the name of the file to whatever you want. By default, also, the initial size of these files will be 1MB; change this value to something in line with your expected database size.

**If you want all new databases in your SQL Server System to possess certain properties (such as initial size or data type), you may specify these properties in your Model database and every custom database you subsequently create will inherit it. (After you are through with the database-creation process, try modifying your Model database, setting its database size to 10MB and its log to 2MB and recreating your custom database, to see how this affects the new database properties.)**

**4.** Now it is time to specify some properties of your yet-to-be-created database (see Figure 7-1). I recommend leaving the Automatically grow the database files option selected. The last option on this screen deals with the file-growth restriction: If you choose to restrict file growth, the file will grow only until it reaches a specified limit. This is an important option because unrestricted file growth can potentially chew up all your hard-drive space. Click Next.

**One of my pet peeves is the option to increase file size by percents. Doing this can result in your running out of space, as you have no control over the number of megabytes allocated once the maximum capacity is reached. If your database occupies 1GB, a 10 percent increase means an increase of 100MB to accommodate only 1MB of new data. Specifying growth in megabytes gives you greater control over space usage. It is also a good idea to specify the maximum possible size for the transaction log so it does not fill up quickly.**

**5.** Essentially, you repeat the same operations for your new database transaction log: choosing the name and initial size. In selecting the initial size (and in using the file-growth option on the next screen) the rule of thumb is to keep log size at approximately 25 percent of data-file size. Click Next.

**6.** The same considerations for Step 4 apply to the option selection for this step. Click Next.

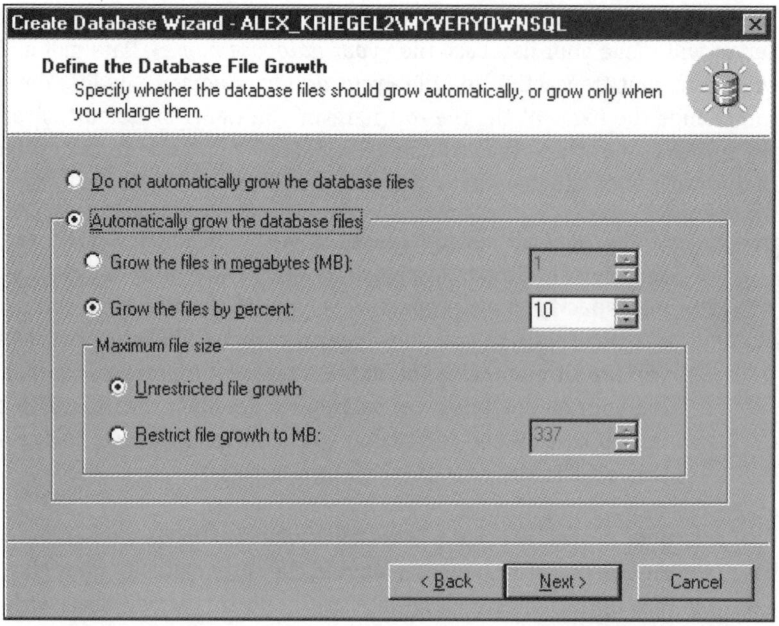

Create Database Wizard - ALEX_KRIEGEL2\MYVERYOWNSQL ☒

**Define the Database File Growth**
Specify whether the database files should grow automatically, or grow only when you enlarge them.

○ Do not automatically grow the database files

◉ Automatically grow the database files

   ○ Grow the files in megabytes (MB):    1

   ◉ Grow the files by percent:    10

   Maximum file size

    ◉ Unrestricted file growth

    ○ Restrict file growth to MB:    337

&lt; Back    Next &gt;    Cancel

**Figure 7-1**
*Set your database properties.*

**7.** Now you see a summary screen displaying all the options you selected in the previous steps. It's a good idea to go through this summary and make sure that the options specified are the ones you want. You can still go back and change them or cancel the whole operation.

After you click Finish, SQL Server will create your database, which you will be able to see on your Enterprise Manager console under the Databases node. If you used the wizard interface, SQL Server will prompt you to create a database maintenance plan; while it is a very good idea to have one, the topic of maintenance plans is beyond the scope of this session and will be covered in Sessions 21, 26, and 27.

**Most of the time SQL Server will succeed. If SQL Server is unable to create your database it will display an error message and an error code you can use to find a more detailed explanation in Books Online (for example, SQL Server displays the error message "There is not enough disk space" and the error code 112 if you attempt to create a 100GB database on a 20GB hard drive).**

If you followed me through this session you should have a brand new database showing under the Databases node on your Enterprise Manager console. Let's take a closer look at all the objects that make up your database.

 **You can create a database simply by issuing a Transact-SQL command from the SQL Query Analyzer window:** create database <database_name>**. The size and all the properties will be the same as those of the Model database, and the default file names will be the same as those that appear in Step 3 of the Create Database Wizard:** *<database_name>*_Data.mdf **and** *<database_name>*_Log.ldf**. The files will be physically located in the default directory of your SQL Server installation under that name.**

At this point all you have is an empty shell ready to be filled with your database content. It contains 19 system tables, roles, and user(s) inherited from the Model database. I will show you how to add your own tables, views, rules, and stored procedures in Sessions 9, 11, and 16.

## *Modifying Database and Transaction Log Properties*

**20 Min. To Go**

You can examine (and modify) the properties of your newly created database by locating the database in your SQL Server Manager console under the Databases node and selecting the Properties option. You'll see a screen like the one shown in Figure 7-2.

There are six tabs on this screen. The first tab, General, displays some information about your database, such as free space and time of last backup. This information is for display only — you cannot modify anything from here. The next tab, Data Files, combines steps 3 and 4 of the Create Database Wizard. Here you can increase allocated space and change file-growth properties.

 **You cannot decrease the size of either the database file or transaction-log file to be less than its initial size when created.**

The Transaction Log tab gives you access to the same options as the Data Files tab, only for transaction-log files.

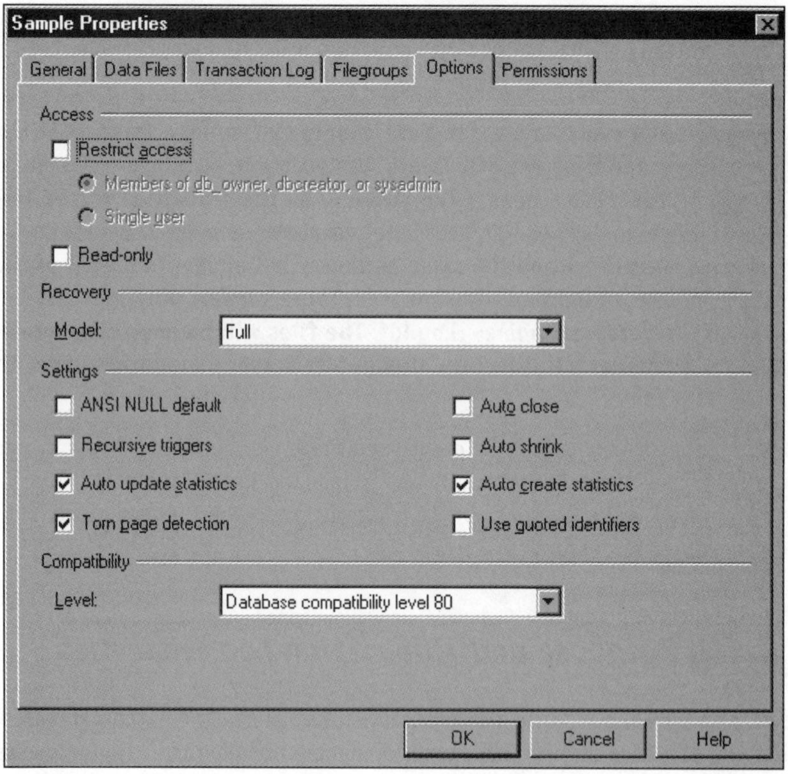

**Sample Properties**

| General | Data Files | Transaction Log | Filegroups | Options | Permissions |

Access

☐ Restrict access

    ○ Members of db_owner, dbcreator, or sysadmin

    ○ Single user

☐ Read-only

Recovery

Model: `Full`

Settings

☐ ANSI NULL default        ☐ Auto close

☐ Recursive triggers       ☐ Auto shrink

☑ Auto update statistics     ☑ Auto create statistics

☑ Torn page detection      ☐ Use quoted identifiers

Compatibility

Level: `Database compatibility level 80`

| OK | Cancel | Help |

**Figure 7-2**
*Adjust your database properties.*

The Filegroups tab displays information about the filegroup a data file belongs to. By default all data files are placed into the PRIMARY group. The idea behind filegroups is to improve performance for large databases (usually over 1GB); secondary files can be placed on different servers and have access to additional resources there.

The Options tab is probably the most important. Here you can restrict access to the database so that only members of a specific group have access, or put the database in single-user mode, thus denying access to anyone but you (which can be useful for troubleshooting).

**These options are for advanced users. You should familiarize yourself with the concepts involved before attempting to modify any of them. I recommend that you at least finish this book first.**

The Recovery option enables you to specify how you intend to recover your database in case of corruption, data loss, server crash, or some other unforeseen disaster. Later, in Sessions 21 and 27, I will explain what your choices are and how to choose the one that's best for you. For now, I recommend leaving the default setting, which is Full. The remaining eight options in the Settings group of the Options tab require more than a basic understanding and you will be better off if you leave them intact for the moment.

SQL Server 2000 provides four levels of compatibility with previous versions of SQL Server. The default is obviously SQL Server 2000 itself (level 80); there are also levels 70, 65, and 60, each representing a major version of SQL Server. The compatibility levels are provided to ensure that legacy applications can still use the database or be ported to it from the previous versions without much hassle. Unless you are planning on using legacy databases, I recommend leaving this option at its default, which is SQL Server 2000 itself.

The last tab on the screen, Permissions, enables you to control the use of your database. With it you can restrict rights to create a table or view, or rights to perform database backup. I cover Permissions in more detail in Session 28.

Once you've changed any of the settings described above, you need to click OK to finalize the change.

## Deleting a Database

**10 Min.
To Go**

Selecting the database node from the Enterprise Manager console and choosing Delete from the right-click menu deletes the database and corresponding log files. You will be asked whether you want to delete the backup and restore the database history; unless you really need this information for future reference, answer yes to remove it. You do not have to restart SQL Server after deleting a database. SQL Server removes data files, transaction-log files, and all database objects (such as tables, rules, and so forth).

You can also drop a database by issuing a Transact-SQL command from the SQL Query Analyzer (covered in Session 9):

```
drop database <database name>[,...n]
```

You have to be in the context of the Master database to execute the query (make sure that the combo box on the Query Analyzer toolbar reads Master); make sure that you are not currently viewing the database you want to delete in the Enterprise Manager and that no clients are connected to it, as you cannot delete a database that is in use. You must also have sufficient permissions in order to drop a database — you must be a member of the sysadmin or dbcreator group. You can drop multiple databases with the same command by specifying a comma-delimited list of the database names from the Query Analyzer window.

**No system database — meaning Master, Msdb, Model, or TempDB — can be dropped; SQL Server effectively prevents it from happening. Hacking your way around this protection is not recommended.**

Be absolutely sure about your decision to delete: all your data will be lost, and you will only be able to restore it if you performed a full backup immediately prior to deleting.

**Done!**

## REVIEW

- The Create Database Wizard makes creating a custom database much easier by guiding you step by step through the whole process.
- You can modify any custom database in a number of ways or drop it altogether.
- Modifying database properties through the Database Properties window is relatively easy but requires a thorough understanding of SQL Server.

## QUIZ YOURSELF

1. What are the three ways of creating a database with SQL Server 2000?
2. Do databases behave in different ways if they are created differently?
3. What is a transaction log? Why do you need one?
4. Why would you want to allow a database file to automatically increase in size?
5. What is the default compatibility level for SQL Server 2000?

# Transact-SQL Programming Language

## Session Checklist

✔ Learning about Transact-SQL

✔ Using the SELECT keyword

✔ Working with JOIN and UNION keywords

✔ Using the INSERT, UPDATE, and DELETE keywords

✔ Knowing about additional Transact-SQL keywords and functions

**30 Min. To Go**

**T**his session will introduce you to the basic concepts of Transact-SQL, with an emphasis on obtaining immediate results. You'll learn the fundamentals of data manipulation and running SQL queries, as well as how to use built-in functions and operators.

## Learning about Transact SQL

Now it is time to take a closer look at the heart of Microsoft SQL Server — Transact-SQL (or T-SQL). I mentioned in Session 5 that T-SQL is a dialect of the standard ANSI SQL supported both by Microsoft and Sybase. It is a programming language used exclusively for communicating with RDBMSes. Though many dialects exist, they all are required to comply with at least entry-level ANSI SQL guidelines.

T-SQL is a third-generation procedural language and, as such, is lacking all the features of the object-oriented programming model found in more advanced languages (such as C++, Java, and Visual Basic). T-SQL is all about data and how to manipulate them; unlike other programming languages, you cannot use it to create stand-alone programs — its statements can only be understood and executed in the context of SQL Server. T-SQL statements can be executed directly through the Query Analyzer utility, passed from the command line, or submitted to SQL Server via a custom client application. T-SQL was designed specifically for querying and modifying data in relational databases, and that is what it does best.

**T-SQL keywords also include built-in functions like COUNT (which returns a number of records) or AVG (which calculates the average for a particular field). One of the new features of SQL Server 2000 is the ability to define your own custom functions, thus expanding the T-SQL vocabulary.**

All T-SQL keywords are grouped into four categories:

- **Data Definition Language (DDL)** — Contains keywords dealing with defining database structures — creating a table or index, or dropping or modifying various objects within SQL Server.

- **Data Manipulation Language (DML)** — Contains keywords for manipulating data.

- **Data Query Language (DQL)** — Contains one keyword — SELECT — that is used to compose queries that extract data from the SQL database.

- **Data Control Language (DCL)** — Contains keywords controlling access to the database objects.

This session is concerned primarily with the DML and DQL groups.

## Using the SELECT Keyword

In previous sessions, you learned about the two sample databases supplied with Microsoft SQL Server 2000 — Pubs and Northwind. Now, it's time to use the data that these databases contain.

Suppose you want to get a list of all authors from the Authors table in the Pubs database, as shown in Figure 8-1.

**authors**
| | |
|---|---|
| 🔑 | au_id |
| | au_lname |
| | au_fname |
| | phone |
| | address |
| | city |
| | state |
| | zip |
| | contract |

**Figure 8-1**
*View the Authors table from the Pubs database.*

The T-SQL command you would use looks like this:

```
SELECT * FROM authors
```

Except for the asterisk (*) — which stands for "every single field in the table" — this command looks a lot like a plain English statement. If you run this statement from the Query Analyzer window, you will see a result set containing all 23 rows in the Authors table and all fields in each row. The result set (sometimes called the *recordset*) represents a virtual copy of the Authors table.

If you know the structure of the table you are querying, you can be more specific:

```
SELECT au_fname, au_fname, phone from Authors
```

The query will partition the underlying table vertically, returning a subset of the 23 Authors records — namely the author's first name, last name, and phone number — and leaving out all other fields.

But while it is useful for producing lists of records, you will sometimes need the SELECT statement to be more precise, more specific. What if the table contains millions of records? To filter through the records, to partition the table horizontally, you can use the WHERE clause.

The syntax of the WHERE clause is very intuitive. Suppose that you want a list of all the authors living in the state of California. The following is the statement that will return the first name, last name, and phone number of every author in the database who lives in California. This query returns only 15 records out of 23 present in the table, as shown in Figure 8-2.

```
SELECT au_fname, au_fname, phone, state from Authors WHERE
state = 'CA'
```

|   | au_fname | au_fname | phone        | state |
|---|----------|----------|--------------|-------|
| 1 | Johnson  | Johnson  | 408 496-7223 | CA    |
| 2 | Marjorie | Marjorie | 415 986-7020 | CA    |
| 3 | Cheryl   | Cheryl   | 415 548-7723 | CA    |
| 4 | Michael  | Michael  | 408 286-2428 | CA    |
| 5 | Dean     | Dean     | 415 834-2919 | CA    |
| 6 | Abraham  | Abraham  | 415 658-9932 | CA    |
| 7 | Ann      | Ann      | 415 836-7128 | CA    |
| 8 | Burt     | Burt     | 707 938-6445 | CA    |

**Figure 8-2**
*Records returned from the Authors table.*

Let's be even more selective. Here is the query that returns one record only:

```
SELECT au_fname, au_lname , phone, state  from Authors WHERE
state = 'CA'
AND  au_fname = 'Cheryl'
```

Of course, if you have more than one Cheryl in your database, and all of them happen to live in California, T-SQL will return more than one record. As you can see, issuing very selective commands requires a thorough knowledge of the table structure.

If you happen to have a table that contains duplicate records, T-SQL enables you to filter them with a DISTINCT keyword: T-SQL will return only the first occurrence of the record, ignoring the rest, as in the following example:

```
SELECT DISCTINCT  au_fname, au_lname , phone, state  from
Authors
WHERE state = 'CA' AND  au_fname = 'Cheryl'
```

So far you've learned query basics: the SELECT statement, the FROM clause, the WHERE clause, and the AND clause; you also learned that * means "all fields in the table," and that if you request specific fields, you must separate them from each other with commas. The following query will select information about all authors in the Pubs database living either in California or in Utah:

```
SELECT au_fname, au_lname , phone, state  from Authors WHERE
state = 'CA'
OR  state = 'UT'
```

What if you do not know what state Cheryl Carson lives in? You can combine several modifiers, such as AND and OR, in the same query.

```
SELECT au_fname, au_lname , phone, state  from Authors WHERE
au_fname = 'Cheryl' AND au_lname =' Carson' AND  (state = 'CA'
OR
state = 'UT')
```

**The uses of the SELECT statement can be much more complex than the samples given in this session. For full SELECT-statement syntax please refer to Books Online or a book specializing in T-SQL.**

As you learn more about T-SQL, you will find more than one way to achieve the results you want. The important thing is to understand your selection criteria and the order in which they are applied.

With the last query, T-SQL will return one and only one record (assuming that you do not have more than one person named Cheryl Carson in your Authors table). The results are quite different if you remove the brackets: Instead of the record pertaining to Cheryl Carson only, you will also receive records for completely irrelevant Utah residents. Why's that? The query is supposed to return all the records for a Cheryl Carson living in the state of California — as well as all the records for Utah residents, regardless of what their names are. If you apply brackets, you instruct SQL Server to return the records for any Cheryl Carsons that happen to live in California or Utah. The lesson here: Be careful what you query for.

You are in total control of the way the records appear in the final result set. If you want to combine one or more fields under a different name, this is the query you use:

```
SELECT au_fname + ',' + au_lname AS FullName, phone, state
from
Authors WHERE au_fname = 'Cheryl' AND au_lname =' Carson' AND
(state = 'CA' OR state = 'UT')
```

The values of the two fields — au_fname and au_lname — will be concatenated under the new field name FullName. The only restriction on this kind of concatenation is that the fields must be of compatible data types — meaning that you cannot concatenate character data and numeric data, for example, to produce one column.

T-SQL is a strongly typed language, which means that prior to using a variable in your code, you must declare it as being of a particular data type. The very basic data types are characters, numbers, and date/time values. SQL Server 2000 also introduces the new data type sql_variant, which can contain any of the basic types. Table 8-1 lists all supported data types.

**Table 8-1**

*SQL Server 2000 Supported Data Types*

| Numeric Data Types | Dates | Binary Data Types | Text Data Types | SQL server Special Data Types |
|---|---|---|---|---|
| decimal, float, smallint, tinyint, bit, int, real, money, bigint, smallmoney | timestamp, smalldatetime, datetime | binary, image varbinary | nchar, text, ntext, nvarchar, varchar, char | uniqueidentifier, sql_variant, sysname, NULL |

Using the correct data type saves resources and helps ward off implicit conversion errors. (Assigning a numeric value to a variable declared as varchar, for example, will result in an error message.)

**You may have noticed that I enclose values for the state and the names in single quotes. This is because T-SQL requires that all data assigned to a variable of character string type be so enclosed. Numbers — integers, doubles, and so on — do not require quotes.**

Now let's order the result set. To get a list of all Californian writers alphabetized by last name, issue the following request:

```
SELECT au_fname, au_lname , phone, state  from Authors WHERE
state = 'CA'
ORDER BY au_lname
```

The result is a list in ascending alphabetical order (from A to Y); with the ORDER BY clause, ascending order is the default. For descending alphabetical order, simply add the following modifier:

```
SELECT au_fname, au_lname , phone, state  from Authors WHERE
state = 'CA'
ORDER BY au_lname DESC
```

You have more options for arranging records in the result set, such as using the GROUP BY and HAVING clauses. These are more advanced options and require an understanding of aggregate functions, which I will explain in Session 10.

**20 Min.
To Go**

## Working with the JOIN and UNION Keywords

So far you have been querying only one table — but the whole point of a relational database is the ability to assemble information from related tables into one result set. Take a closer look at the Pubs database diagram, shown in Figure 8-3. I've selected four tables: Authors, Titles, Publishers, and TitleAuthors.

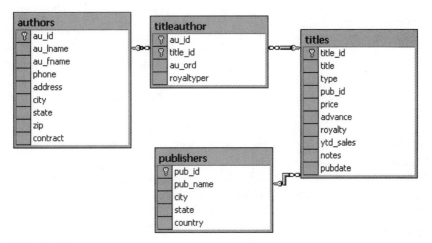

**Figure 8-3**
*Four selected tables from the Pubs database.*

The tables Authors and Titles are in a many-to-many relationship, because an author may have written more than one book, and a book may have been written by more than one author. The table AuthorTitles resolves this N:N relationship, replacing it with a one-to-many relationship between itself and each of the related tables. The table Publishers is related to the table Titles in a one-to-many relation-ship, because one publisher can publish many titles. In Figure 8-1 you can see this relationship diagram defined by primary and foreign keys in the related tables.

### The JOIN keyword

To enable you to assemble information from different tables into one result set, T-SQL provides you with the keyword JOIN. Five types of joins are at your disposal: INNER JOIN (also called NATURAL JOIN), LEFT OUTER JOIN, RIGHT OUTER JOIN, FULL OUTER JOIN, and CROSS JOIN. You choose which one to use when assembling information from one or more tables, based on the information you require.

When you join two tables with an INNER JOIN you are asking for matching data from both tables: For each row in one table there must be one row in the second table. Suppose you want to know what publisher published which title. You can use a command like the following:

```
SELECT  *  FROM  publishers INNER  JOIN titles ON
titles.pub_id =
   publishers.pub_id
```

The result set is comprised of rows from both Publishers and Titles. Of course, you could be more selective, as in the following example:

```
SELECT  *  FROM  publishers INNER  JOIN titles ON
titles.pub_id =
   publishers.pub_id WHERE titles.title = ' The Gourmet Microwave '
```

An OUTER JOIN will ask for additional rows from one of the tables even if no matching rows exist in the other table; fields returned from the table where no matching records exist will contain NULLs. This is where the RIGHT and LEFT keywords come in handy. LEFT OUTER JOIN will return all records for the table mentioned in the FROM clause — that is, all matching records from the JOINed table plus NULL records where no matching records were found. RIGHT OUTER JOIN does the opposite — the table mentioned in the FROM clause will be the one containing NULLs.

 **NULL values are not zero; they are a special data type indicating absence of any value in the field. When SQL Server evaluates the content of the fields, one NULL is never equal to another NULL unless you turned off the database option ANSI NULLS.**

The following query returns a result set, made up of 23 records, wherein rows 19 through 23 contain some data for the fields from Publishers and NULLs for the fields borrowed from Titles. This is because these five records represent publishers that have not published any books yet, and whose pub_id fields consequently have no matches in the Titles table.

```
SELECT * FROM publishers LEFT OUTER JOIN titles ON
   publishers.pub_id = titles.pub_id
```

While a publisher might not have published a single book yet, a published book must have at least one publisher: RIGHT OUTER JOIN, therefore, will yield results identical to those returned by INNER JOIN.

FULL JOIN will return all records in both tables only where they match.

CROSS JOIN will return a result set containing every possible combination of the rows in both tables. The following query will produce a result set consisting of 144 rows: the table Publishers contains 8 rows and the table Titles 18 rows, and 8 times 18 equals 144.

```
SELECT * FROM publishers CROSS JOIN titles
```

**There are two ways to define a JOIN between two (or more) tables — one that was introduced in SQL-89 and one that was introduced in the newer version SQL-92. Both are supported in SQL Server 2000, though there is strong indication that the old syntax has to go. The preceding query can be rewritten as follows:**

```
SELECT * FROM publishers WHERE publishers.pub_id =
titles.pub_id
```

**For the purpose of clarity this book will use the new syntax exclusively.**

After you learn how to join two tables, you can proceed to joining multiple tables.

Suppose you want to find all the titles published by authors living in California. Some of the required information is in the Authors table and some is in the Titles table: The query you use to extract it is a JOIN query. The JOIN query returns 17 records:

```
select T.title,A.au_lname,A.au_fname from titles as T
join titleauthor as TA on T.title_id = TA.title_id join authors
A
on TA.au_id = A.au_id where A.state = 'CA'
```

This is three-way inner join wherein table names are aliased for better readability — Titles is aliased to T, Authors to A, and TitleAuthors to TA. You can just as easily use the full table names.

**Though there is no limit on the number of the tables you can join in one query, use your common sense and keep joins to a minimum. Any more may have a negative effect on SQL Server performance.**

### The UNION keyword

The UNION keyword combines the results of two or more queries into a single result set. The following query produces a single-column result set of 40 records, the results from the second query being appended to the results from the first:

```
SELECT  title from titles UNION SELECT au_lname from authors
```

By default, the UNIONized result set will remove all duplicate rows; to include all records, use the ALL keyword. The following query returns 41 records. The previous query eliminated one duplicate record in the case of two people — Anne and Albert — with the last name Ringer.

```
SELECT  title from titles UNION ALL SELECT au_lname from authors
```

**10 Min.
To Go**

## Using the INSERT, UPDATE, and DELETE Keywords

Now that you have mastered the SELECT statement, INSERT, UPDATE, and DELETE are a breeze. Unlike SELECT, these keywords actually change the data in the table — and for this reason, you should exercise particular caution in using them.

### Using the INSERT keyword

INSERT inserts data into the table. To insert data into a table you must know not only the structure but also the data type of each field in this table. See Figure 8-4.

| Column Name | Data Type | Length | Allow Nulls |
|---|---|---|---|
| pub_id | char | 4 | |
| pub_name | varchar | 40 | ✓ |
| city | varchar | 20 | ✓ |
| state | char | 2 | ✓ |
| country | varchar | 30 | ✓ |
| | | | |
| | | | |

**Figure 8-4**
*The structure of the Publishers table from the Pubs database.*

Suppose that you want to add a new publisher to the Publishers table. I know that the columns to be filled are pub_id, pub_name, city, state, and country (see

Figure 8-1). The syntax for the INSERT statement looks like one of the following examples:

```
INSERT INTO PUBLISHERS (pub_name, pub_id, city, state ,country)
VALUES ('Alex Publishing','9912','Vancouver','WA','USA')
```

or

```
INSERT INTO PUBLISHERS VALUES  ('9912','Alex
Publishing','Vancouver','WA','USA')
```

You can omit the list of fields if the values are supplied in the same order in which the fields occur in the table.

If you look closely at the Publishers table structure in Figure 8-4, you'll notice a field called Allow Nulls; a check mark signifies that these fields allows NULL values, meaning that the INSERT query does not have to supply any values because NULL is assigned by default. The ability to allow NULLs is a useful feature — when you create a record you might not know the country of the publisher, or the state.

```
INSERT INTO PUBLISHERS (pub_id) VALUES ('9913')
```

After this T-SQL statement executes, the rest of the fields will be filled with NULLs waiting for UPDATE. It is important to pay attention to data types as well as to data range. For example, attempting to insert a five-character value into the field defined as char (4) — a character field allowing four characters — results in an error; attempting to insert a numeric value in a character field results in an error; attempting to insert out-of-range values such as 100,000 into an integer field results in an error.

## Using the UPDATE keyword

UPDATE modifies existing data. In the previous INSERT sample you inserted pub_id 9913 into the Publishers table and left all the other fields NULL; now imagine that you would like to update this record with some additional information.

By their nature UPDATE queries tend to be highly selective and — unless you want to change the value of each and every record in your table — should use the WHERE clause.

The following simple statement will change the value of the field pub_name to 'New Publisher' for every record in the Publishers table.

```
UPDATE Publishers SET pub_name = 'New Publisher'
```

If it is your intention to update only a single record, the following statement is more appropriate:

```
UPDATE Publishers SET pub_name = 'New Publisher' WHERE
pub_id = '9913'
```

One query can update more than one field at the same time, as in the following code:

```
UPDATE Publishers SET pub_name = 'New Publisher',
city='Portland',
    state ='OR' WHERE pub_id = '9913'
```

## Using the DELETE keyword

The DELETE keyword is very similar to UPDATE. As its name implies, it removes one or more records from the table. You must also be very selective when using it, unless you want to remove all records from the table. The following query deletes all records from the Publishers table:

```
DELETE   publishers
```

And this one removes only the record that you've just updated:

```
DELETE publishers WHERE pub_id = '9913'
```

As in the case of the UPDATE keyword, you can modify this query with calculated values, joins, and so forth.

**All these statements can be — and usually are — very complex if you use all the optional arguments. This brief introduction is by no means an exhaustive discussion of the proper syntax and usage for each of these statements, but rather a sample of some useful scenarios appropriate for beginners.**

## Knowing about Additional T-SQL Keywords and Functions

You can use the following keywords in your T-SQL queries right away:

- LIKE — When you know only some of your search criteria you can use pattern-matching with this keyword and wildcard characters (see Table 8-2).

- IS (NOT) NULL — Use this keyword to search the database for records in which a certain field is or is not NULL.

- RTRIM — It is not uncommon for data to contain trailing blank spaces. In the T-SQL world the values "Cheryl" and "Cheryl    " are not the same.

- LTRIM — LTRIM is essentially the same as RTRIM, except that it deals with leading blank spaces, such as in the value "    Cheryl."

**Table 8-2**
*Transact-SQL Wildcard Examples*

| Wildcard | Description | Query Example | Output |
|---|---|---|---|
| % | Consider any number of characters, before or after the sign | SELECT au_fname fromAuthors WHERE state = 'CA' and au_fname LIKE 'C%' | Cheryl Charlene |
| _ | Consider only one character in place of the underscore | SELECT au_fname<br><br>from Authors WHERE state = 'CA' and au_fname LIKE '_heryl' | Cheryl Sheryl |
| [ ] | Consider any single character within the specified range ([A-Y]) or set ([ABCYX]) | SELECT au_fname from Authors WHERE state = 'CA' and au_fname LIKE '[CS]heryl' | Cheryl Sheryl |
| [^] | Consider any single character that is not within the specified range ([^A-Y]) or set ([^ABCYX]) | SELECT au_fname from Authors WHERE state = 'CA' and<br><br>au_fname LIKE '[^C]heryl' | Sheryl |

**Done!**

---

## REVIEW

- Transact-SQL is a strongly typed programming language you need to master in order to query and manipulate data in the SQL Server relational database.
- Transact-SQL consists of keywords and operators that you combine with logic to produce code.
- INNER, OUTER, and CROSS JOINs help you to combine, update, or delete data from two or more tables.
- A Transact-SQL query can contain wildcards if the exact selection criteria are not known.

---

## QUIZ YOURSELF

1. What is Transact-SQL and how does it correspond to other SQL implementations?
2. What would you use the WHERE clause for?
3. What would you use the DISTINCT keyword for?
4. What is the difference between an INNER JOIN and an OUTER JOIN?
5. What keyword would you use with the UPDATE statement?
6. Why is it usually a good idea to specify the WHERE clause when issuing UPDATE and DELETE commands?

9

# T-SQL and SQL Query Analyzer

## Session Checklist

✔ Learning about T-SQL and SQL Query Analyzer

✔ Creating, altering, and dropping databases with T-SQL

✔ Creating, altering, and dropping tables with T-SQL

✔ Getting information about your SQL Server

✔ Working with Query Analyzer templates and the Object Browser

**30 Min.
To Go**

S QL Query Analyzer provides you with a way of executing ad hoc Transact-SQL (T-SQL) queries against a SQL Server database. You're going to learn how to use it with T-SQL batch commands to create, modify, and destroy various SQL Server objects (such as tables and databases). SQL Server provides you with a number of useful utilities such as the Object Browser, which you can use to facilitate developmental and administrative tasks.

## Learning about T-SQL and SQL Query Analyzer

If there were no way to execute them, T-SQL programs would be nothing more than an exercise in logic — amusing but useless. SQL Query Analyzer is a client utility that enables you to execute Transact-SQL statements and displays the results; it also enables you to analyze query performance.

You can start the SQL Query Analyzer in three ways: from the Programs ➪ Microsoft SQL Server startup menu, from the Tools menu in the Enterprise Manager console, or from the MS-DOS command-line prompt (with the command isqlw.exe).

Once Query Analyzer has started it will prompt you for a login and password; either supply this information or, if you have set up SQL Server to use Windows Authentication, just click OK. See Figure 9-1.

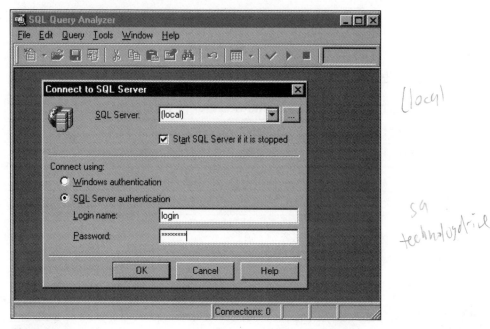

**Figure 9-1**
*Connecting Query Analyzer to SQL Server 2000.*

Try running several queries from the previous session to see whether they really produce the results they're supposed to. Enter the query shown in Figure 9-1 and press F5 to execute it (or click the small green triangle on the toolbar). Chances are that your screen will show something like what's shown in Figure 9-1. If it does not, check the drop-down list on the toolbar to make sure that your database context is Pubs and run the query again. See Figure 9-2.

```
SQL Query Analyzer                                                    _ □ ✕
File   Edit   Query   Tools   Window   Help
  ⌂ ▾ ⌂ ⊟ ⬚ │ ⅄ ⬚ ⬚ ⬚ ⬚ ⍾ │ ⋂ │ ⬚ ▾ │ ✓ ▸ ▪ │ ᴍ pubs       ▾ │ ⬚ ⬚ ⬚ │ ⬚ ⬚

Query - ALEX_KRIEGEL2\MYVERYOWNSQL.pubs.TEKLOGIX-VAN\akriegel - Untitled1*    _ □ ✕
  SELECT * FROM AUTHORS                                                        ▲


                                                                              ▼
◄                                                                          ►

     au_id          au_lname       au_fname       phone          address              city ▲
  1  172-32-1176   White          Johnson        408 496-7223   10932 Bigge Rd.       Menlo
  2  213-46-8915   Green          Marjorie       415 986-7020   309 63rd St. #411     Oakla
  3  238-95-7766   Carson         Cheryl         415 548-7723   589 Darwin Ln.        Berke
  4  267-41-2394   O'Leary        Michael        408 286-2428   22 Cleveland Av. #14  San
  5  274-80-9391   Straight       Dean           415 834-2919   5420 College Av.      Oakla ▼
◄                                                                          ►

 ▦ Grids  ▤ Messages
Query batch completed.  ALEX_KRIEGEL2\MYVERYOW!  TEKLOGIX-VAN\akriegel (54)  pubs  0:00:00  23 rows  Ln 1, Col 22
                                                                  Connections: 1
```

**Figure 9-2**
*Displaying the results of a T-SQL query.*

The results of the query are displayed in a table; you can use the Query menu on the toolbar to display them in a grid or in text form. You can also use the Query menu to save the results in a file.

Let's analyze what you see. The query requested all records from the Author table and 23 rows were returned. The topmost row in the results pane (shown in Figure 9-2) shows the names of the fields in the Authors table: au_id, au_fname, and so on. If you selected the Grid view option there are two tabs on the results pane: Grid and Messages. If you're displaying results in text Grid and Messages are displayed in the same pane.

The number of tabs on the results pane will vary depending on the execution mode you select. *Execution mode* refers to the type and amount of information you wish to collect about the query being executed; some of these modes require an advanced understanding of SQL Server and are better left alone for now.

**The Query Analyzer editor differentiates among T-SQL keywords, variables, and comments by coloring them differently. The palette and font are totally adjustable — if you prefer a different font or color scheme you can make the change by right-clicking inside the query pane and choosing Font from the pop-up menu.**

> **You can maintain several distinct connections to SQL Server through Query Analyzer windows, because each window in SQL Query Analyzer opens its own connection.**

Now that you have a tool I encourage you to go through all the queries you were presented with in the previous session and verify their accuracy. While you're doing that I suggest looking into the Query Execution Plan, one of the execution mode options. In short, the Query Execution Plan shows you all the steps the SQL Server Query Engine takes to process a query and return results. It shows you the total cost of each step, each operation performed, and so on, which can be very helpful in query optimization. I will cover it in more detail in Session 26; here I just want to point out that such an option exists.

## Creating, Altering, and Dropping Databases with T-SQL

In the previous session you learned about Data Query Language (DQL) and Data Manipulation Language (DML); now take a look at the basic Data Definition Language (DDL) statements.

### Creating databases

Using DDL syntax you can create and destroy virtually any object in SQL Server 2000 — DEFAULT, PROCEDURE, FUNCTION, SCHEMA, VIEW, and TRIGGER, to name just a few. Though different in their usage they all follow the same syntax:

```
CREATE <object type> <object name>
```

followed by the specifics of the particular object. The same rule applies to destruction:

```
DROP <object type> <object name>
```

In Session 7, you learned about creating a SQL Server database using a wizard; now take a look at the hardcore T-SQL that actually did the job.

While creating a database with all the options from T-SQL might be a daunting task, fortunately almost all of these options can be defaulted. A simple statement like the following would do the job:

```
CREATE DATABASE  MyDatabase
```

Leaving everything to its default might make your life easier in the short run, but can create problems in the future. With the preceding query you have no control over where the physical database files will be located, what the maximum size of the database and its log will be, how the database will grow, and so on. Using a simple template can help you to stay in control.

The basic syntax for creating a database is as follows:

```
CREATE DATABASE SampleDatabase
ON
( NAME = MyDatabase,
   FILENAME = 'C:\program files\MyData\mydatabasefile.mdf',
   SIZE = 10MB,
   MAXSIZE = UNLIMITED,
   FILEGROWTH = 1MB)
LOG ON
( NAME = MyDatabase_LOG,
   FILENAME = 'C:\program files\MyData\mydatabaselog.ldf',
   SIZE = 5MB,
   MAXSIZE = 25MB,
   FILEGROWTH = 5MB )
GO
```

You may want to change the path to change the location, which is fine as long as you make sure that the path is valid and the directories exist.

This T-SQL query creates a database called SampleDatabase with an initial size of 10MB and potential unlimited growth in increments of 1 MB. The physical file mydatabasefile.mdf will be placed into the directory C:\Program Files\MyData\; its log file will be created with an initial size of 5MB and will be limited to 25MB in increments of 5MB. You can specify many other options when creating a database; full database-creation syntax is available from SQL Server Books Online.

## Altering databases

You can add or remove files and filegroups from an existing database as well as change the name of the database, the names of files and filegroups, or even the size of a data file. The basic syntax is as follows:

```
ALTER DATABASE SampleDatabase
ADD FILE
(
 NAME = MyDatabase1,
```

```
FILENAME ='c:\program files\MyData\mydatabasefile2.ndf',
SIZE = 10MB,
MAXSIZE = 50MB,
FILEGROWTH = 1MB
)
```

## Dropping databases

The syntax for deleting a database is very simple:

```
DROP DATABASE  SampleDatabase
```

You can delete multiple databases at once by supplying a comma-delimited list of the databases to destroy.

```
DROP DATABASE  SampleDatabase, SampleDatabase1, SampleDatabase3
```

**Once you have dropped a database it disappears from the Enterprise Manager and the physical database files are deleted. Your only chance to restore it is by using full backups (covered in Session 18).**

# Creating, Altering, and Dropping Tables with T-SQL

Adding tables to your database is easy with the wizard and not much more difficult with raw T-SQL.

## Creating tables

Once you've decided on the table structure you can assemble T-SQL statements to bring your table into existence, as in the following example:

```
CREATE TABLE MyTable (
    Field1    int  PRIMARY KEY,
    Field2    char(10) NOT NULL),
    Field3    datetime
)
```

You need to specify fields' names and data types as well as whether certain columns can accept NULL as a valid value (by default a field does accept NULLs). Though you can use this table immediately after running a statement in the Query Analyzer to create it, there is a lot of room for improvement: You can specify a FOREIGN KEY, an index, computed fields, constraints, rules, default values, and more. These features will be covered in sessions 10, 16, and 26.

The table created with the preceding statement is stored permanently in your database and you can view it in the Tables collection of the Enterprise Manager. But sometimes you will need to create a table that you will soon discard. You can create a temporary table with an almost identical query:

```
CREATE TABLE #MyTable (
    Field1    int  PRIMARY KEY,
    Field2    char(10) NOT NULL),
    Field3    datetime
)
```

The pound sign (#) as the first character specifies that the table is temporary. Temporary tables can be either local or global, the difference being the degree of visibility: Local tables are accessible only to the connection in which they were created, while global tables are accessible to all processes in all current connections. The global temporary-table identifier is a double pound sign as the first two characters of the table name, as in ##MyTable.

Both local and global temporary tables are physically created in the TempDB database.

## Altering tables

To modify an existing table you can use the ALTER statement. With the following statement you can add or remove fields in the table, and add, drop, or disable constraints. (To modify a table you need to have the privileges of the database owner or administrator.)

```
ALTER TABLE MyTable ADD Field4 VARCHAR(10) NULL
```

To remove a field from the table, use the following command:

```
ALTER TABLE MyTable DROP COLUMN Field4
```

Some restrictions apply when you are adding fields to a table. This is the when a table already contains data; when rules exist; or if constraints or triggers are bound to the table. For the complete syntax, consult Books Online.

### Deleting tables

Deleting a table is just as easy as deleting an entire database:

```
DROP TABLE  MyTable
```

Temporary tables have a different life span from regular tables: If a temporary table is not explicitly dropped it will be dropped as soon as the last task referencing it is completed.

## Getting Information about Your SQL Server

**10 Min. To Go**

SQL Server provides you with a number of system functions that you can use to retrieve some important information about it. You can type these statements directly into the query window and see the results in the Messages tab, as shown in Figure 9-3. The following is a list of the most common functions; there are many more.

- SELECT ←NGUAGE displays the name of your SQL Server language.
- SELECT @@SERVERNAME displays the name of the SQL Server for the current connection.
- SELECT @@VERSION displays information about Microsoft SQL Server — version, build, edition, and so on.
- SELECT @@TRANCOUNT displays the number of open transactions for the current connection.
- SELECT @@ERROR displays an error number giving you a clue about the source of an error and the reason it occurred.

**I'll discuss SELECT@@TRANCOUNT in greater detail in Session 14.**

Cross-Ref

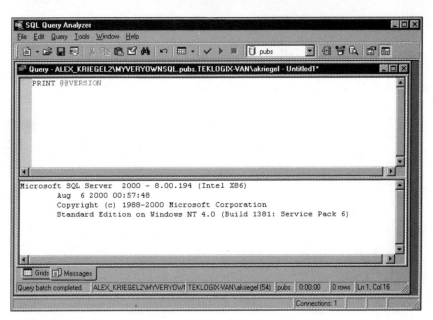

**Figure 9-3**
*Displaying return results of the system function.*

## Working with the Query Analyzer Templates and the Object Browser

SQL Server comes with a number of useful templates that will save you time in creating T-SQL programs. The templates are canned T-SQL framework solutions that you can modify for your own use. You can get to the Templates dialog either from the toolbar of the SQL Query Analyzer or from its Edit menu. Templates are available for every occasion: for creating databases, creating tables, managing indexes, moving databases from server to server, and more.

The Object Browser (see Figure 9-4) is another important feature provided to make your life easier. In addition to the Templates browser it also includes a full list of supported T-SQL functions and all supported system data types. The Object

Browser also provides a full description of the functions and their accepted parameters. Once you've decided which function to use, you can transfer its text (declaration and arguments) into the current pane of the Query Analyzer or a new pane. To do this, select the appropriate option from the right-click menu — it sure does reduce the amount of typing you have to do.

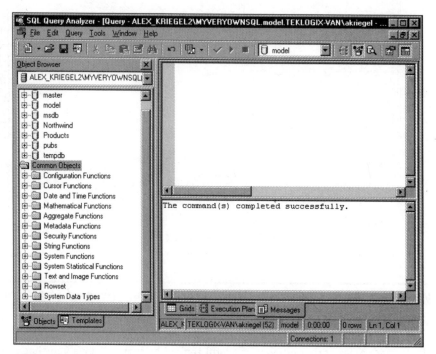

**Figure 9-4**
*SQL Server's Object Browser and templates.*

*Done!*

# REVIEW

- SQL Query Analyzer enables you to execute T-SQL queries directly against SQL Server and analyze the results.

- You can use T-SQL to create, modify, and delete various objects in SQL Server 2000, such as databases and tables.

- SQL Server 2000 contains a vast collection of system functions that you can use in your T-SQL code to perform specific tasks and retrieve system properties.
- Query Analyzer templates and the Object Browser provide you with an easy way to locate and use specific system functions, and reduce the amount of typing you have to do.

## QUIZ YOURSELF

1. What is the SQL Query Analyzer?
2. What parameter(s) is/are not optional when you're creating a database with T-SQL statements?
3. Where in SQL Server are temporary tables placed upon creation?
4. Is it possible to modify a table after it has been created?
5. How do you invoke the Object Browser?
6. What are system functions?

# Programming with T-SQL

## Session Checklist

✔ Declaring and using T-SQL variables

✔ Using control-of-flow statements

✔ Exploring T-SQL operators

✔ Working with aggregate functions

✔ Running subqueries

✔ Using the CASE function

**30 Min.
To Go**

**T**his session is about programming SQL Server 2000 using its own built-in language, Transact-SQL. You will learn how to produce working programs using T-SQL, as well as when and how to use variables, T-SQL operators, conversions, and aggregate functions.

## Declaring and Using T-SQL Variables

The concept of a variable is central to programming and T-SQL is no exception. A variable is a conceptual placeholder that can contain data and to which you, the programmer, can assign these data at will. Until a value is assigned to the variable, the variable is empty. For strongly typed languages like T-SQL, the assigned value of the variable must be of the same or a compatible data type.

In T-SQL, as in many programming languages, a variable must be declared prior to use. The syntax for declaring a variable is simple:

```
DECLARE @Counter    int
DECLARE @FirstName   varchar(25)
```

This declares a local variable named @Counter of type integer and a local variable @FirstName of type varchar, which is capable of holding up to 25 characters. You can declare several variables on the same line, as in the following example:

```
DECLARE @FirstName     varchar(25),  @Counter int
```

All local variables are preceded by the commercial at sign (@).

This example brings up another important concept — *scope of variables*. The variable declared in a stored procedure or a batch job is visible within it. You may find some literature that refers to names preceded by the double at sign (@@) as *global*, but in reality these are system functions that you learned about in the previous session. No true global variables exist in T-SQL, which means that you cannot share variables between connections.

 **See Session 11 for a discussion of stored procedures.**

The main function of variables is to store intermediate data, keep a counter for the loop, or return a single value from the stored procedure. You assign a value to a variable with code such as the following:

```
SET @Counter = 1
SET @FirstName = 'Alex'
```

If the assigned value is a result of a query, the syntax is different, as follows:

```
SELECT @FirstName = au_fname FROM authors where au_lname =
'Carson'
```

You need to understand what it means if a query returns more than one row. If the table contains more than one record in which the last name of the person is Carson, then the last record's au_fname value will be assigned to the variable @FirstName. For example, the following query, executed in the context of the Pubs database, returns two records in ascending alphabetical order (the default): first 'Albert' and then 'Anne'.

```
SELECT au_fname FROM authors WHERE au_lname = 'Ringer'
```

The query

```
SELECT @FirstName = au_fname FROM authors where au_lname =
'Ringer'
```

will put 'Anne' into the variable @FirstName.

T-SQL provides support for many different data types. It is important to use the correct data type in order to prevent errors. When dealing with financial data you may want to use the highest-precision numeric data type to avoid rounding errors, while for an inventory count you may want to use integers to speed up processing and consume fewer system resources.

Variables can be converted to different data types either explicitly or implicitly; no data type can be converted to *every* other data type, but every data type can be converted to *some* other data type.

### Implicit conversion

Implicit conversion is taken care of by SQL Server itself. It occurs either when a variable of one data type is assigned to another variable of a compatible data type, or when an operation, such as comparison, requires both variables to be of the same type. In either case you must understand the potential ramifications of an implicit conversion, which might introduce subtle, hard-to-catch bugs into your T-SQL program. Consider a situation wherein you have two variables, one of the float type and another of the integer type. The float-type variable holds a value representing your account, with all cents represented as digits after the decimal point, as follows:

```
DECLARE     @AccountValue       money
DECLARE     @IntermediateHolder     int
SET  @AccountValue = 1234.56
SET  @IntermediateHolder = @AccountValue
```

At this point SQL Server implicitly converts @AccountValue into an integer and @IntermediateHolder hereafter contains 1,234 dollars — your 56 cents are gone forever if you use @IntermediateHolder for future calculations.

## Explicit conversion

In order to convert from one type to another you need to use the special conversion functions CAST and CONVERT. These functions behave similarly, but CAST is preferable to CONVERT: It complies with SQL-92 standards, so you can use it when porting your SQL code to other vendors' products.

```
CAST ( expression AS data_type )
CONVERT ( data_type [ ( length ) ] , expression [ , style ] )
```

Here are some examples of explicit conversion. If for some reason you want to convert all postal codes from the Authors table into numbers, you use the following statement:

```
SELECT CAST (zip AS int) FROM authors
```

It might not be obvious why you would want to turn data represented as a character string into numbers. Consider the following: The ZIP field is of the varchar type and you cannot do arithmetic with characters, but you need to add up all the ZIP codes from the Authors table — your boss requires it for his astrological research. You can do this using CAST and the aggregate function SUM (covered later in this session). The result, by the way, is 1,904,317.

The following query using CONVERT will produce exactly the same result. You do not have to specify the length of the data for the basic type, as it is implied by default.

```
SELECT  SUM(CONVERT ( int , ZIP))  FROM authors
```

When converting date/time into strings you may want to add a third argument — style — to produce results of a specific format (such as *dd/mm/yyyy*). For the full syntax of this argument see Books Online.

Some data types cannot be converted into each other. Figure 10-1, taken from Microsoft SQL Server Books Online, specifies which data types can be converted to which others — implicitly or explicitly.

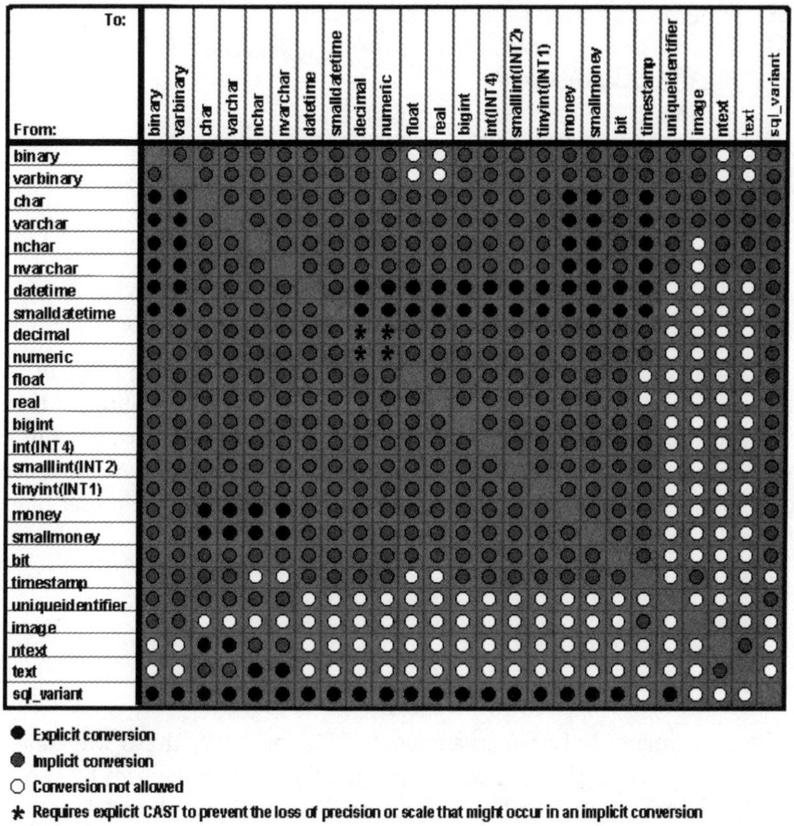

The following table (Figure 10-1) lists the data-type conversion options. The columns represent the "To:" types and the rows represent the "From:" types.

Columns (To:): binary, varbinary, char, varchar, nchar, nvarchar, datetime, smalldatetime, decimal, numeric, float, real, bigint, int(INT 4), smallint(INT 2), tinyint(INT 1), money, smallmoney, bit, timestamp, uniqueidentifier, image, ntext, text, sql_variant

Rows (From:): binary, varbinary, char, varchar, nchar, nvarchar, datetime, smalldatetime, decimal, numeric, float, real, bigint, int(INT 4), smallint(INT 2), tinyint(INT 1), money, smallmoney, bit, timestamp, uniqueidentifier, image, ntext, text, sql_variant

Legend:

- ● Explicit conversion
- ◉ Implicit conversion
- ○ Conversion not allowed
- ✱ Requires explicit CAST to prevent the loss of precision or scale that might occur in an implicit conversion

**Figure 10-1**
*Data-type conversion options.*

## Using Control-of-Flow Statements

Control-of-flow statements direct the execution path based on some condition.

A BEGIN...END statement defines a block that executes as one; it is usually followed by a WHILE, IF, or IF...ELSE statement.

The classic example is the IF...ELSE construct. Somewhere in your HR department database there might a T-SQL that runs once a year to update your salary in the Salaries table, using as its criterion your Social Security number:

```
DECLARE @increase  money
DECLARE @salary    money
```

```
SET @increase = $1000
SELECT @salary = salary FROM salaries WHERE ssn='123456789'
 IF @salary < $100000
    BEGIN
        SET @salary = @salary + @increase
        UPDATE salaries SET salary = @salary WHERE ssn =
'123456789'
    END
 ELSE
    PRINT 'HAVE A NICE DAY'
```

Often you need to organize a loop construct to scroll through a range of possible values. T-SQL provides the WHILE construct for this purpose. Suppose that management decides to give everybody a bonus — within its means, of course; management does not want the total of all employees' salaries to exceed a cool million dollars. So it will do incremental salary increases until the preset limit is met.

```
WHILE (SELECT SUM(bonus) FROM salaries) <= $1000000
BEGIN
    UPDATE salaries SET bonus = salary * 0.02
END
```

In the preceding code I used an aggregate function, SUM, that I will come back to later in this session. The loop will incrementally increase bonuses by two percent of the annual salary for all employees until the limit is reached. The check condition of the WHILE loop must evaluate to Boolean — true or false.

The loops can be nested: While updating bonuses you can also increase the number of vacation days, again based on some upper or lower limit.

To give you more control over the execution of a loop T-SQL provides two additional keywords to go with the WHILE statement: BREAK and CONTINUE.

BREAK triggers an immediate exit from the innermost WHILE loop and jumps to the line after END statement. If you are using nested loops you will need to use the BREAK statement for every loop in order to get out completely.

CONTINUE immediately returns you to the WHILE condition; not a single statement following CONTINUE will be executed.

RETURN is used in stored procedures (covered in the next session). It causes execution to stop immediately and returns results to the calling procedure or the client.

WAITFOR introduces a delay in the execution. The following statement will suspend execution until 6:15 p.m.; a statement on the next line will be executed after this time.

```
WAITFOR TIME '18:15'
```

You can also suspend the process for a certain amount of time, in the following example, it's five seconds:

```
WAITFOR DELAY '000:00:05'
```

One of the most maligned flow-control statements is the infamous GOTO:

```
IF @salary < 10000
    GOTO ask_for_raise
    many more statements here
ask_for_raise:
    UPDATE salaries SET salary = @salary * 0.1
```

This block of code will jump unconditionally to the label ask_for_raise (which you specify by adding a semicolon after the name), no matter where in the T-SQL program the block is located.

This keyword has been unanimously condemned by every professional programmer — for a reason. It causes a jump from the current statement to the place in your SQL program where it finds the specified label. It is easy to argue that frequent use of this keyword greatly reduces clarity and may lead to spaghetti code — hard to read, impossible to maintain. Nevertheless, I vouch for its validity when applied judiciously. For example, if one validation fails and you wanted to bypass all other validations, and you had several such validations in your procedure, would it not make sense to use GOTO to go to a CLEANUP label on condition of a failure?

## Exploring T-SQL Operators

**20 Min. To Go**

Once you've got variables you need tools in order to perform operations on them. SQL Server uses the following categories of operators:

- Arithmetic operators
- Comparison operators
- Logical operators
- Assignment operators

- String concatenation operators
- Unary operators

You have been using some of them for quite a while. Using bitwise operators requires a thorough understanding of programming concepts and low-level computer operations; I will touch on this subject only briefly.

## Arithmetic operators

Table 10-1 introduces five arithmetic operators you can use with your T-SQL programs.

**Table 10-1**
*Arithmetic Operators*

| Operator | Description |
| --- | --- |
| + | Addition |
| - | Subtraction |
| * | Multiplication |
| / | Division |
| % | Modulo (returns the integer remainder of a division) |

## Comparison operators

You use the comparison operators shown in Table 10-2 to evaluate expressions or specify selection criteria.

**Table 10-2**
*Comparison Operators*

| Operator | Description |
| --- | --- |
| = | Equal to |
| > | Greater than |
| < | Less than |

| Operator | Description |
|----------|-------------|
| >= | Greater than or equal to |
| <= | Less than or equal to |
| <> | Not equal to |
| ! = | Not equal to (SQL-89 standard) |
| ! < | Not less than (SQL-89 standard) |
| !> | Not greater than (SQL-89 standard) |

Examples of using comparison operators are shown throughout this session.

## Logical operators

Logical operators evaluate to true or false following the rules of Boolean algebra — they are, in fact, Boolean operators. The full list of the logical operators is given in Table 10-3.

**Table 10-3**
*Logical Operators*

| Operator | Description |
|----------|-------------|
| ALL | True if all of a set of compared values evaluates to true |
| AND | True if both expressions evaluate to true |
| ANY | True if any one of a set of compared values evaluates to true |
| BETWEEN | True if the value is within a specified range |
| EXISTS | True if a subquery (introduced later in this session) returns any records |
| IN | True if the result is equal to one in a list |
| LIKE | True if the result matches a pattern |
| NOT | Reverses the value of any other logical operator (such as NOT IN) |
| OR | True if either logical expression evaluates to true |
| SOME | True if some of a set of compared values evaluates to true |

The compared values or set of compared values is evaluated based on the operators' order of precedence.

### The assignment operator

Transact-SQL only has one assignment operator, and you've probably guessed it already — it's the equals sign (=). You use it when assigning values to variables or specifying column headings.

### The string concatenation operator

String concatenation is an operation you'll find yourself performing over and over again. Luckily, it is very intuitive — T-SQL uses the plus sign (+) to concatenate strings. You can use it in SELECT statements like the following:

```
SELECT au_fname + ',' + au_lname FROM authors
```

You can also use it to produce console output:

```
DECLARE @MyString  VARCHAR(40)
SET @MyString = 'concatenating' + ' ' + 'strings' + ' is ' +
'easy'
PRINT @MyString
```

### Unary operators

The unary operators listed in Table 10-4 work only on a numeric type of the variable. They enable you to use negative and positive numbers. The default for a number is positive — a number without a negative sign is considered positive.

**Table 10-4**
*Unary Operators*

| Operator | Description |
|----------|-------------|
| + | The number is positive |
| - | The number is negative |

The following sample creates two variables, assigns an integer value to one of them, and assigns the negative value of the first variable to the second.

```
DECLARE @Num1          int
DECLARE @Num2          int
SET @Num1 = 5
SET @Num2 = -@Num2
PRINT CAST(@Num2 AS VARCHAR(2))
```

In Books Online you also will find the bitwise unary operator (~), which performs the logical NOT operation.

## Operator precedence

*Precedence* determines the order in which operators will be executed. Pay special attention to the precedence of operators when assembling complex queries, because the order of execution affects the final results. Here are the operators, in order of precedence:

- + (positive), - (negative), ~ (bitwise NOT)
- * (multiply), / (divide), % (modulo)
- + (add), + (concatenate), - (subtract)
- =, >, <, >=, <=, <>, =, >, < (comparison operators)
- ^ (bitwise exclusive OR), & (bitwise AND), | (bitwise OR)
- NOT
- AND
- ALL, ANY, BETWEEN, IN, LIKE, OR, SOME
- = (assignment)

**You can influence the order of precedence by using parentheses, which causes the operators to be executed in the exact sequence you specify. Consider, for example, (x \* y - z) versus x \* (y - z).**

## Working with Aggregate Functions

I used some aggregate functions earlier in this session while explaining how to control flow statements. The syntax and usage of the aggregate functions is fairly intuitive. The general syntax is as follows:

```
<function's name> ( [ ALL | DISTINCT ] expression )
```

- DISTINCT tells the query to ignore duplicate values, and ALL is a default (for applying the function to all values).
- SUM returns the total of all the values in a numeric field, as in the example used earlier in this session:

  ```
  SELECT SUM(bonus) FROM salaries
  ```

- AVG returns the average of all the values in the numeric column:

  ```
  SELECT AVG(bonus) FROM salaries
  ```

- COUNT returns the number of records in the group:

  ```
  SELECT COUNT( DISTINCT au_lname) FROM authors
  ```

- COUNT(*) tells Transact-SQL to select all records fulfilling the condition.
- MAX returns the highest value in the column:

  ```
  SELECT MAX(bonus) FROM salaries
  ```

- MIN returns the lowest value in the column:

  ```
  SELECT MAX(bonus) FROM salaries
  ```

You can apply aggregate functions only to numeric columns, because aggregate functions can accept only numeric values as arguments.

**10 Min.
To Go**

## Running Subqueries

I mentioned earlier that you can use subqueries in logical expressions. The concept of a subquery is really simple — it's a query within a query, or a query within a query within a query, and so on *ad infinitum*. You'll typically use subqueries when the WHERE clause contains a selection criterion that must be calculated or selected on the fly from a table (usually an unrelated lookup table). The following query prepares a result set of all authors living in states wherein tax is lower than two percent:

```
SELECT  *  FROM  authors WHERE  state IN (SELECT state FROM
states
   WHERE tax < 2)
```

As you can see, the second query — the subquery, that is — returns a list of the states wherein tax is lower than two percent, and the first query selects only those authors who live in the states on this list. A statement in a subquery evaluates before the query: This means that states were selected before the search for authors began. If you can find a relationship between tables it is easy to rewrite the query with an equivalent JOIN statement.

You can use subqueries with UPDATE, DELETE, and INSERT statements.

**If you can use a JOIN operation instead of a subquery, I recommend using it; subqueries, though useful, are expensive in terms of system resources.**

## Using the CASE Function

In T-SQL the CASE function compares two or more values and returns some predefined result. Consider the following sample in which your boss wants a suggestion based on overall employee performance.

```
SELECT  Emp_FirstName + ',' + Emp_LastName,  suggestions =
   CASE rating
      WHEN  'excellent' THEN  'deserves a bonus'
      WHEN  'good'  THEN  'needs to improve'
      WHEN  'poor'  THEN   'ready to be fired'
      ELSE  'no suggestions'
   END
FROM employees
```

**To those who program in any other language, the CASE statement of T-SQL can be somewhat confusing. It is not equivalent to the CASE you might know from C or Visual Basic, but it is similar to the IIF function. For example, consider the following: variable = IIF( expression, true part, false part). In plain English, this means that if the expression yields true then the true part will be returned; otherwise, false part is assigned to the variable.**

No restrictions exist on the number of CASE statements you can have in your SELECT statement. You can apply CASE to every field (column) you wish to return in your result set.

**Done!**

## REVIEW

- Variables are the data holders you can use in your T-SQL programs to store various data types; a variable must be declared of a specific type and used to store data of this type.

- Some types can be converted into others implicitly, while others need to be converted explicitly.

- Control-of-flow statements enable you to control the program's execution path based on certain conditions.

- T-SQL supports a wide range of operators: Use them carefully, paying attention to precedence.

- Transact-SQL provides a number of aggregate functions for computational queries; an aggregate function computes a single value for a single column from a number of records returned.

- Subqueries always execute before the parent query; use them to specify selection criteria based on another selection.

- The CASE statement is a great tool for formatting returned data without resorting to row-by-row processing.

## QUIZ YOURSELF

1. Why do we need different types of data?
2. Can you share global variables between connections?
3. What is an implicit conversion? An explicit conversion?
4. How do you exit a loop construct?
5. Which operator takes the highest precedence?
6. Can you use aggregate functions on a column of the varchar data type?

# PART

# II

## Saturday Morning

1. What is a relational database and how is it different from a flat file or a spreadsheet?
2. What is referential integrity?
3. How is data integrity enforced in RDBMS?
4. What is the difference between a key and an index?
5. What databases are supplied with every SQL Server installation?
6. What is the purpose of the Master database in SQL Server?
7. Which SQL Server system database is a template database?
8. How do you resolve many-to-many relationships in RDBMS?
9. What is data normalization?
10. What is the purpose of the first normal form?
11. What components must you define for every database created in SQL Server?
12. How do you create a database with T-SQL?
13. What is the T-SQL syntax for deleting a database?
14. Which databases cannot be deleted from SQL Server?
15. How are SQL Server databases physically stored under Windows 2000?
16. What is the internal language of SQL Server 2000?
17. How do you execute T-SQL statements?
18. What is a variable? How do you declare one?
19. What value could be assigned to VARCHAR datatype.

20. What are the four basic queries in SQL?
21. What are the main control-of-flow T-SQL constructs?
22. What are the different types of joins and what do they do?

# PART

# III

## *Saturday Afternoon*

# Creating and Using Stored Procedures

## Session Checklist

✔ Creating stored procedures

✔ Commenting Transact-SQL code

✔ Handling errors

✔ Using different types of stored procedures

✔ Renaming and dropping stored procedures

**30 Min.
To Go**

**M**icrosoft SQL Server enables you to store compiled T-SQL statements as a special database object known as a *stored procedure*. Stored procedures in SQL Server are very similar to the procedures in other programming languages, though there are some important differences you should be aware of.

## Creating Stored Procedures

The T-SQL statements that you learned to write and execute in Sessions 8, 9, and 10 were compiled before being executed. The major difference between an interpreted program and a T-SQL program is that the latter is compiled all at once before it runs, whereas the former is compiled line by line. The difference between a stored procedure and T-SQL statements in the Query Analyzer window is that, unlike the stored procedure, the T-SQL batch is compiled and optimized *every* time it runs. As you may imagine, compilation is a time-consuming operation that will hinder performance.

Like standard functions, stored procedures can accept input parameters and return values to the calling procedure or batch as output parameters only; a function can return a value. Stored procedures can also return a status value, which can only be of the integer data type; this value is normally used to report success or failure of the procedure (0 for success and 1 for failure); a function's return value can be of any data type.

Functions are usually compiled into an executable and distributed; stored procedures are meaningless outside SQL Server.

The T-SQL statements that make up the body of a stored procedure can perform database operations like INSERT, DELETE, UPDATE, and SELECT as well as call another stored procedure(s).

Here is the basic syntax for a stored procedure:

```
CREATE PROCEDURE  <PROCEDURE NAME>
```

A stored procedure consists of a batch of T-SQL statements compiled under a specific name and adhering to specific rules. The following is a simple stored procedure named MyStoredProcedure that returns the total number of authors in the table Authors, which is contained in the Pubs database. It accepts no input parameters and returns an integer. Make sure that the code is executed in the context of the Pubs database.

```
CREATE PROCEDURE  MyStoredProcedure AS
    DECLARE @count_authors int
    SELECT @count_authors = COUNT(*) FROM authors
RETURN @count_authors
```

You can execute this batch from the Query Analyzer window or use the SQL Server visual interface.

You also can create a stored procedure through a visual interface shown in Figure 11-1. (Select a Stored Procedures node for a given database and then select New Stored Procedure from the right-click menu.) This interface enables you to do some useful things such as check the correctness of the syntax or save the stored procedure as a template for all future stored procedures you may create there.

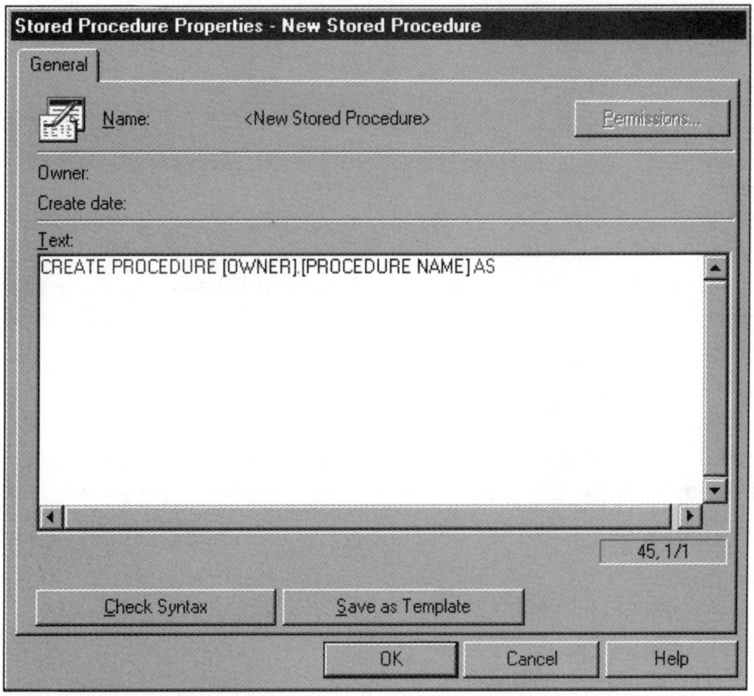

**Figure 11-1**
*Create a new stored procedure.*

Once you have created the stored procedure you can execute it from the SQL Query Analyzer window using the following syntax:

```
EXECUTE MyStoredProcedure
```

You can use a shorthand version: PROC instead of PROCEDURE and EXEC instead of EXECUTE.

In order to see the results this procedure returns you need to elaborate a bit: You must place a return value into a variable in the calling procedure. MyStoredProcedure returns an integer value that is subsequently assigned to the @result variable:

```
DECLARE @result int
EXECUTE @result = MyStoredProcedure
PRINT CAST(@result as varchar(5))
```

You cannot print an integer value in the Messages window without converting it into a text value first: use the CAST function to do that.

The following is an example of a stored procedure that accepts an input parameter of a string type and returns an integer:

```
CREATE PROCEDURE  MyStoredProcedure  @State AS
   DECLARE @count_authors int
   SELECT @count_authors = COUNT(*) FROM authors where
state=@State
RETURN @count_authors
```

To find the number of authors living in the state of California you use the following syntax:

```
DECLARE @result int
EXEC @result = MyStoredProcedure('CA')
```

The stored procedure can accept input parameters and return a value with output parameters (note the difference between stored-procedure return values and output parameters). Here is the syntax for a stored procedure returning parameters:

```
CREATE PROCEDURE  MyStoredProcedure
@state varchar(2),@count_authors int OUTPUT AS
    SELECT @count_authors=COUNT(*) FROM authors where state=@state
RETURN 0
```

The calling-statement syntax has changed — you need to send a variable into the stored procedure for the output parameter, as shown here:

```
DECLARE @result int
EXECUTE MyStoredProcedure 'CA', @result OUTPUT
```

 **You still have to convert between data types in order to print the output value; if a return parameter is varchar however, you can print it without conversion.**

**20 Min.
To Go**

## Commenting Transact-SQL Code

With the ability to create increasingly complex Transact-SQL programs comes the responsibility to comment your code. While comments might not be important in a single-line statement, they become of paramount importance in a complex stored procedure or batch implementing business logic. The reason for commenting code is simple — maintainability. Keep in mind that down the road, months or years from now, you or somebody else will have to make changes in the stored procedure to reflect changing business rules, and that without clear comments about what the stored procedure is expected to produce, and why a certain block of code was written, this will be very time-consuming. Comments in SQL Server come in two flavors: double-dash format and block format. A double dash in front of the line excludes it from the compilation process and therefore renders it non-executable as an inline comment, as shown in the following example:

```
CREATE PROCEDURE  MyStoredProcedure
- -  returns total count for authors in specific state
@state varchar(2),@count_authors int OUTPUT AS
        SELECT @count_authors=COUNT(*) FROM authors where state =
@state
RETURN 0
```

You can use block comments when more than one line of comments is required: Use the opening and closing slash/asterisk combination, as follows:

```
/* put your comments here
and continue for as many lines
as you wish as long as you remember to close
it with */
```

## Error Handling

Programming and debugging are two parts of the same process. Virtually all code ever written has needed to be debugged. Unfortunately, even the most thoroughly debugged and tested code might throw an exception under some unforeseen circumstances. It is well worth the effort to provide your program with the ability to trap an exception, handle it, and gracefully recover.

An *exception* is an error in a program that usually results in abnormal termination of the program unless special efforts have been taken to handle the error.

How do you know that an exception had occurred in your program — before the computer crashes, that is? Whenever your T-SQL code executes you can inquire about errors using the @@ERROR SQL Server function shown in the next example (0 indicates an error-free state):

```
    IF @@ERROR <> 0
BEGIN
            PRINT 'AN ERROR HAS OCCURRED'
        END
```

If you execute an error while generating a batch or stored procedure from within the Query Analyzer window, SQL Server will give you quite a bit of information about each error it detects. Table 11-1 lists some information you might expect about an error.

**Table 11-1**
*Components of SQL Server Errors Reported to Clients*

| Component | Description |
| --- | --- |
| Error number | The unique number assigned to this error |
| Error message | Concise information about the possible cause of the error |
| Severity | The seriousness of the error |
| State code | Additional information that you can use to diagnose a problem (the same error might have one or more causes, depending on the state of the system) |
| Procedure name | The name of the stored procedure that raised the error |
| Line number | The location; the line number of the T-SQL statement that generated the error |

Not all the information in the preceding table is available to you at all times; you may need to dig a little to get a coherent picture of what has happened.

If you trap the error to analyze it in a calling procedure then you may want to get all your error information from the master.dbo.sysmessages table; all the @@ERROR function returns is an integer representing the error code. Try executing the following code in the Query Analyzer:

```
SELECT  * FROM master.dbo.sysmessages WHERE error = 8134
```

Here is the result you will get:

```
error      severity    dlevel  description                          msglangid

-------    --------     ------  --------------------------          ---------
8134       16           0       Divide by zero error encountered     1033
```

(1 row(s) affected)

You also can define an error of your own based on some business-logic criterion specific to your application. You can do it by placing the RAISERROR statement anywhere in a stored procedure or batch. The general format is as follows (the first three arguments are required; those in brackets are optional):

```
RAISERROR (custom error message OR error message ID, severity
level, state, [argument (...n)], WITH [options...])
```

Here is an example of a custom error message, severity 3, state 5:

```
RAISERROR ('Guess what? An Error!!', 3,5)
```

Use your best judgment in selecting severity levels for your custom messages. Severity levels 0 to 19 are considered informational; they are used to report execution status or return some trace message. For example, level 10 reports status, levels 11–16 are for errors that can be corrected by user, level 18 is for non-fatal internal errors, and so on. Levels 20 to 25 indicate fatal errors from which the application cannot recover: Level 23 indicates a database-integrity problem, and level 24 indicates hardware failure. For a full list of severity levels please consult Books Online.

**It is easy to get carried away by defining a high custom level of severity; keep in mind, though, that if the severity level specified is 20 or higher, the client connection to the server is terminated after the error is returned. Also, the error is logged in both the error log and the application log.**

Again, you can hardcode in your stored procedure all the parameters that RAISERROR requires, or add your custom data to the sysmessages table using the system stored procedure sp_addmessage. The RAISERROR statement is very powerful and provides you with many options for formatting error information to supply as many details as possible. I encourage you to explore its full capabilities and take advantage of them.

Keep in mind that every application that accesses data in SQL server goes through layers of connectivity interfaces provided with SQL Server. Each layer may raise its own errors, such as OLE DB Provider, ODBC Driver, Enterprise Manager, Net Libraries, and so on. These errors will not be in the sysmessages table; look them up in the MSDN (Microsoft Developers Network) Library or in the documentation supplied with the application.

## Using Different Types of Stored Procedures

**10 Min.
To Go**

The following are the three categories of stored procedures:

- Temporary
- Nested and recursive
- System

I'll describe each in the following sections.

### Temporary stored procedures

As you may have guessed, a stored procedure can be temporary just as a table can be temporary, and just like a table the temporary stored procedure can be both local and global. The similarity extends to syntax as well:

```
CREATE PROCEDURE  #MyStoredProcedure
```

The preceding code creates a local temporary stored procedure; the following code creates a global temporary stored procedure:

```
CREATE PROCEDURE  ##MyStoredProcedure
```

Any connection with sufficient privileges has access to the global stored procedure; a temporary local stored procedure is visible within the context of the connection with which it was created. The life span of a local temporary stored procedure is the same as that of the connection, whereas a global temporary stored procedure exists as long as the current SQL Server session. Once the server is restarted all temporary stored procedures are gone.

## Nested and recursive stored procedures

A stored procedure can call another stored procedure, which in its turn can call yet another stored procedure, and so on for a total of up to 32 nested levels. No limit exists to how many stored procedures you can call from within a given stored procedure.

A stored procedure is a stored procedure and there is no reason why it cannot call itself. This is called *recursion* and refers here to a programming technique in which an output parameter is used as input for the next cycle (a call to itself) until a certain condition is met. The same nesting-levels rule applies to recursive stored procedures: They can call themselves for a total of up to 32 nested levels.

You can also use recursive stored procedures as an alternative to cursors (introduced in Session 13). The following example uses recursion to calculate a factorial and populate the Factorials table; it assumes the existence of such a table with two fields (Number and Result) of type integer:

```
CREATE PROCEDURE usp_FindFactorial
(
    @Number    int,
    @Result    int
) AS
-- e.g. 5! = 5 * 4 * 3 * 2 * 1
-- multiply result
SET @Result = @Result * @Number
-- decrement number
SET @Number = @Number - 1
-- check that you get the value and limit of recursions is not
-- exceeded
IF @@NESTLEVEL <=32
    BEGIN
        IF @Number = 1
            BEGIN
INSERT INTO Factorials (Number,Result)
VALUES((@@NESTLEVEL+1),@Result)
            RETURN 0
                END
        ELSE
        -- not yet, continue multiplication
        EXEC usp_FindFactorial @Number, @Result
    END
GO
```

You call the preceding stored procedure from the SQL Query Analyzer with the following syntax to calculate the factorial of 5. The values will be stored in the Factorials table:

```
EXEC  usp_FindFactorial 5,1
```

This example will not work for numbers greater than 12 (it is limited by data-size restriction), but it serves to illustrate the principle.

**A stored procedure written in T-SQL has all the strengths and weaknesses of SQL itself. Sometime you need to access functionality beyond what is provided by SQL Server and T-SQL. Microsoft SQL Server enables you to invoke an extended stored procedure implemented as a Dynamic Linked Library (DLL), usually in C/C++. Extended stored procedures comply with the same calling conventions as regular stored procedures.**

## System stored procedures

Microsoft SQL Server 2000 uses stored procedures extensively: It comes with a number of precompiled system stored procedures to assist you in performing various tasks that are difficult or dangerous to perform directly (such as querying system tables).

The system stored procedures are stored in the Master database. Microsoft SQL Server 2000 comes with 930 canned system stored procedures.

Every system stored procedure starts with the prefix sp_ and is callable from any database without a fully qualified path; similarly, any custom stored procedure with the prefix sp_ that is stored in the Master database can be executed from any database within a given SQL Server installation.

**I'll discuss system stored procedures at greater length in Session 23.**

## Renaming and Dropping a Stored Procedure

Once created, a stored procedure can be renamed. The easiest way to rename a stored procedure is from the same menu you would invoke when creating a new stored procedure through the Enterprise Manager interface. Behind the scenes the following Transact-SQL system stored procedure is executed:

```
sp_rename  <OldName>,  <NewName>
```

## The Advantages and Disadvantages of Using Stored Procedures

The following are the major advantages of using stored procedures:

- T-SQL statements for the stored procedure are compiled and optimized only once, and thus execute quickly.

- Stored procedures introduce the benefits of structured programming to the otherwise unstructured Transact-SQL. Dividing the logic and implementing it in a number of stored-procedure modules makes debugging and making changes easier, because you can recompile one stored procedure without affecting another (as long as you do not change the input and output parameters).

- Several applications can reuse a single stored procedure: You can create your own library of stored procedures and use these precompiled and presumably bug-free modules to build your application.

- A built-in security mechanism enables you to assign privileges for executing particular stored procedures.

- Stored procedures consume relatively few resources, both in terms of network traffic for distributed applications (compare the transfer of tens of lines of T-SQL statements to the transfer of a single line representing the name of the stored procedure), and in terms of memory and system resources for compilation and optimization.

The following are the major disadvantages of using stored procedures:

- Once you are using a stored procedure control over database logic is no longer with a client application; you will need administrative privileges to create or modify a stored procedure.

- The business logic of the client application becomes dispersed among separate objects — applications and stored procedures — which makes maintaining the logic somewhat difficult.

*faste*

**Part III—Saturday Afternoon**
**Session 11**

You can execute this system stored procedure directly from the Query Analyzer.

To remove a stored procedure from the procedures collection for any given database you follow the same conventions you would follow for any other database object: Select the right-click menu option Delete, or direct the execution of the underlying T-SQL statement and issue the following command:

```
DROP  PROCEDURE   MyStoredProcedure
```

Be aware that renaming a stored procedure does not change the name inside any other stored procedure that is used to call that stored procedure by its old name: Unless you manually replace the old name with the new one, this can cause errors. Similarly, dropping a stored procedure does not remove references to it from any calling procedure or client application.

*Done!*

## REVIEW

- Stored procedures are compiled blocks of Transact-SQL Statements stored within SQL Server under unique names.
- You use different types of stored procedures in different situations.
- It is important to comment your stored procedures for maintenance purposes.
- You need to properly handle any error your stored procedure may produce.

## QUIZ YOURSELF

1. Is a stored procedure interpreted or compiled?
2. How do you return results from a stored procedure?
3. What is the syntax for inserting inline comments into T-SQL code?
4. Why do you need error-handling code in your stored procedures?
5. What are the advantages of using stored procedures as opposed to T-SQL batch statements?

# Trigger Happy

## Session Checklist

✔ Introducing triggers

✔ Managing triggers

**30 Min.
To Go**

**T**riggers are a powerful SQL Server mechanism for implementing complex business logic and maintaining database integrity. In this session you are going to learn about the different types of triggers and their implementations, and how to create and use them. You will also learn when and when not to use triggers, and about some alternatives.

## Introducing Triggers

Triggers are in virtually all RDBMSes as a means of enforcing business logic in a relational database. In essence a trigger is no different from a stored procedure (see Session 11). What makes a trigger different from a stored procedure is how it executes: Unlike a stored procedure, which you have to call by name, a trigger executes (fires) automatically in response to some event.

**Triggers are one of the advanced features of SQL Server and ought to be implemented with caution, as there are so many options and conditions to be taken into account. This session is only a brief introduction to the most essential aspects of triggers.**

A trigger is created for a specific base table or view and cannot exist without one. Three events can fire a trigger: an UPDATE, DELETE, or INSERT statement executed on the table that the trigger is associated with. Each of these events fires a specific trigger designed specifically for it, and this enables you to apply complex business logic to the data being INSERTed, DELETEd, or UPDATEd.

Once you read past Session 16 you will be able to compare triggers to SQL Server constraints (such as CHECK constraints or FOREIGN KEY constraints) and decide which is more efficient in any given situation; for now triggers are the only thing you have learned about that is capable of validating data against rules that make your database a system.

There are four types of triggers:

- AFTER
- INSTEAD OF
- Recursive
- Nested

Though a trigger creating T-SQL statements can be very complex if all the options are specified, the basic syntax for creating a trigger is as follows:

```
CREATE TRIGGER <trigger name> ON <table name>
    AFTER|FOR UPDATE,INSERT,DELETE
AS
<Transact SQL statements>
```

**As you may have noticed, you can use two keywords for AFTER triggers: AFTER and FOR. These keywords are identical in their action and I speculate that FOR is provided only for compatibility with previous versions of SQL Server. AFTER is a default type of SQL Server trigger.**

Another type of trigger, INSTEAD OF, has a slightly different syntax, reflecting its specific status:.

```
CREATE TRIGGER <trigger name> ON <table name>
    INSTEAD OF [UPDATE,INSERT,DELETE']
AS
<Transact SQL statements>
```

You can create triggers through the Query Analyzer or the Enterprise Manager's console, much as you would create a stored procedure. The only difference is that the trigger is tied to a particular table. From the Tables collection select a table you'd like to create a trigger for; then from the right-click menu select All Tasks ⇨ Manage Triggers, as shown in Figure 12-1. 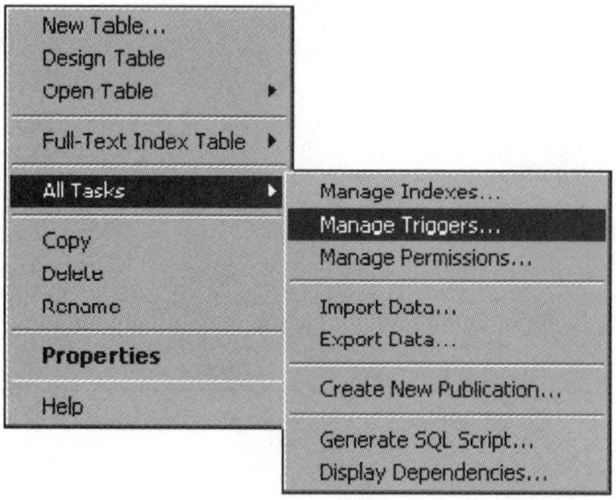

**Figure 12-1**
*Managing triggers through the Enterprise Manager interface.*

In the following sections we'll look at these and other triggers in more detail.

## AFTER triggers

There were only two types of triggers available with earlier versions of SQL Server — FOR and AFTER. These types of triggers began working after data in the table was modified; as I mentioned before, though featuring different keywords, these triggers are identical in their action. They are fully supported in SQL Server 2000 as well.

Let's say that in your database there is a table into which you record data about your employees' salaries, and that you do not want to give your employees raises of more than twenty percent at a time. You can control this action with a trigger. In Figure 12-2, I show you how to create a trigger using the Enterprise Manager console (you can run the same code from the Query Analyzer):

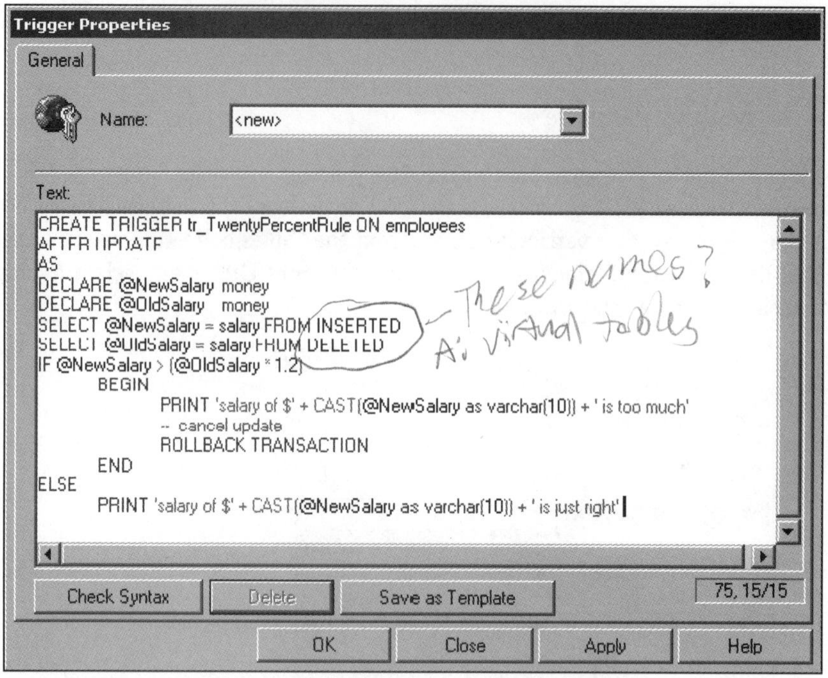

**Figure 12-2**
*Creating, modifying, and deleting triggers.*

If you are updating the record from the Query Analyzer window the appropriate message will be printed; alternatively, you can choose to raise an error to a calling application or just silently log this error into a table. This Transact-SQL code uses the concept of transaction. Though I will discuss transactions later (in Session 16), it is important to understand now that the operation (INSERT in my sample) and the trigger comprise a single block that either succeeds or fails as a whole; ROLL-BACK TRANSACTION rolls back the whole transaction, nullifying the update — the data in the Employees table will remain as it was before the update.

SQL Server also introduces two virtual tables, INSERTED and DELETED, for use with triggers. When data is about to be modified by insertion, updating, or deletion there is no guarantee that the operation will be completed: Some business logic implemented as constraints (Session 15) or triggers may prevent this. SQL Server creates INSERTED and DELETED automatically whenever a particular action occurs. The DELETED table contains rows as they were prior to the modification, and the INSERTED table contains modified rows, as does the base table itself (remember, the trigger fires *after* data is modified). The number of rows in each table matches exactly the number of rows affected by the T-SQL statement.

**These tables are to be used for information only; you cannot directly access them to modify data.**

Now, the preceding sample implies that only one row at the time will be updated. This is not always the case. You can update one row at a time with the modified records by organizing a loop or using a *cursor* (covered in Session 13). From the trigger's code you can access any other table.

**I use PRINT statements in the trigger to make the results more visual, assuming that you execute all UPDATE statements from the Query Analyzer. Normally triggers are not supposed to print messages or otherwise visually manifest their action.**

You can define a single AFTER trigger to respond to UPDATE, DELETE, or INSERT actions, or you can define one trigger per action. You can even define multiple triggers for the same action, as long as they have different names.

The sequence in which the same-action triggers are executed is usually determined by the sequence in which they were created; you can partially override this default by using a system stored procedure, sp_settriggerorder, as shown in the following code:

```
EXECUTE sp_settriggerorder  trg_UpdateAction2, first, 'update'
EXECUTE sp_settriggerorder  trg_UpdateAction1, last, 'update'
```

Using this stored procedure you can only specify which trigger will be executed first and which will be executed last; the rest of the triggers will execute in the order in which they were created.

**20 Min. To Go**

## INSTEAD OF triggers

INSTEAD OF triggers are new to SQL Server 2000. They can perform some validating action *before* any data are inserted into the table, and are normally used to implement updates on views that normally do not support updates.

Unlike with AFTER triggers, there can be only one INSTEAD OF trigger for each INSERT, UPDATE, or DELETE. The INSTEAD OF UPDATE, INSTEAD OF DELETE, and INSTEAD OF INSERT triggers will be executed before any AFTER triggers get a chance, effectively preventing them from being executed — ever.

You can encrypt triggers or stored procedures to prevent anyone from looking into your source code. Just add the modifier WITH ENCRYPTION right before the AS keyword.

## Recursive triggers

A trigger can call itself *recursively* (if the database option that allows it is set to true). For example, if a FOR UPDATE trigger contains an UPDATE statement for the base table, this trigger will be called again as this UPDATE executes, and again, and yet again. The maximum number of recursive calls is 32, which is also the maximum nesting depth. While a valid programming tool, recursive triggers can be tricky to write and you should exercise caution in using them.

Besides implementing business logic, triggers are mainly used to enforce referential integrity (see Session 5). Though the best way to maintain referential integrity is normally to use the FOREIGN KEY constraint, triggers and stored procedures become a viable alternative in some situations. Check out Books Online or some advanced books on SQL Server 2000 for some examples of such situations.

## Nested triggers

Triggers can be nested. They follow the same rules defined for stored procedures and cannot exceed 32 levels. One example of nested triggers can be a table whose FOR UPDATE makes an INSERT into the same table, thus invoking a FOR INSERT trigger, which in turn invokes a FOR DELETE trigger. It is possible that one trigger will invoke another that in turn invokes the first one, causing a so-called *indefinite loop*. Because of the maximum depth of nesting levels, this loop will stop after 32 cycles. The SQL Server 2000 default setting allows nested triggers. You can disable this option on the Server-level right-click menu by selecting Properties followed by an option on the Server Settings menu, or by executing the following system stored procedure:

```
exec sp_configure 'nested triggers', 0
```

**Disabling nested triggers will automatically disable recursive triggers, regardless of the setting you may have in your database. Recursive triggers are a special kind of nested triggers.**

## Managing Triggers

**10 Min. To Go**

The easiest way to manage triggers is through a visual interface (see Figure 12-1). You can view, modify, or delete a trigger. Behind the scenes, SQL Server will assemble and execute a batch of T-SQL statements; you can, of course, also create and execute these statements yourself.

Triggers are powerful, built-in tools for implementing business rules in the SQL Server database as well as for enforcing referential integrity. I strongly recommend reading Session 16, "Understanding Transactions and Locks," before attempting any real-life implementations.

### Creating triggers

To create a trigger, simply run the code shown in Figure 12-2 from a Query Analyzer window.

### Dropping (deleting) triggers

To drop/delete a trigger, use the following syntax:

```
DROP TRIGGER <trigger name>
```

You can drop more than one trigger at the same time by specifying a list of triggers. Dropping a trigger does not affect its base table.

**You can remove a trigger by dropping it or by dropping the table that it is associated with. When a table is dropped, all associated triggers are also dropped.**

## Modifying triggers

The easiest way to modify a trigger is to drop it and then create another one under the same name. If, for whatever reason, you need to preserve the trigger's internal ID (a unique number under which the trigger is listed among system objects), you can use the ALTER TRIGGER statement. The T-SQL code following the AS keyword will replace the original code :

```
ALTER TRIGGER tr_TwentyPercentRule ON employees
    AFTER UPDATE
AS
    PRINT    'NO MORE RULES'
```

**You can quickly view the information about triggers defined on a table by using the system stored procedure sp_helptrigger. The syntax is as follows: exec sp_helptrigger <table name>**

**Done!**

## REVIEW

- Many different types of triggers exist; each has a different use.
- You manage triggers as you would any other SQL Server database objects: either with T-SQL commands or through the Enterprise Console manager.

## QUIZ YOURSELF

1. What is a SQL Server trigger?
2. How is a trigger different from a stored procedure?
3. What are the SQL Server trigger types?
4. In response to what events would a trigger be fired?

# *Introducing Cursors*

## *Session Checklist*

✔ Using different types of cursors

✔ Understanding the scope of cursors

✔ Setting cursor concurrency options

✔ Choosing the right cursor

**T**his session introduces Transact-SQL cursors, a very powerful programming tool for data manipulation. You will learn about different types of cursors, their advantages and disadvantages, programming considerations affecting cursors, and how to choose the right cursor for any given job.

**30 Min.
To Go**

## *Understanding Cursors*

In the SQL Server environment sets are the most efficient means of accessing or modifying data, and you should use them whenever possible. For everything else there is a *cursor*. Cursor is an extension provided by SQL Server to enable you to work with result sets returned by SELECT statements — one row at the time. From examples in previous sessions you should have a general idea of what will be returned by the following statement on the Pubs database:

```
SELECT * FROM authors WHERE state = 'CA'
```

This statement returns a result set of 15 rows. This is the result set you are working with and there is no way to access a single row within this result set without losing the rest of the rows. That is, unless you are using a cursor. If you want to update each record in a table differently, you either have to run a different query for each row, or use a cursor.

You can request a cursor in SQL Server in two ways: inside the server itself by using Transact-SQL statements, or via a client application by using one of the supported interfaces, such as Microsoft Active Data Objects, ODBC (Open Database Connectivity), OLE DB (the latest database interface from Microsoft), or DB-Library (a low-level programming interface to SQL Server). In this session I will concentrate mainly on server-side cursors created with Transact-SQL.

The basic syntax for declaring a simple cursor is similar to a standard T-SQL batch statement:

```
DECLARE  cur_California CURSOR FOR
SELECT * FROM authors WHERE state = 'CA'
```

Since the primary reason for opening a cursor is to scroll it, all cursors are scrollable (that is, you can navigate from record to record sequentially). In the interest of preserving system resources the default scrolling is forward-only; if you need to scroll backward, you open a specific type of cursor. (I'll go into more detail about cursor types later in this session.)

Once a cursor is declared you need to OPEN it so it can be populated with records:

```
OPEN cur_California
```

Once the cursor is open you can access the data by scrolling the cursor. In order to retrieve a row from a cursor you have to FETCH it as shown here:

```
FETCH NEXT FROM cur_California
```

FETCH instructs SQL Server to retrieve a single row from the result set contained in the cursor. Once you've examined the content of this row it is time to move on as follows:

```
WHILE @@FETCH_STATUS = 0
BEGIN
```

The following code is executed as long as the previous FETCH succeeds:

```
    FETCH NEXT FROM cur_California
END
```

You have to organize a loop to scroll the cursor and you also need to know when to stop. The system function @@FETCH_STATUS will let you know when you reach the end of the cursor: 0 means that a row was successfully FETCHed, and anything else means that the FETCH NEXT statement failed. Once you are through with the cursor you need to explicitly close and destroy it:

```
CLOSE   cur_California
DEALLOCATED. cur_California
```

**Note**

**Closing and de-allocating cursors is very important. An open cursor takes up a lot of memory that will not be freed until the cursor is closed and de-allocated; nor will you be able to open another cursor with the same name.**

If you run all the T-SQL statements introduced earlier in this session as a batch from the Query Analyzer window, in your Results pane you will see 15 separate rows as opposed to a single result set of 15 rows.

In the preceding sample you FETCHed the whole row. It is possible to FETCH only the fields (columns) you are interested in; you can also declare a cursor on a join. You can use any valid T-SQL SELECT statement to produce a cursor.

Here is an example of creating and scrolling a cursor containing records of the last names and first names of the authors living in California, ordered alphabetically by last name:

```
USE Pubs
DECLARE  @FirstNameVARCHAR(20)
DECLARE  @LastName VARCHAR(20)

DECLARE  cur_California CURSOR FOR
SELECT au_lname,au_fname FROM authors WHERE state = 'CA' ORDER BY
au_lname
OPEN cur_California

FETCH NEXT FROM cur_California INTO  @FirstName, @LastName

WHILE @@FETCH_STATUS = 0
BEGIN
PRINT  @LastName+ "," + @FirstName
```

The following code is executed as long as the previous FETCH succeeds:

```
        FETCH NEXT FROM cur_California INTO  @FirstName, @LastName
END

CLOSE  cur_California
DEALLOCATE  cur_California
```

The result of this batch executed from the Query Analyzer will be a comma-delimited list of all authors' first and last names.

## Using Different Types of Cursors

**20 Min.
To Go**

According to your particular needs you may choose one of the four following types of cursors:

- Scrollable cursors
- Static cursors
- Dynamic cursors
- Keyset cursors
- Forward-only cursors

You specify the type of cursor you want through a specific modifier in the declaration statement, as shown here:

```
DECLARE  cur_California CURSOR STATIC FOR
SELECT au_fname, au_lname FROM authors  WHERE state = 'CA'
```

I discuss each type of cursor in the following sections.

### Scrollable cursors

So far you have only scrolled the cursor forward. Forward-only is the default for any cursor type that opens for which no options are specified. To get a scrollable cursor that scrolls both ways, you should ask for one:

```
DECLARE  cur_California CURSOR SCROLL FOR
SELECT au_fname, au_lname FROM authors  WHERE state = 'CA'
```

Now you can move backward and forward. You can navigate a cursor using the FETCH command.

- FETCH PRIOR — Moves to the previous record in the result set.
- FETCH FIRST — Moves to the first record in the result set.
- FETCH LAST — Moves to the last record in the result set.
- FETCH ABSOLUTE *number* — Retrieves a specific position within the result set (FETCH ABSOLUTE 4, for example, retrieves the fourth record from the beginning.) The number you specify must be a positive integer.
- FETCH RELATIVE *number* — Works like FETCH ABSOLUTE, with the exception that the count starts from the current row: If you are on the fourth record in your result set FETCH RELATIVE 3 will take you to the seventh row from the beginning. The number you specify must be a positive integer.

**You should always check @@FETCH_STATUS to verify that the record was retrieved. At the beginning of the result set FETCH PRIOR does not yield any results and @@FETCH_STATUS is -1; when you are trying to fetch a row that was deleted after the cursor was opened, @@FETCH_STATUS is -2. The value of @@FETCH_STATUS is global to all cursors created on a particular connection, meaning that all cursors you happen to create and that have not yet been destroyed will affect its value.**

## Static cursors

Static cursors represent snapshots of the data: Once created, a static cursor does not reflect any subsequent changes to the underlying data. Static cursors in SQL Server are always read-only. They are the least resource-intensive scrollable type of cursor.

## Dynamic cursors

Dynamic cursors, as their name implies, never lose a contact with the data from which they were created. Every modification (INSERT, UPDATE, or DELETE) is visible through this cursor — that is, if it has been made through the cursor itself or committed to the database by other clients (to see uncommitted modifications made by others to the same set of data requires more advanced techniques). The dynamic cursor is always scrollable.

### Keyset cursors

KEYSET cursors behave almost exactly like DYNAMIC cursors, with the exception that the KEYSET cursors are — well — keyset-based. A *keyset* is a unique set of columns that the cursor's SELECT statement contains, and only these values are guaranteed to be there while you are scrolling the cursor. When you OPEN the cursor the list of all key values is created in TempDB, a workbench for all databases in the SQL Server system. The keyset membership is fixed — after the cursor is OPENed, only the data present at that moment will be available for viewing.

### Forward-only cursors

The forward-only cursor does not support scrolling, which means that you can only use FETCH NEXT — there's no going back. The cursor is not built upon executing the OPEN statement; the FETCH NEXT command fetches the row directly from the database.

## Understanding the Scope of the Cursors

By default, the cursor is global for the connection it was created with. This means that unless you close and de-allocate the cursor, you can use it throughout every T-SQL batch you execute on the connection. While this is certainly a convenient feature, you must be careful not to keep the cursor open longer than necessary. This is because SQL Server will generate an error if a T-SQL block or batch tries to open the same cursor before you close it. If you forget to de-allocate the cursor it will be hanging around until the connection to the SQL Server is closed.

If you want to create a local version of a cursor you must explicitly state this at the database-settings level by setting CURSOR_DEFAULT to LOCAL (it is set to GLOBAL by default), or specifying it in the declaration of the cursor, as in the following example:

```
DECLARE  cur_California CURSOR LOCAL FOR
SELECT * FROM authors WHERE state = 'CA'
```

Local cursors are visible only within the batch with which they were created and last only as long as it takes that batch to execute; they are implicitly de-allocated afterwards.

> **If you need to perform another cursor operation while scrolling a cursor, feel free. Unlike nested stored procedures or triggers, cursors are not limited to any nesting depth. Just keep in mind that the @@FETCH_STATUS function is global for the whole connection and that both cursors will affect it.**

**10 Min. To Go**

## Setting Cursor Concurrency Options

Concurrency can become an issue in a fast-paced environment wherein many users are working on the same data set. How can users be sure that their changes are not being accidentally overridden by other users? By preventing anyone from modifying the record until you're done — in other words, by placing a lock on it — you can protect your changes. If you think that there's a good chance that somebody else will try to modify the data while you are working with them, you may try other options.

SQL Server 2000 supports four concurrency options:

- **READ_ONLY** — Use this option when you need only to see the data, not to modify it; this option uses the least system resources.

- **OPTIMISTIC WITH VALUES** — Use this option when you do want to update your data but estimate that the chances that a second user might try to update the same record at the same time are very slim: Any other user will get an error notification upon trying to update values that you've just changed.

- **OPTIMISTIC WITH ROW VERSIONING** — Use this option when you are still optimistic and prepared to take your chances, but want to make sure that only the whole row can be updated, not just some fields within it.

- **SCROLL_LOCK** — Use this option when you trust no one: Nobody can modify a thing in the result set affected by your cursor until you are through with it.

Unless you are using a cursor within a transaction (see Session 16), the cursor does not lock the records it was created against. This means that while you are scrolling your cursor somebody else can modify the underlying data. Depending on the type of cursor you are using you might not be aware of the changes until you close the cursor and reopen it. DYNAMIC cursors let you see the changes as they come — but you must take precautions in order to manipulate them correctly. By placing a lock on the underlying records you effectively deny anyone access to the records while you are working with them. You can lock the whole result set specified by the SELECT criteria, as in the following example:

```
DECLARE cur_California CURSOR SCROLL SCROLL_LOCK FOR
SELECT * FROM authors WHERE state = 'CA'
```

This will prevent other users from modifying the data, although they will still be able to view it.

No strict rules determine which concurrency option you should choose in any given situation. You need to take into consideration the desired throughput, frequency of updates, available system resources, system load, and so on.

## Choosing the Right Cursor

You have a wide range of opinions when you are deciding which cursor to use or even whether to use cursors at all. The choices can be overwhelming but they do not have to be. Consider these priorities and the tradeoffs they entail:

- For data consistency, consider locking records.
- For system performance, consider using the STATIC or READ_ONLY option.
- For code maintainability, ask yourself this: Is my code too complex and convoluted?

You will certainly come up with your own set of priorities. As a rule of thumb, if you can avoid using cursors — do it. If you do need to perform row-by-row operations, then consider your options: use the STATIC cursor with the READ_ONLY option when you only want to look at the data, the DYNAMIC cursor when you need to be aware of changes in the underlying data, and the SCROLL_LOCK cursor when you need to shield your data from any intrusion while you are working on them.

**Done!**

---

### REVIEW

- Cursors are powerful tools in your Transact-SQL toolbox that operate row by row.
- The four different types of cursors differ in terms of how they communicate with the data they were created for. You need to choose an appropriate type of cursor for the task at hand.

- Cursors can be either global or local. You can set the visibility scope of the cursor through database properties or through the cursor declaration. The default setting is GLOBAL.
- When using cursors you need to pay attention to concurrency issues: Other users can modify the underlying records while you are working on the data set.

---

## QUIZ YOURSELF

1. How are cursors different from T-SQL batch statements?
2. What are the four basic types of cursors?
3. What is the purpose of the @@FETCH_STATUS system function?
4. What is the default scope of a cursor? How can you change it?
5. Why should you care about concurrency issues?

14

# *Understanding Indexes*

## *Session Checklist*

✔ Using indexes

✔ Designing an index

✔ Creating and deleting an index

✔ Managing an index

**30 Min.
To Go**

**Y**ou can greatly improve database performance by designing and implementing proper indexes. In this session you will learn about the different types of indexes and general index-design considerations, as well as how to optimize and manage an index.

## *Using Indexes*

An index in the database does not differ much from an index in the phone book. It serves the same purpose: speeding up the search process. Imagine flipping through each and every page to find a particular phone number in a thousand-page phone book with randomly assembled phone numbers and then think of finding the same number quickly in a phone book wherein the records are organized alphabetically by last name. This is the difference an index can make to your database performance.

You create an index for a table or a view. You can create it either for a single column or for a combination of columns. Indexes are stored separately from tables, which increases overall database size. Information about every index defined for the tables in a particular database is stored in the sysindexes system table for that database. You can create an index for virtually any data type except bit, ntext, text, and image.

SQL Server automatically creates an index for the table's primary key. The total number of indexes you can define for a single table is 250 (this includes one *clustered* index and 249 *non-clustered* indexes — I'll explain the distinction later in this session).

Give careful consideration to the column(s) you choose for an index: A properly selected index can increase performance tenfold, while a poorly selected index can actually slow down your database.

## Clustered indexes

When you create a clustered index for a table the data in this table are physically ordered around this key. This explains why you can have only one clustered index: Once your phone book is ordered alphabetically by last name you cannot order it by first name — at the same time.

When you create a clustered index all the rows in the table must be shuffled to reflect that index. This operation is fairly resource-intensive and requires some free swap space on your hard drive; also, be aware that all previously declared non-clustered indexes will be dropped.

A clustered index is usually created on a primary key, though you have the power to override this default behavior and create a clustered index on any named column. The only requirement is that the values in the column be unique; if the values are not unique the efficiency of the index will be greatly diminished, because SQL Server will create a secondary index on the rows that have duplicates in the primary index.

A clustered index is particularly efficient for frequent searches for a specific value: The table is physically sorted (clustered) on the column containing this value, or for the ranges of values, because rows containing the values within a range will be grouped together.

### Non-clustered indexes

A non-clustered index is merely a pointer to the row containing data. It corresponds to the index of a textbook: You find the keyword and then go to the specified page. Non-clustered indexes do not affect the order of the rows in the table. When you make a request for a particular column, SQL Server searches through the index, finds the actual records and goes directly there. This is not as efficient as searching with a clustered index but is still far superior to looking through the table record by record in search of a value. A non-clustered index is especially helpful when the query is searching for an exact value.

You can create multiple non-clustered indexes for different columns or combinations of columns and use them in different queries.

**SQL Server 2000 enables you to define an index on computed columns. This is rather an advanced feature: Refer to Books Online for a discussion of the computed-columns indexes.**

**20 Min. To Go**

## Designing an Index

While it is always a good idea to have indexes — a clustered index and one or more non-clustered indexes — you should give some consideration to the design issues. Not all indexes are created equal: Some will speed up operations while others might slow it down. In order to choose proper columns for indexing you must have intimate knowledge of the database structure and business logic. Ask these questions when it comes to choosing columns: Which data are accessed? How often? Are the data in the table static or do they change all the time? Is the value unique? Is it too long?

Ideally, you should run SQL Server Profiler to determine what types of queries are run against your database, and then use the Index Tuning Wizard, which suggests the columns to use for the index (these techniques will be described in Session 26, which deals with tuning and optimization).

Until you gain some experience in using the Index Tuning Wizard, some simple rules can help you make a choice. You should create an index (either clustered or non-clustered) for the following items:

- Large tables containing more than one hundred rows
- Frequently searched-for columns
- Columns used in aggregate functions
- Columns used in GROUP BY and ORDER BY clauses
- Columns used in JOIN queries

You should not create an index for:

- Small tables
- Columns rarely or never used in queries
- Columns containing long strings of data
- Columns in which values are updated frequently

If you have a primary key in your table (and it is a good idea to have one) you already have a clustered index: the same applies if you have defined a UNIQUE constraint (see Session 15). You should create a clustered index on frequently searched unique keys, columns with strong selectivity (a large count of unique values), and columns used by several different queries.

The prime candidates for non-clustered indexes are foreign keys, columns used in the WHERE clause, columns used in aggregate functions, and columns returning small result sets.

## Creating and Deleting an Index

Like most SQL Server database objects, an index can be created in two ways: with Transact-SQL statements, or visually, through a wizard (which creates the equivalent T-SQL statements for you).

To create an index visually using the wizard, follow these steps:

1. Select Enterprise Manager ⇨ Tools ⇨ Create Index Wizard. The Welcome screen briefly explains the other steps you will follow while creating the index. Click Next.

2. The next screen asks you to select a database and a table for which you wish to create an index. (I have selected Pubs and Titles in Figure 14-1.) Click Next.

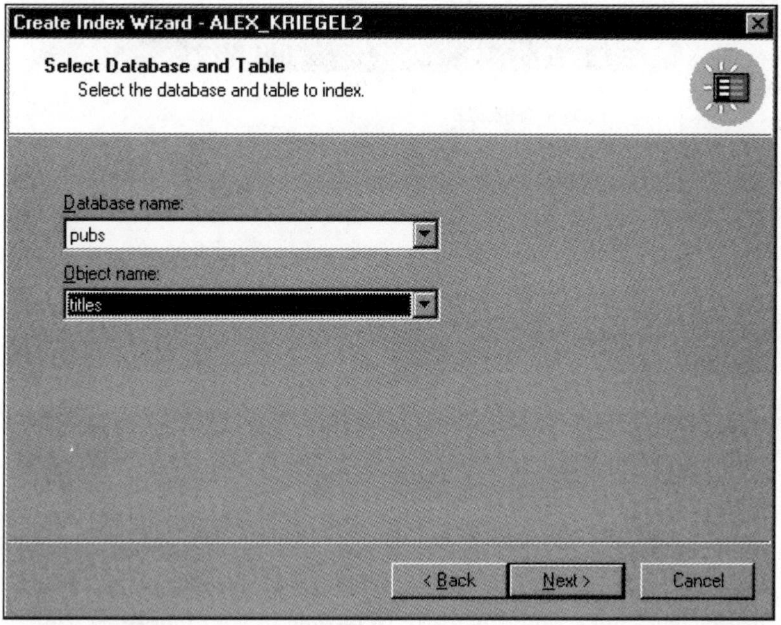

**Figure 14-1**
*Selecting a database and a table.*

3. The next screen displays all the information about existing indexes for the selected table (see Figure 14-2). Make sure that you are not attempting to create an index on the same columns. Click Next.

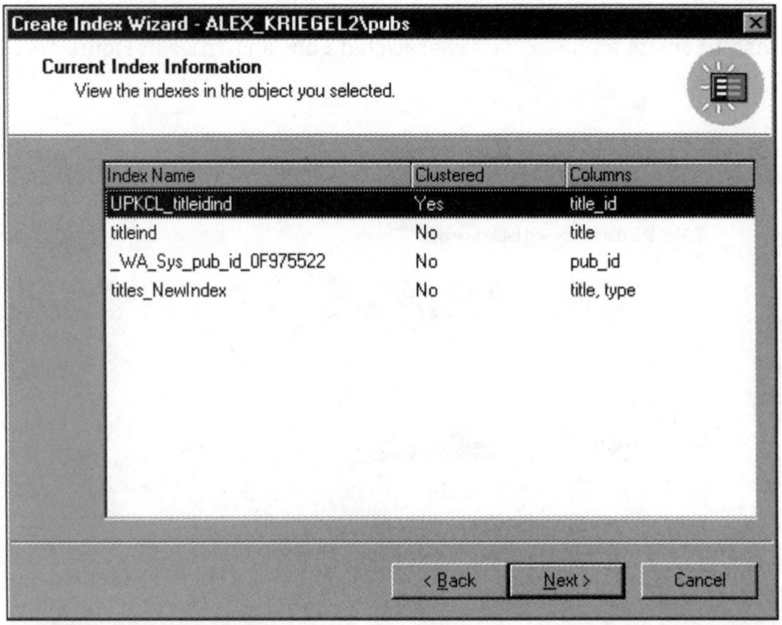

**Figure 14-2**
*Inspecting existing indexes.*

4. The next screen displays the structure of the selected table. You can choose the columns you would like to include in your index (see Figure 14-3) as well as the sort order (ascending or descending, ascending being the default). Click Next.

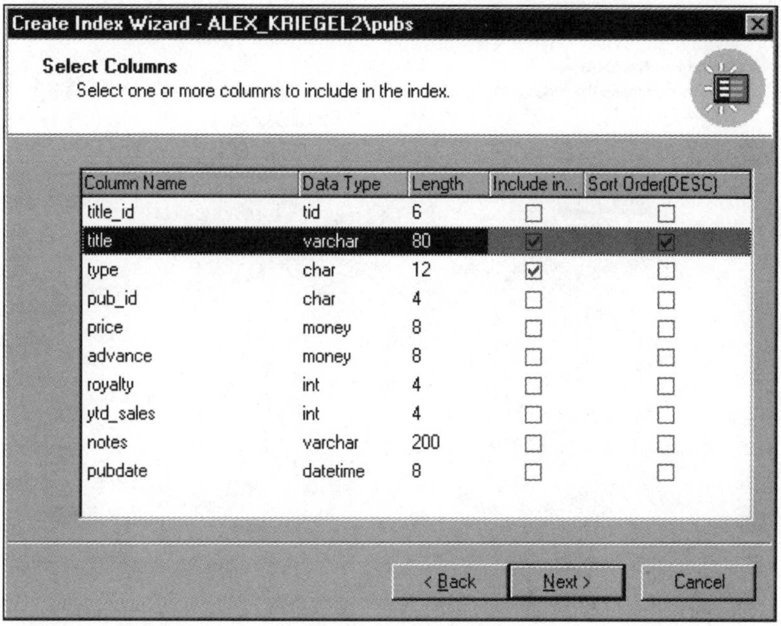

**Figure 14-3**
*Selecting columns and sort order.*

5. The next screen enables you to specify the index options: clustered or non-clustered, unique or non-unique, default or custom fill factor (see the Note in this section). Figure 14-4 shows this screen. Click Next.

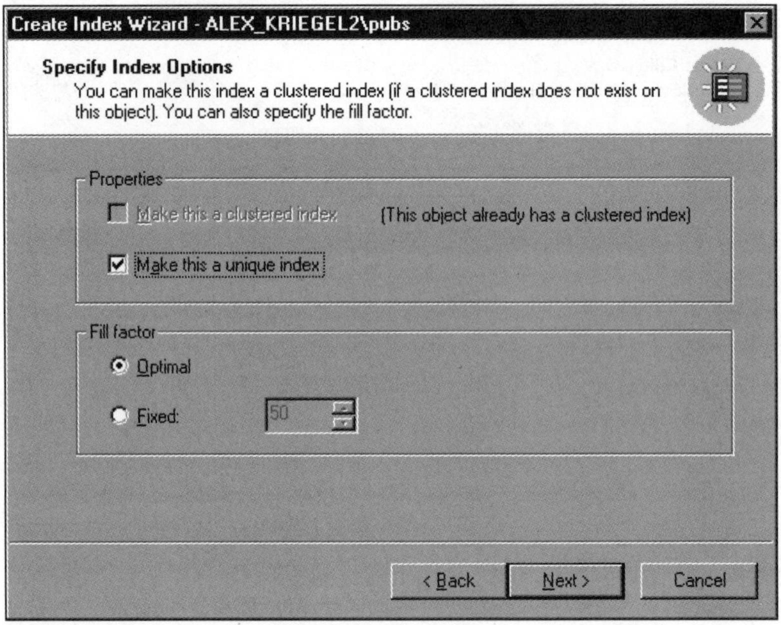

Create Index Wizard - ALEX_KRIEGEL2\pubs ☒

**Specify Index Options**
You can make this index a clustered index (if a clustered index does not exist on this object). You can also specify the fill factor.

Properties

☐ Make this a clustered index   [This object already has a clustered index]

☑ Make this a unique index

Fill factor

◉ Optimal

○ Fixed:   50

< Back   Next >   Cancel

*Figure 14-4*
*Specifying the index options.*

**The fill factor specifies how full the page should be before another page is allocated for the growing index. The fill factor option is provided for fine-tuning; in the majority of situations you should use the default.**

6. Every object in SQL Server is supposed to have a name (see Figure 14-5). Name your index and, if more than one column is used for the index, select the order in which the columns will appear. Click Finish.

**I suggest using some kind of descriptive name (such as *titles_id_nc_title_type*) for your indexes. This will help you remember the columns for which you created the index, whether the index is clustered or non-clustered, whether it is created or primary, and so on.**

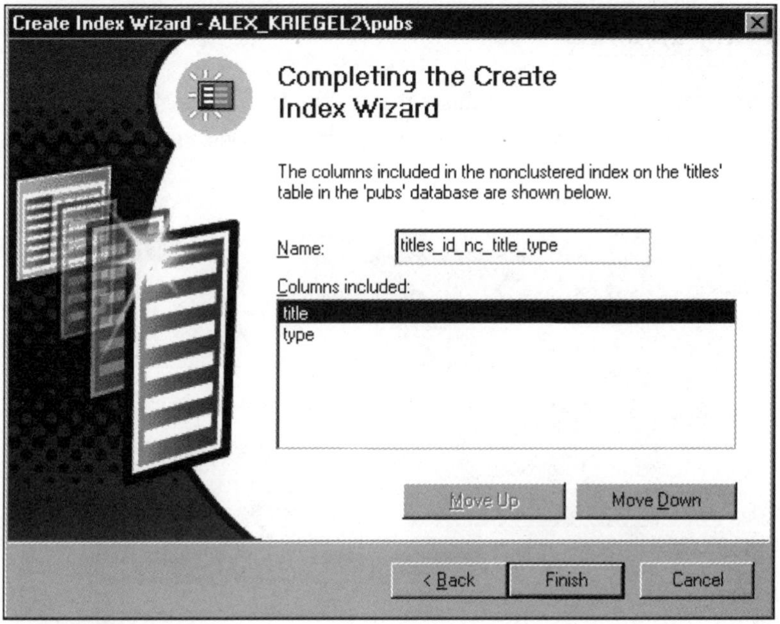

**Figure 14-5**
*Creating the index.*

You also can create the same index using pure Transact-SQL by issuing the following commands:

```
CREATE  NONCLUSTERED INDEX titles_id_nc_title_type
ON titles (title,type)
```

The full syntax for creating an index is more complex: You can specify many options, such as FILLFACTOR, IGNORE_DUP_KEY, and more. Refer to Books Online for the complete list of options.

To remove an index you can execute a Transact-SQL statement like the following:

```
DROP INDEX titles.titles_id_nc_title_type
```

Note that the index name is preceded by the table name for which this index was created. To drop indexes created with PRIMARY KEY and UNIQUE constraints, you must first drop the constraints (see Session 15). To drop the index from the Enterprise Manager console, refer to "Managing an Index," the next section in this session.

**10 Min.
To Go**

## Managing an Index

Once your index is created you manage it from the Enterprise Manager console. Select a table and from the right-click menu select Manage Indexes (see Figure 14-6).

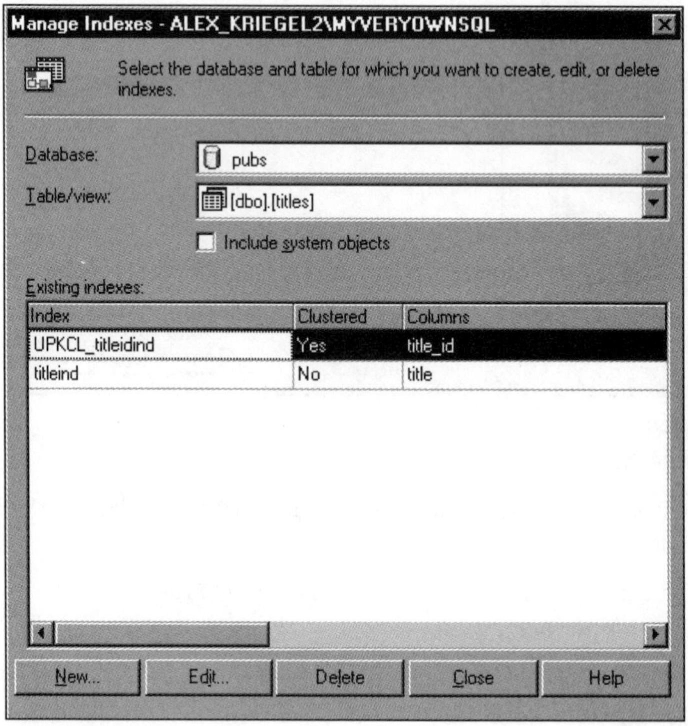

**Manage Indexes - ALEX_KRIEGEL2\MYVERYOWNSQL**

Select the database and table for which you want to create, edit, or delete indexes.

Database: pubs

Table/view: [dbo].[titles]

☐ Include system objects

Existing indexes:

| Index | Clustered | Columns |
|---|---|---|
| UPKCL_titleidind | Yes | title_id |
| titleind | No | title |

New...    Edit...    Delete    Close    Help

**Figure 14-6**
*Managing indexes.*

From the Manage Indexes window you can rename the index, change its options (such as fill factor), or delete (drop) it altogether.

You also can use system stored procedures to retrieve information about indexes on a particular table, as shown here:

```
USE Pubs
EXEC sp_helpindex Titles
```

Finally, you can use the system stored procedure sp_rename to rename the index with the following syntax:

```
sp_rename 'titles.sample_index', 'titles.new_index','INDEX'
```

SQL Server will display the following message: "Caution: Changing any part of an object name could break scripts and stored procedures." You'll receive a report of the status and find out whether or not the object was renamed.

**Done!**

## REVIEW

- Indexes created for a particular table can greatly speed up queries on that table.
- You can create one clustered and up to 249 non-clustered indexes for a table.
- SQL Server automatically creates a clustered index for a primary-key column; it is good practice to have a primary key defined for virtually every table.
- You must be very careful when selecting the columns for which to build an index, as a poor choice can slow down the query.
- You can create an index either with the Create Index Wizard or with raw Transact-SQL; both methods produce identical results.
- Once you have created an index, you can manage it through the Index Manager or by using system stored procedures.

## QUIZ YOURSELF

1. What is an index and why do you need it?
2. How many indexes can be created for a table?
3. What's the difference between clustered and non-clustered indexes?
4. What columns should you consider for a clustered index?
5. In what situations do you not want an index on your table?

# *Rules, Defaults, and Constraints*

## *Session Checklist*

✔ Enforcing data integrity

✔ Understanding NULL values

**30 Min.
To Go**

**M**aintaining integrity is the paramount goal of any database administrator. SQL Server provides you with a number of different mechanisms with which to enforce different types of integrity. In this session you will learn about constraints and how to use them to insure the integrity of your data.

## *Enforcing Data Integrity*

Relational databases are all about data, and in order to be useful data must maintain its integrity, which refers to the quality of the data. If a table contains invalid data it is said to have lost its integrity.

## Types of integrity

These are the four different types of integrity you can enforce in SQL Server:

- **Entity integrity** — Refers to a row in the table. Every row represents an entity whose integrity is maintained by means of indexes and constraints. Entity integrity basically ensures that every column in the row is unique; if a PRIMARY KEY or UNIQUE constraint is applied then the row must be unique within that table.
- **Domain integrity** — Refers to the data itself: they must be valid and in the correct format. SQL Server enforces domain integrity through the use of data types, CHECK constraints, rules, and DEFAULTs.
- **Referential integrity** — What makes RDBMS. Referential integrity ensures the consistency of key data across the database. You enforce it with PRIMARY KEY and FOREIGN KEY constraints (see Session 5).
- **User-defined integrity** — A part of your business logic enforced by all the aforementioned constraints, rules, and defaults, as well as triggers and stored procedures.

## Types of constraints

These are the six types of constraints:

- PRIMARY KEY constraints
- FOREIGN KEY constraints
- UNIQUE constraints
- CHECK constraints
- RULE constraints
- DEFAULT constraints

Each of these is discussed in the following sections.

### PRIMARY KEY constraints

In Session 5 you learned about the PRIMARY KEY and FOREIGN KEY constraints. You can define a primary key on a column or a group of columns; a table can have only one primary key and by definition the key must be unique. This requirement precludes the use of NULL as a value in any column that contains the primary key.

When a primary key is specified SQL Server creates a unique index on this column(s), which prevents you from inserting a duplicate record. If you do try to insert a duplicate record SQL Server will generate an error. For example, if you try to insert a duplicate record into the Authors table of the Pubs database from the Query Analyzer, you will see this message:

```
Violation of PRIMARY KEY constraint 'UPKCL_auidind'. Cannot insert
duplicate key in object 'authors'. The statement has been
terminated.
```

You can create a primary key and a table at the same time or add the primary key later. Again, you can either go through the Enterprise Manager (by selecting Design Table from the right-click menu on the table node) or directly issue Transact-SQL commands. T-SQL gives you several ways to specify PRIMARY KEY constraints; here is an example of the most basic method:

```
CREATE TABLE SampleTable
(
    Sample_ID       varchar(5)  NOT NULL PRIMARY KEY,
    Sample_Key      varchar(10)
)
GO
```

To modify a PRIMARY KEY constraint you need to drop it and recreate it again, as in the following example:

```
ALTER TABLE [dbo].[SampleTable] DROP CONSTRAINT
[PK__SampleTable__6C190EBB]
GO
```

SQL Server generates a name for the constraint, thus ensuring that the name will be unique.

In relational databases a primary key in one table is often referenced by a foreign key in another table. In this case, you cannot drop the PRIMARY KEY constraint without dropping the FOREIGN KEY constraint first.

### FOREIGN KEY constraints

Recall that FOREIGN KEY constraints are a means of enforcing referential integrity. SQL Server 2000 enables you to specify what action to take if a FOREIGN KEY constraint is violated. You can specify NO ACTION, meaning that no custom action is to be taken if a violation occurs when trying to delete a record; a deletion is prevented and an error message is returned to a client application. Alternatively, you can specify CASCADE to propagate the deletions to all the rows referenced by this key. This feature is new to this version of SQL server (though it is similar to the cascading in Microsoft Access).

Here is a sample of FOREIGN KEY constraint declaration:

```
CREATE TABLE SampleTable
(
   Sample_ID  varchar(5) NOT NULL PRIMARY KEY,
Sample_Key varchar(10)NOT NULL REFERENCES OtherTable(Sample_Key)
                     ON UPDATE NO ACTION ON DELETE CASCADE
)
GO
```

The parent table, OtherTable, contains the primary key Sample_Key; if a record in SampleTable (referencing the primary key in OtherTable) is deleted, then the record in OtherTable also has to go — no orphaned records are allowed. The Sample_Key column in SampleTable is specified as NOT NULL, meaning that for each record in the parent table at least one record must be stored in the child table.

 **A theoretical limit of 253 exists for foreign keys declared for a table. I recommend declaring as few foreign keys as possible for good performance.**

## UNIQUE constraints

The UNIQUE constraint and the PRIMARY KEY constraint are essentially the same. The idea behind the UNIQUE constraint is that you can enforce the uniqueness of columns in the table without their having to be part of a primary key, as shown here:

```
CREATE TABLE SampleTable
(
   Sample_ID  varchar(5)  NOT NULL PRIMARY KEY,
   Sample_Key  varchar(10),
   CONSTRAINT sample_key_unique UNIQUE (Sample_Key)
)
GO
```

The same rules apply to the UNIQUE constraint as to the primary key: no NULL values, the ability to include more than one column, and so on.

### CHECK constraints

The CHECK constraint enforces domain integrity by applying specific business logic to the value that can be entered into the column. Like all the constraints I mentioned earlier in this chapter you can create it either during or after table definition. The following sample creates a table, SampleTable, with two columns and a constraint on the column Sample_Key that restricts the possible values for this column to letters only:

```
CREATE TABLE SampleTable
(
  Sample_ID  varchar(5)  NOT NULL PRIMARY KEY,
  Sample_Key  varchar(1),
  CONSTRAINT sample_key_check CHECK([Sample_Key] LIKE '[A-Z]')
)
```

The CHECK constraint sample_key_check will raise an error every time you attempt to insert an invalid value — in this case anything that is not a letter.

You can modify an existing table to add a CHECK constraint, like this:

```
ALTER TABLE SampleTable ADD CONSTRAINT
sample_key_check CHECK([Sample_
Key] LIKE '[A-Z]')
```

When applying a CHECK constraint to a table with existing data you may choose not to check those data against the constraint, as shown here:

```
ALTER TABLE SampleTable WITH NOCHECK ADD CONSTRAINT
sample_key_check2 CHECK ([Sample_Key] LIKE '[1-3]')
```

By default (if WITH NOCHECK is specified) all existing data are checked against the constraint. SQL Server will raise an error if the constraint is violated.

Sometimes you need to disable a constraint temporarily: the following T-SQL statement will do that.

```
ALTER TABLE SampleTable NOCHECK CONSTRAINT sample_key_check
```

As with most SQL Server objects you can choose to use T-SQL or the visual interface of the Enterprise Manager to create or destroy constraints (choose Design Table from the right-click menu in the Tables node).

Figure 15-1 shows the properties for a constraint on the Publishers table from the Pubs database. This constraint ensures that the values entered into column pub_id fall within a certain range.

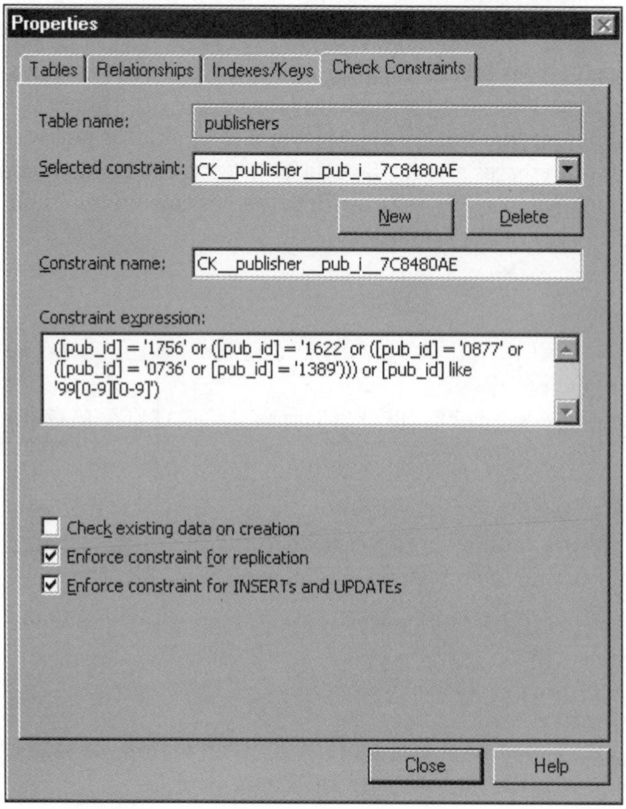

**Figure 15-1**
*Modifying a CHECK constraint on a table.*

You can define multiple CHECK constraints for the same table: they will be applied in the order in which you create them. No limit exists on the number of CHECK constraints you can specify for a column.

## RULE constraints

RULE constraints act very much like CHECK constraints, the only difference being that they are applied to multiple tables at once. In the previous examples, if the column Sample_Key were present in more than one table it would make perfect sense to create a RULE instead of modifying each and every table in the database that happened to contain this column.

You can access the Rules node from the Enterprise Manager; it is global for the entire database. Select New Rule from the right-click menu in the Rules node to bring up the Rule Properties window. The rule shown in Figure 15-2 will reject any attempts to insert values that do not fall into the certain range values.

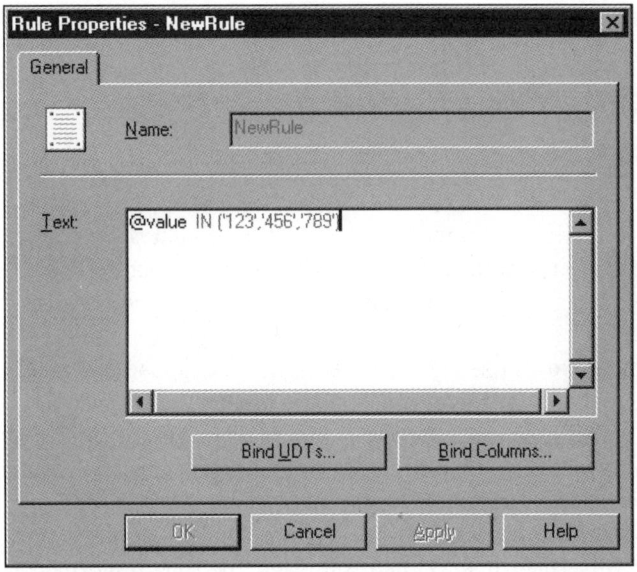

**Rule Properties - NewRule**

General

Name: NewRule

Text: @value IN ('123','456','789')

Bind UDTs...    Bind Columns...

OK    Cancel    Apply    Help

*Figure 15-2*
*Changing the rules.*

The column name is represented by the @value variable. Once you have created a rule you can bind it to a column in the tables; the name of the column is not important as long as the logic of the rule can be applied to it. You can select multiple columns in multiple places. Binding a rule to a column produces the same results as creating CHECK constraints for that column.

## DEFAULT constraints

A DEFAULT constraint enables you to specify the value that will be assigned to the column if an INSERT statement has nothing to assign to it. The value you assign can be a constant or a result of a system function. As with all the constraints you have learned about so far, you can add DEFAULT constraints to the table definition, as shown here:

**10 Min.
To Go**

```
CREATE TABLE SampleTable
(
   Sample_ID    varchar(5)   NOT NULL PRIMARY KEY,
   start_date   datetime     DEFAULT (getdate())

)
GO
```

You can also alter the existing table like this:

```
ALTER TABLE SampleTable WITH NOCHECK ADD
CONSTRAINT  DF_start_date DEFAULT (getdate()) FOR [start_date]
```

This T-SQL statement adds a default constraint to the column start_date; the system function getdate() will return a current date to be assigned to this field whenever an INSERT statement is executed on the SampleTable and no value is specified for this field.

A DEFAULT constraint works like a RULE constraint: it is applied to a single column only but can be defined for the entire database and bound to specific columns. Although DEFAULT constraints help maintain data integrity while simplifying the client application's job, they need to be applied judiciously. Consider a scenario in which your application inserts some data into a database and one of the columns maintains the date and time of insertion. What if you insert data remotely from a different time zone? Should you insert the time from the computer on which you run your client application, or the time from your database server? The answer depends on the business logic of your application.

Also, you need to watch out for possible conflicts with other constraints. Consider this syntax:

```
CREATE TABLE SampleTable
(
   Sample_ID  varchar(5)   NOT NULL PRIMARY KEY,
   start_date  datetime     NOT NULL DEFAULT NULL

)
GO
```

It defines a table with the column start_date, which must not contain NULL values with DEFAULT constraints that assign NULL to this column if no value is specified in the INSERT query. SQL Server will have no problems creating such a table, but any insert statement relying on DEFAULT will fail and return the error message "column does not allow nulls."

## Understanding NULL Values

When data are inserted into the table and neither a value nor a DEFAULT constraint is specified for a field, SQL Server 200 enters NULL into that field by default. NULL is a special value assigned to a field in a table when no value is specified. NULL is not zero; though it is not a data type per se, you may consider it a special case of the data type. Let's say that you enter a job ID and job description into some Jobs table that contains the columns job_id, description, and salary, but that you have not yet determined the salary level for the job in question. SQL Server will assign the value NULL to that field. The query returning all jobs that have not yet been assigned salary levels looks like this:

```
SELECT job_id, description FROM  Jobs WHERE salary IS NULL
```

The opposite — a query returning all jobs to which a salary has been assigned — looks like this:

```
SELECT job_id, description FROM  Jobs WHERE salary IS NOT NULL
```

When using NULL in a query you must consider the database setting ANSI NULLs default, which determines how NULL values are evaluated in the Transact-SQL query. According to the SQL-92 standard (ANSI), NULLs on any comparative statement (<> or =) against the field containing NULL evaluates to false.

When ANSI NULLs option is set to OFF, SQL Server can compare NULLs: For example, if the value in compared fields is NULL, the fields evaluate to true.

---

### REVIEW

- Constraints play an important role in maintaining the integrity of the database.
- You can use different types of constraints to maintain data integrity.
- You can specify constraints at the table-definition level or add them later, using either T-SQL statements or the Enterprise Manager console.
- You can modify a constraint after it has been created; some constraints have to be dropped and recreated in order for this to work.
- NULL is not zero; the way in which NULL is evaluated depends on the database settings.

*Done!*

## Quiz Yourself

1. What are the four integrity types supported by SQL Server 2000?
2. What kind of integrity is enforced by the PRIMARY KEY constraint?
3. What kind of integrity is enforced by the FOREIGN KEY constraint?
4. How does the UNIQUE constraint differ from the PRIMARY KEY constraint?
5. How many CHECK constraints can you define for a column?
6. What is the scope of the RULE constraint?
7. What values can you use for the DEFAULT constraint?

# Understanding Transactions and Locks

## Session Checklist

✔ Understanding transactions

✔ Setting isolation levels

✔ Learning about SQL Server locks

✔ Exploring lock types

✔ Dealing with deadlocks

**30 Min.
To Go**

Transactions are used in applications where maintaining data consistency is of importance. This session is all about transactions and the mechanisms that SQL Server uses to support them. SQL Server locks protect data in multiuser environments and are used in conjunction with transactions to ensure data consistency.

## Understanding Transactions

By now you are already used to retrieving and modifying data through Transact-SQL batches or stored procedures. These methods do work flawlessly and the results do not bring any surprises — in a world where you are the only user of the database, where nothing ever interrupts the power supply, and where your computer hardware never fails. You might yet get there; but for now you should be concerned with the real world.

What turns your regular T-SQL batch statements into a transaction is their ability to pass what is referred to as the ACID test. ACID is an acronym for:

- **Atomicity** — Either all changes are made, or none.
- **Consistency** — All data involved must be left in a consistent state upon completion of the transaction; a database must maintain its integrity.
- **Isolation** — One transaction must not be aware of any modifications to the data by any other transaction; it must either see the data in the original state or after the other transaction has been completed.
- **Durability** — The results of the completed transaction must be preserved in the database no matter what.

You might wonder how to implement all of these requirements; fortunately, this is something the SQL Server takes care of for you. In order to run a T-SQL batch as a transaction you need to BEGIN TRANSACTION and, assuming that everything goes well, COMMIT TRANSACTION.

Say you want to withdraw some money from a bank: The transaction is supposed to check how much you have in your account, subtract the required sum, and put the money into your hands. At no point during this transaction should there be an inconsistent state wherein, for example, you get the money without the same amount being deducted from your account or — even worse — the money is deducted from your account without making it into your hands.

The following code is intentionally simple, created just to demonstrate the concept behind transactions; actual code implementing this operation would be much more complex and dependent on the particular business logic that the bank uses.

```
BEGIN TRANSACTION tWithdrawal
    BEGIN
     -- initialize @TotalSavings variable
    SET @TotalSavings = 0
    -- verify that the client has enough money for withdrawal
    SELECT @TotalSavings = account_value FROM savings WHERE
    account_id = '12345'
    IF @TotalSavings >= @RequestedAmount
    BEGIN
        -- subtract money from the client's account
     UPDATE savings SET account_value = (@TotalSavings -
@RequestedAmount) WHERE account_id = '12345'
```

```
-- send notice to the bank machine to release requested        --
amount of money; implemented as a stored procedure ----------
sp_releasemoney
        -- details of implementation are irrelevant at this point,
        -- assumes that it returns 0 on success and 1 on failure
        execute @Status = sp_releasemoney @RequestedAmount
        IF @Status = 0
            BEGIN
-- client's got his/her money; the amount was deducted ----- from
his/her account
                COMMIT TRANSACTION tWithdrawal
            END
        ELSE
        -- something went wrong, undo all the changes
                ROLLBACK TRANSACTION tWithdrawal
        END
ELSE
    -- there is no enough money or user does not exist
    ROLLBACK TRANSACTION tWithdrawal
END
```

Once a BEGIN TRANSACTION statement is issued no data modifications are permanent until the COMMIT TRANSACTION statement is issued; the ROLLBACK statement rolls back all the changes made during the course of the transaction up to the last statement.

**Note**

**Every transaction is a named transaction. You must specify the name in the BEGIN TRANSACTION statement, but you can omit it in either the COMMIT or ROLLBACK statement.**

This is as close as you can get to ensuring atomicity within SQL Server, short of divine intervention. Evolved mechanisms of ensuring isolation and durability (such as replication, mirroring, and so forth) exist, and data consistency will be ensured by the constraints applied to the database.

The following T-SQL statements are not allowed in transactions.

- ALTER DATABASE
- BACKUP LOG
- CREATE DATABASE
- DROP DATABASE

- DUMP TRANSACTION
- DISK INIT
- LOAD DATABASE
- LOAD TRANSACTION
- RECONFIGURE
- RESTORE DATABASE
- RESTORE LOG
- UPDATE STATISCTICS

The next two sections discuss the three following types of transactions:

- Explicit transactions
- Implicit transactions
- Distributed transactions

## Explicit and implicit transactions

Any transaction that you start, end, or roll back using BEGIN TRANSACTION, COMMIT TRANSACTION, or ROLLBACK TRANSACTION is an *explicit transaction*. The code in the preceding section is a sample of an explicit transaction.

*Implicit transactions* are more subtle and complex. SQL Server automatically starts an implicit transaction when it encounters one of the following T-SQL statements (grouped according to functionality):

- SELECT, INSERT, UPDATE, DELETE
- ALTER TABLE
- TRUNCATE TABLE
- OPEN, FETCH
- GRANT, REVOKE

Imposing a transaction on these statements is just plain common sense, because data might be left in an inconsistent state should the statement fail. You have the power to turn the implicit-transactions mode off by issuing a T-SQL statement at the beginning of your batch, as follows:

```
SET IMPLICIT_TRANSACTIONS OFF
```

To turn the implicit-transactions mode back on, use the following statement:

```
SET IMPLICIT_TRANSACTIONS ON
```

SQL Server autocommits every T-SQL statement by default if no errors were encountered during execution; you can override this default behavior by starting an explicit transaction.

**Explicit transactions can be *nested* — that is, you can begin a transaction within a transaction. Only the outermost transaction, which envelops all other transactions, can commit results; if you call COMMIT from any other level, SQL Server will simply ignore it.**

### Distributed transactions

Two types of distributed transactions exist: transactions that run across two or more databases within a single SQL Server, and transactions that involve two or more servers. The first type of distributed transaction is managed internally by SQL Server, which hides the nature of the transaction: To the client it appears to be a standard transaction. The second type, cross-server distributed transactions, is inherently more complex and follows stricter rules. The coordination of the transactions in this case is performed by a transaction coordinator such as Distributed Transaction Coordinator (MSDTC), the one supplied by Microsoft, shown in Figure 16-1. If you want to process distributed transactions, this service must be running.

**Figure 16-1**
*Running Microsoft Distributed Transaction Coordinator.*

The BEGIN TRANSACTION statement does not differ much from that of a local transaction, but the COMMIT phase is a wee bit different. In order to minimize the effects of a possible network failure, the COMMIT in distributed transactions is managed in two phases. In the first phase (called the Prepare phase), the DTC sends a message to all resource managers involved to prepare to commit. Upon receiving this message, the resource manager saves the state of the transaction and notifies the DTC of either success or failure. Only if all involved parties report success does the DTC send the second-phase (called the Commit phase) message to actually commit the transaction. Each resource manager involved attempts to commit the transaction and report the status of its attempts to the DTC. If any resource manager reports failure the transaction is rolled back for each of them; otherwise, the transaction is completed.

You can start a distributed transaction explicitly, as follows:

```
BEGIN DISTRIBUTED TRANSACTION tWithdrawal
```

You can also start a transaction on a linked server, a remote server registered with your Enterprise Manager Console; the syntax you use is identical to that which you would use for a local transaction and it will be up to the DTC to attend to the details of implementation.

**In case of failure you can use a ROLLBACK command on part of the transaction, rather than affecting the whole thing. At any time after a BEGIN TRANSACTION statement you may use the SAVE TRANSACTION *<name>* statement to set the rollback point. When issuing the ROLLBACK command using the saved-point name, you roll back to this saved point and not to the beginning of the transaction. Consult Books Online for more details.**

**20 Min.
To Go**

## Setting Isolation Levels

SQL server provides fine granularity when it comes to what a particular transaction can and cannot see. This granularity is closely connected to locking, which I discuss later in this session. Setting the isolation level prevents the surprises that can occur when two or more transactions are working on the same data.

Following the SQL-92 standard, SQL Server allows transactions to run at four isolation levels:

- **Read uncommitted** — The lowest isolation level, which ensures only that the transaction does not read physically corrupt data.

- **Read committed** — Allows the transaction to see the data after they are committed by any previous transactions. This is the default isolation level for SQL Server 2000.

- **Repeatable read** — Ensures just that: Reading can be repeated.

- **Serializable** — The highest possible level of isolation, wherein transactions are completely isolated from one another.

Table 16-1 outlines the behavior exhibited by transactions at the different levels of isolation.

**Table 16-1**
*Data Availability at Different Isolation Levels*

| Isolation Level | Dirty Read | Non-Repeatable Read | Phantom Read |
|---|---|---|---|
| Read uncommitted | Yes | Yes | Yes |
| Read committed | No | Yes | Yes |
| Repeatable read | No | No | Yes |
| Serializable | No | No | No |

*Dirty read* refers to the ability to read records that are being modified; since the data are in the process of being changed, dirty reading may result in unpredictable results.

*Phantom read* refers to the ability to "see" records that have already been deleted by another transaction.

 **When designing transactions keep them as short as possible, as they consume valuable system resources.**

## *Introducing SQL Server Locks*

Locking is there to protect you. It is highly unlikely that you have the luxury of being the only user of your database. It is usually a case of tens, hundreds, or — in case of the Internet — thousands of concurrent users trying to read or modify the data, sometimes exactly the same data. If not for locking, your database would quickly lose its integrity.

Consider a scenario wherein two transactions are working on the same record. If locking is not used the final results will be unpredictable, because data written by one user can be overwritten or even deleted by another user.

Fortunately, SQL Server automatically applies locking when certain types of T-SQL operations are performed. SQL Server offers two types of locking control: *optimistic concurrency* and *pessimistic concurrency*.

Use optimistic concurrency when the data being used by one process are unlikely to be modified by another. Only when an attempt to change the data is made will you be notified about any possible conflicts, and your process will then have to reread the data and submit changes again.

Use pessimistic concurrency if you want to leave nothing to chance. The resource — a record or table — is locked for the duration of a transaction and cannot be used by anyone else (the notable exception being during a deadlocking situation, which I discuss in greater detail later in this session).

**By default, SQL Server uses pessimistic concurrency to lock records. Optimistic concurrency can be requested by a client application, or you can request it when opening a cursor inside a T-SQL batch or stored procedure.**

## Exploring Lock Types

The following basic types of locks are available with SQL Server:

- **Shared locks** — Enable users to read data but not to make modifications.
- **Update locks** — Prevent deadlocking (discussed later in this session).
- **Exclusive locks** — Allow no sharing; the resource under an exclusive lock is unavailable to any other transaction or process.
- **Schema locks** — Used when table-data definition is about to change — for example, when a column is added to or removed from the table.
- **Bulk update locks** — A special type of lock used during bulk-copy operations (Bulk-copy operations are discussed in Session 17).

Usually SQL Server will either decide what type of lock to use or go through the lock-escalation process, whichever its internal logic deems appropriate.

**Lock escalation converts fine-grained locks into more coarsely grained locks (for example, from row-level locking to table-level locking) so the lock will use fewer system resources.**

You can override SQL Server's judgment by applying lock hints within your T-SQL batch or stored procedure. For example, if you know for sure that the data are not going to be changed by any other transaction, you can speed up operation by specifying the NOLOCK hint:

```
SELECT account_value FROM savings WITH (NOLOCK)
```

**Other useful hints include ROWLOCK, which locks the data at row level (as opposed to at the level of a full table), and HOLDLOCK, which instructs SQL Server to keep a lock on the resource until the transaction is completed, even if the data are no longer required. Use lock hints judiciously because: they can speed your server up or slow it down, or even stall it. Use coarse-grained locks as much as possible, as fine-grained locks consume more resources.**

Another option you may want to consider when dealing with locks is setting the LOCK_TIMEOUT parameter. When this parameter is set the lock is released after a certain amount of time has passed, instead of being held indefinitely. This setting applies to the entire connection on which the T-SQL statements are being executed. The following statement instructs SQL Server to release its lock after 100 milliseconds:

```
SET LOCK_TIMEOUT 100
```

You can check the current timeout with the system function @@LOCK_TIMEOUT.

## Dealing with Deadlocks

Strictly speaking, deadlocks are not RDBMS-specific; they can occur on any system wherein multiple processes are trying to get a hold of the same resources.

In the case of SQL Server, deadlocks usually look like this: One transaction holds an exclusive lock on Table1 and needs to lock Table2 to complete processing;

**10 Min. To Go**

another transaction has an exclusive lock on Table2 and needs to lock Table1 to complete. Neither transaction can get the resource it needs, and neither can be rolled back or committed. This is a classic deadlock situation.

SQL Server periodically scans all the processes for a deadlock condition. Once a deadlock is detected, SQL Server does not allow it to continue *ad infinitum* and usually resolves it by arbitrarily killing one of the processes; the victim transaction is rolled back. A process can volunteer to be a deadlock victim by having its DEADLOCK_PRIORITY parameter set to LOW: the client process usually does this and subsequently traps and handles the error 1205 returned by SQL Server.

Deadlocks should not be ignored. The usual reason for deadlocks is a poorly designed stored procedure or poorly designed client application code, although sometimes the reason is an inefficient database design. Any deadlock error should prompt you to examine the potential source.

The general guidelines for avoiding deadlocks, as recommended by Microsoft, are as follows:

- **Access objects in the same order** — In the previous example, if both transactions try to obtain a lock on Table1 and then on Table2, they are simply blocked; after the first transaction is committed or rolled back, the second gains access. If the first transaction accesses Table1 and then Table2, and the second transaction simultaneously accesses Table2 and then Table1, a deadlock is guaranteed.

- **Avoid user interaction in transactions** — Accept all parameters before starting a transaction; a query runs much faster than any user interaction.

- **Keep transactions short and in one batch** — The shorter the transaction the lesser the chance that it will find itself in a deadlock situation.

- **Use a low isolation level** — In other words, when you need access to only one record on a table, there is no need to lock the whole table. If the read committed is acceptable, do not use the much more expensive serializable.

**Done!**

## REVIEW

- Transactions are T-SQL statements executed as a single unit. All the changes made during a transaction are either committed or rolled back. A database is never left in an inconsistent state.

- ACID criteria are applied to every transaction.

- Transactions can either be implicit or explicit. SQL statements that modify data in the table are using implicit transactions by default.

- Distributed transactions execute over several servers and databases. They need a Distributed Transaction Coordinator (DTC) in order to execute.
- Isolation levels refer to the visibility of the changes made by one transaction to all other transactions running on the system.
- A transaction can place several types of locks on the resource. Locks are expensive in terms of system resources and should be used with caution.

- Avoid deadlock situations by designing your transactions carefully.

---

## Quiz Yourself

1. What does the acronym ACID stand for?
2. What are two possible outcomes of a transaction?
3. What is the difference between explicit and implicit transactions?
4. What SQL Server component do distributed transactions require in order to run?
5. What are the four isolation levels supported by SQL Server 2000?
6. What are the two forms of concurrency locking offered by SQL Server 2000?
7. What is a deadlock?

# PART

# III

## *Saturday Afternoon*

1. How does a stored procedure differ from a T-SQL batch?
2. Where is a stored procedure stored?
3. What is the scope of the stored procedure?
4. What is the scope of the @@ERROR system function?
5. What is a nested stored procedure?
6. What are the advantages and disadvantages of using stored procedures?
7. How is a trigger different from a stored procedure? From a T-SQL batch?
8. What events can a trigger respond to?
9. What are the two virtual tables SQL Server maintains for triggers?
10. What does the INSTEAD OF trigger do?
11. What is a SQL Server cursor?
12. What are the four different cursor types?
13. What is concurrency and how does it apply to cursors?
14. What is an index in the context of SQL Server?
15. What is the difference between a clustered and a non-clustered index?
16. How many clustered indices can you define for one table? Non-clustered?
17. Would it be a good idea to create an index on a table that always contains 10 records? Why or why not?
18. What columns would you use for a non-clustered index?
19. What are the four types of integrity?
20. What types of integrity are enforced by a foreign-key constraint?

21. When can you add the CHECK constraint to a table?
22. In order for a RULE to be functional what do you need to do after it is created?
23. What is a NULL in SQL Server? How does it differ from zero?
24. What is a transaction?
25. What do the letters in the acronym ACID stand for?
26. What are explicit and implicit transactions?
27. What are the two types of concurrency?
28. What are the four isolation levels?
29. What is locking escalation? When does it occur?
30. What is a deadlock? How do you avoid deadlocks?

# PART

# IV

## Saturday Evening

# Data Transformation Services

## Session Checklist

✔ Learning about Data Transformation Services

✔ Importing and exporting data through DTS

✔ Maintaining DTS packages

✔ Using the Bulk Copy command-line utility

**30 Min.
To Go**

**T**his session deals with SQL server mechanisms for moving data among different, sometimes heterogeneous data sources. Data Transformation Services provide you with a powerful interface that is flexible enough to transform data while moving them.

## Introducing Data Transformation Services

Data Transformation Services (DTS) were introduced in SQL Server 7.0 and improved in the current version of SQL Server 2000. They were designed to move data among different SQL Servers (especially those with different code pages, collation orders, locale settings, and so on), to move data among different database systems (for example, between ORACLE and SQL Server), and even to extract data from non-relational data sources (such as text files and Excel spreadsheets).

The DTS components installed with SQL Server are DTS wizards and support tools. The important part of Data Transformation Services is the database drivers — small programs designed to provide an interface with a specific data source, such as an ASCII text file or Access database. These drivers come as OLE DB providers (the latest Microsoft database interface) and Open Database Connectivity (ODBC) drivers.

The basic unit of work for DTS is a DTS package. A DTS package is an object under SQL Server 2000 that contains all the information about the following:

- Data sources and destinations
- Tasks intended for the data
- Workflow procedures for managing tasks
- Data-transformation procedures between the source and the destination as needed

SQL Server 2000 provides you with DTS wizards to help you create packages for importing and exporting the data, and with DTS Designer to help you develop and maintain the packages.

You can also use DTS to transfer database objects, create programmable objects, and explore the full advantages of ActiveX components (COM objects).

## Importing and Exporting Data through DTS

Creating a DTS package can be a daunting task. I recommend that you stick to the basics for now and explore DTS's more advanced features once you've gained some experience.

To create a simple DTS Export package using the DTS Import/Export Wizard, follow these steps:

**1.** Select DTS Export Wizard from the Tools ⇨ Wizards menu.

**You can access the DTS Import/Export Wizard in several different ways. You can choose Start ⇨ Program Files ⇨ Microsoft SQL Server ⇨ Import and Export Data; you can go to the Enterprise Manager Console, right-click on the Data Transformation Services node, and choose All Tasks; or you can even enter dtswiz from the prompt on the command line.**

Let's say you want to export data from your SQL Server into a plain comma-delimited file. Figure 17-1 shows the screen after the one that greets you into the Import/Export Wizard. The dialog prompts you to select the data source, authentication (security mode for establishing a connection to this source), and database (since your data source is RDBMS in this case).

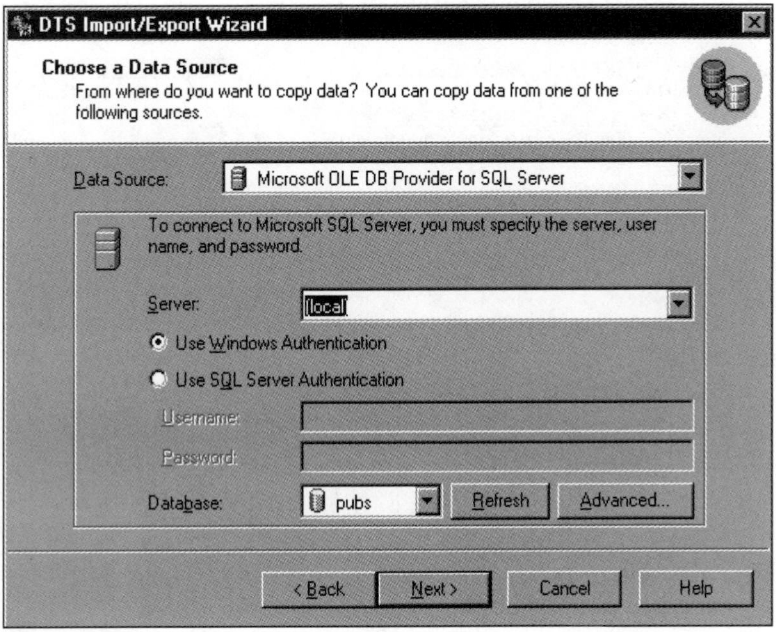

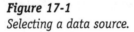

*Figure 17-1*
*Selecting a data source.*

2. Select your local server (you can use this wizard to import or export data from any server you have access to on your network) and the Pubs database. Click Next.

3. The next screen (shown in Figure 17-2) prompts you to select a destination. Initially, it will be almost identical to the screen shown in Figure 17-1. The specifics of the screen you see depend on the data source you selected. Select Text File as a data source (your screen should now look

exactly like the one shown in Figure 17-2) and enter the name of the file in which you wish to save the data. You can browse for a specific file or type in the name and the absolute path. Click Next.

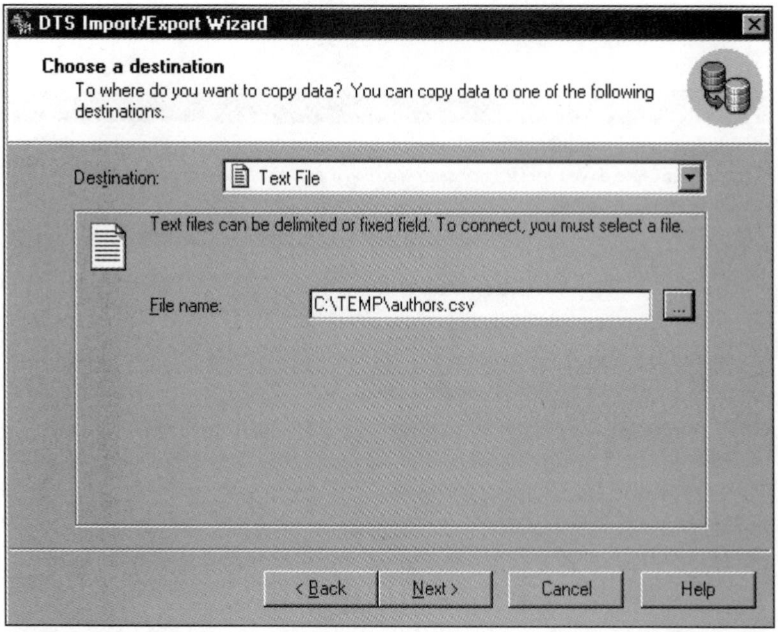

**Figure 17-2**
*Selecting a destination for the data.*

From the screen you see in Figure 17-3 you can either export a single table or specify a T-SQL query of which the results will be saved into the specified file. Of course, choosing to export data into a file prevents you from transferring database objects like indexes, constraints, and such; only data and data structure will be exported.

4. Specify the Authors table as the one you want to export, and then select the destination file format — (ANSI or UNICODE), the row delimiter, the column delimiter, and the text qualifier. You also can decide whether or not the first row will represent column names for the exported table. The default column mapping (which you can change in the Transformation dialog) will be that of the source: that is, the au_id column of the source will be mapped to the au_id column of the destination.

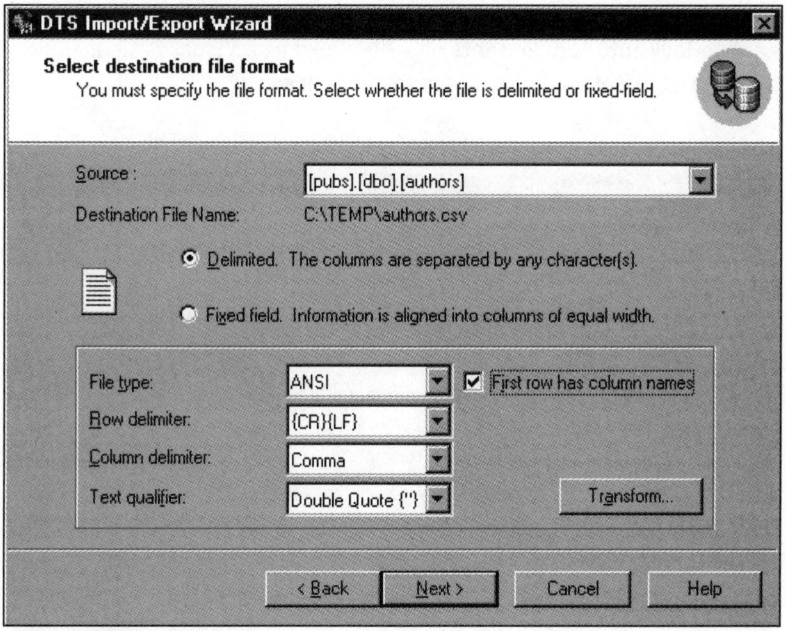

**Figure 17-3**
*Specifying the format of the data in the destination file.*

The Transform button takes you to a screen wherein you can specify additional data transformation for each column being exported. For example, you can specify that every number be converted into a string of type varchar, or instruct the package to ignore columns or to export them under a different name. You can also apply an ActiveX script — usually written in VBScript — to implement more complex transformation rules. Transform is an advanced feature and deserves a book of its own: Here I just mention its existence and encourage you to explore it — carefully. Click Next.

5. From the dialog shown in Figure 17-4 you can select whether you want to run this package immediately or schedule it for future (possibly recurrent) execution. You can also save the package here if you wish. The Save option is probably the most confusing one: It takes advantage of SQL Server's ability to preserve the script in a variety of formats. The important point to remember here is that saving with SQL Server or SQL Server Metadata Services saves the package as an object inside the SQL Server, while the two other options (Structured Storage File and Visual Basic File)

save the package outside it. If you are familiar with Visual Basic you may want to look into the contents of a file saved as a Visual Basic module to see what is really happening behind the scenes.

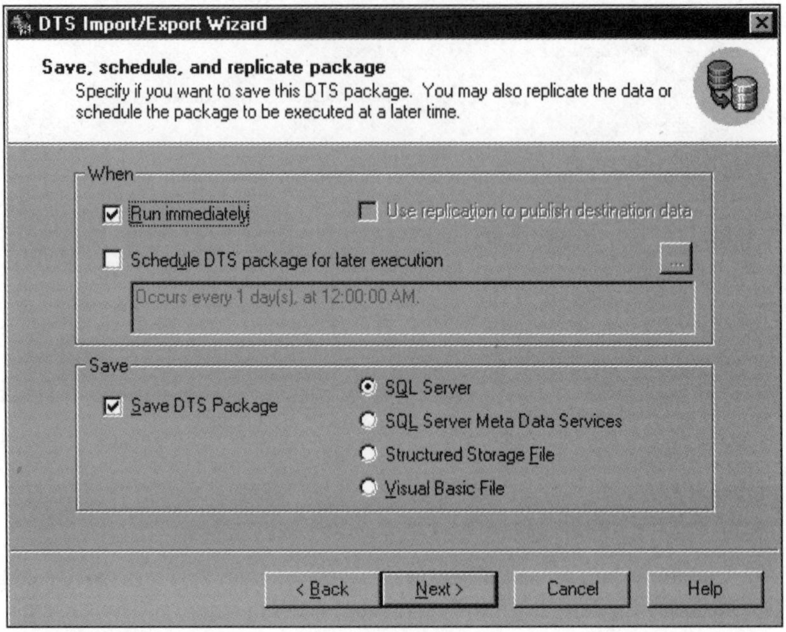

**DTS Import/Export Wizard**

**Save, schedule, and replicate package**
Specify if you want to save this DTS package. You may also replicate the data or schedule the package to be executed at a later time.

When
☑ Run immediately          ☐ Use replication to publish destination data

☐ Schedule DTS package for later execution          [...]

Occurs every 1 day(s), at 12:00:00 AM.

Save
☑ Save DTS Package          ◉ SQL Server
                            ○ SQL Server Meta Data Services
                            ○ Structured Storage File
                            ○ Visual Basic File

[ < Back ]  [ Next > ]  [ Cancel ]  [ Help ]

**Figure 17-4**
*Saving and scheduling the package.*

**Using Meta Data Services is beyond the scope of this book. This is an advanced topic, which involves tracing the lineage of a particular package and cataloging the metadata of the databases referenced in the package.**

6. If you schedule the package it will also be automatically saved. Let's say you wish to save the package with SQL Server and run it immediately. Click Next.

7. The next screen will prompt you for the name and description of the package you are about to create. Select some descriptive name: As you accumulate a number of packages they might help you maintain your sanity. You also may choose to protect your package from unauthorized use with passwords: one for the owner, one for the user (the owner can modify the

package while the user can only run it). Scheduling a recurring task is self-explanatory: The options enable you to schedule the execution daily, weekly, or monthly. You can schedule multiple executions within one day, and specify the start and expiration date.

8.  The last screen will present a summary of all your choices. From here you still can go back and change your selections. When you click Finish, SQL Server will save your package and then run it. If you followed all the steps properly and the export was successful, you should receive the following message: "Successfully copied 1 table(s) from Microsoft SQL Server to Flat File."

**You can open the resulting file in Notepad or Microsoft Excel and view the way in which the exported data were saved.**

Following similar steps you may move the data among various data sources. The import procedure is very similar to the export procedure.

## Maintaining DTS Packages

**20 Min. To Go**

Once a package has been created you can modify it, extend its functionality, add and delete packages, and so on. To edit a data package you use the DTS Designer.

This tool enables you to visually design new packages and modify existing ones. The interface (shown in Figure 17-5) borrows heavily from other Microsoft Visual Studio tools. Tasks and connections are represented by small icons in the toolbox; you assemble a package by dragging the icons and dropping them into the designer pane, where they are treated as objects. Once you have done this you can right-click an object and select the Properties option to customize it.

The DTS Designer tries to hide as much complexity as possible from you. However, if you plan to use it for anything but trivial tasks, you'll need an understanding of the process as well as some experience.

**All local packages are assembled under the Local Packages node of Data Transformation Services.**

If you open the package you just created in this session (select the pop-up menu option Design Package), you'll see that it is represented by two connection objects — one SQL Server (source) and one flat file (destination). Examining their properties will reveal all the specifications you made during the creation process. The fat arrow pointing from the source to the destination is also an object — a Task object. Its properties maintain all the transformation procedures, data description, and such; it is quite enlightening to explore its five-tab property sheet (available from the right-click menu).

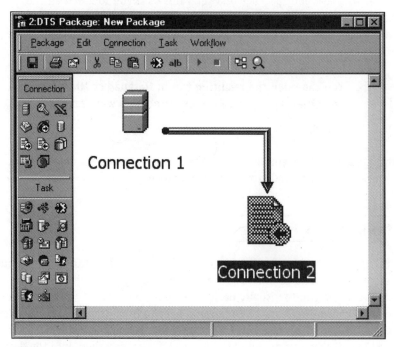

**Figure 17-5**
*Exploring DTS Designer.*

Designing and modifying the package requires intimate knowledge of the processes and data involved as well as some basic programming skills. Until you acquire these, I recommend using the simpler (though just as powerful) Import /Export Wizard interface.

## Using the Bulk Copy Command-Line Utility

In the dawning era of SQL Server, the Bulk Copy Program (BCP) was the one and only tool to use to get data in and out of the SQL Server database. The tradition

**10 Min.
To Go**

continues virtually unchanged. The BCP utility is included with every SQL Server installation. It is best used for importing data from a flat file into SQL Server, and exporting data from SQL Server into a flat file.

This program uses the low-level DB-Lib interface of SQL Server (the one that C programmers use to code their client programs); for SQL Server 7.0 and 2000 it uses ODBC (Open Database Connectivity). As a result it is extremely fast and efficient. Its main drawback is rigid, arcane, unforgiving syntax. It is also gives you relatively few options for transferring data between heterogeneous data sources.

The basic syntax for BCP is as follows:

```
Bcp pubs..authors out authors.txt  -c -U sa -P password
```

This essentially means "Export data from the Authors table in the Pubs database into a flat file named authors.txt, the user ID is -sa and the password is password." The parameter -c specifies that data will be exported to a non–SQL Server destination (ASCII file).

To import data with BCP, use this syntax:

```
Bcp pubs..authors in authors.txt  -c -U sa -P password
```

When you're importing data with BCP constraints will be enforced, though triggers will not be fired.

**Command-line arguments for BCP are case-sensitive: -c and -C represent different parameters.**

BCP supports three different modes of data format:

- Character mode (-c) is used for importing from or exporting to an ASCII text.
- Native mode (-n) is a SQL Server proprietary binary format; it is used when both the source and the destination are SQL Server databases.
- Wide mode (-w) is used for importing from or exporting to a UNICODE text.

**You can incorporate BCP commands into MS-DOS batch files or VBScript files (extension .vbs, executed in Windows Scripting Host) to create powerful data import/export procedures. You also can schedule the execution of these procedures with the NT/Windows 2000 *at* service.**

Part IV—Saturday Evening
Session 17

BCP supports about 40 different parameters and switches, and as you find your-self more involved with DBA daily routines you will decide for yourself which ones you find most useful. Please refer to Books Online for the full list of these switches and their uses.

**One of the important parameters to use with BCP is a compatibility-level switch. When you're importing into SQL Server 7.0/2000 data that were exported in a native format out of an earlier version of SQL Server, this switch tells BCP to use compatible data types so the data will be readable. To make the data compatible set the -6 switch.**

*Done!*

## REVIEW

- Data Transformation Services (DTS) is a powerful mechanism for moving data and objects in and out of different data sources .

- The easiest way to create and schedule DTS packages is through the Import/Export Wizard.

- You can maintain, modify, and enhance a DTS package using DTS Designer, a visual-development environment provided by SQL Server.

- The BCP utility is a small legacy utility that enables you to import and export data to and from SQL Server and some other data sources.

## QUIZ YOURSELF

1. What are two methods of importing and exporting data with SQL Server?
2. What can be transferred using Data Transformation Services?
3. What are acceptable destinations for data being transferred from SQL Server?
4. How can you transform data while transferring it from the source?
5. What is BCP and what can you use it for?
6. How can you schedule a BCP import/export execution?

# SQL Server Backup

## Session Checklist

✔ Implementing backup and recovery planning

✔ Using different backup strategies

✔ Selecting a recovery mode

✔ Restoring a database

✔ Managing backups

I n this session I'll discuss the SQL Server backup and recovery procedures. You will learn about the different backup methods, the various recovery models, and how to create, perform, and restore a backup.

## Implementing Backup and Recovery Planning

Before you can begin to set up a backup procedure, you need to determine which databases need to be backed up, how often they should be backed up, and more. You should consider the following questions when creating a plan:

- **What type of database are you backing up?** User databases will need to be backed up frequently, while the system database will not. The master database will only need to be backed up after a database is created, configuration values are changed, or any other activity is performed that changes this database. If the master database becomes corrupt the whole server ceases to function.

- **How important is the data?** A development database may be backed up weekly, while a production database should be backed up at least daily.

- **How often are changes made to the database?** The frequency of change will determine the frequency of backups. If the database is read-only there is no reason to back it up frequently. A database that is updated constantly should be backed up much more often.

- **How much downtime is acceptable?** Mission-critical databases will have to be up and running almost immediately. In these cases you need to back up to disk rather than to tape. You may even have to use multiple backup devices.

- **What are your off-peak hours?** The best time to back up is when database usage is low. This will allow the backup to complete in the shortest time possible. You must always schedule your backups carefully.

## Using Different Backup Strategies

When backing up a database you will need to use a variety of techniques to ensure a full and valid database recovery in the event of a failure.

The basic types of backups include the following:

- **Complete database backup** — Backs up the entire database, including all objects, system tables, and data. The backup also incorporates all changes logged to the transaction log up to the time of completion of the backup. This ensures that you can recover the complete state of the data up to the time the backup finishes.

- **Differential backup** — Backs up all data that have changed since the last complete backup. This kind of backup runs much faster than a full backup.

You can use a differential backup only in conjunction with a full backup, and it is not allowed on the Master database.

- **Transaction-log backups** — When you back up a transaction log, the backup contains the changes that have occurred since the last transaction-log backup. After completion the log is flushed of all transactions. This type of backup records the state of the transaction log when it starts, unlike the two previous backups, which record the state of the log when they end.

- **File and file-group backup** — Enables you to back up specific database files and file groups rather than the entire database.

## Complete database backups

The easiest way to perform a backup is to go through the Backup Wizard and follow these steps:

1. Select Enterprise Manager Tools ⇨ Wizards. Then, from the Management node on the general wizards menu, select Backup Wizard.

   The welcome screen describes the steps you are about to be guided through. Click Next.

2. Choose a database to back up from the drop-down combo box. Only databases managed by this instance of Enterprise Manager will appear there. Select a database and click Next.

3. You are prompted for the name and description of your yet-to-be-created backup. You will need this name down the road in order to manage your backups. Specify the requested information and click Next.

   On this screen (shown in Figure 18-1) you need to select the type of backup you wish to perform. Click Next.

   This screen (shown in Figure 18-2) requires further explanation. If you have a tape device installed, by all means use it; this is the most common way to preserve frequent backups. The second choice is a file; select it and the backup will be saved on your drive — local or remote.

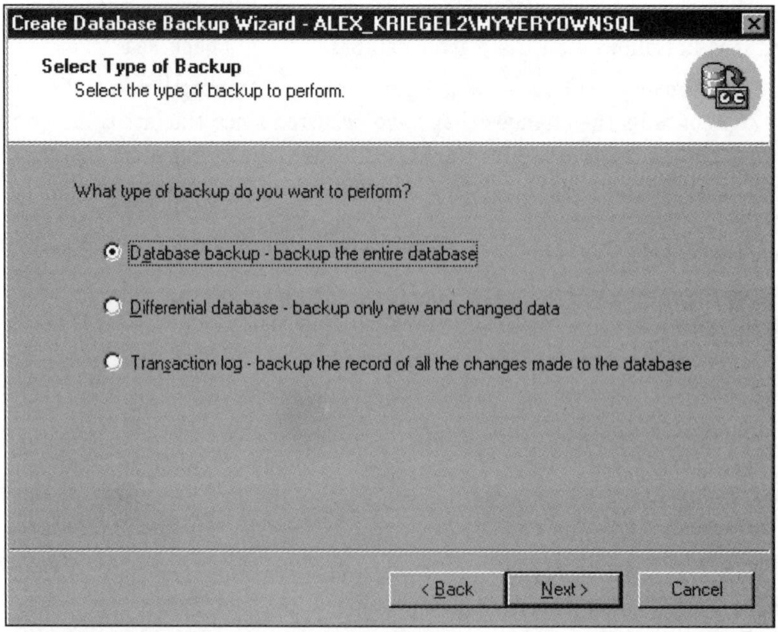

*Figure 18-1*
*Selecting backup type.*

4. Next you must choose a backup device. In its simplest form a backup device is a structured storage file stored on your hard drive or tape; the only difference between it and a backup file is that while organizing devices, inside it you may create a logical device to be referred to. The device has a name under which SQL Server knows it: By this name SQL Server stores information about the physical location of the backup device. It is much easier to keep track of Employees_Backup than it is to keep track of C:\dir1\dir2\dir3\emp1.bak. If you have no devices defined for the system, select New Backup Device from the drop-down Backup Device combo box; you will be prompted to create a new device. Alternatively, you can create a new backup device from the Enterprise Manager console Management/Backup node.

The Properties area of the screen shown in Figure 18-2 asks you how you wish to handle your sequential backups. If a backup already exists you can either overwrite it or append it to the existing file. Your choice depends on your business needs, considerations presented earlier in the section "Implementing Backup and Recovery Planning," the amount of free space you have, and so on. Also, make sure to check Read and Verify Data Integrity of Backup After Backup; this will ensure that your backup is valid and readable. Click Next.

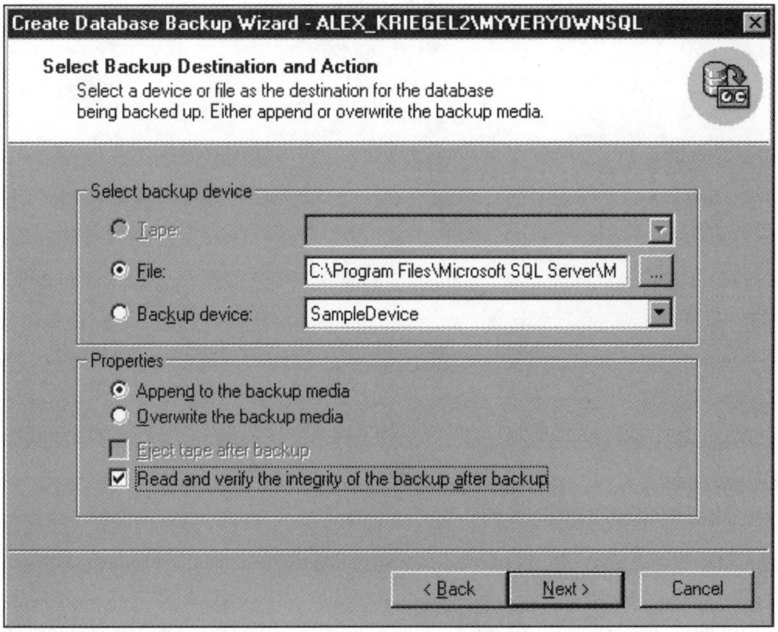

**Figure 18-2**
*Setting backup properties.*

5. If you have chosen to overwrite the backup media option, the next screen will prompt you for media initialization. You may choose to keep the old option (this is the default) or re-initialize. Click Next.

   If you selected Append To the Backup Media from the screen shown in Figure 18-2, this option also appears after you click Next and come to the screen you see in Figure 18-3. Here you can to check the Media Set option (otherwise a backup may be written into the wrong place), and to schedule a backup to be performed periodically. The Backup Set Expiration option will be enabled if you selected Overwrite the backup media from the screen shown in Figure 18-2. Click Next.

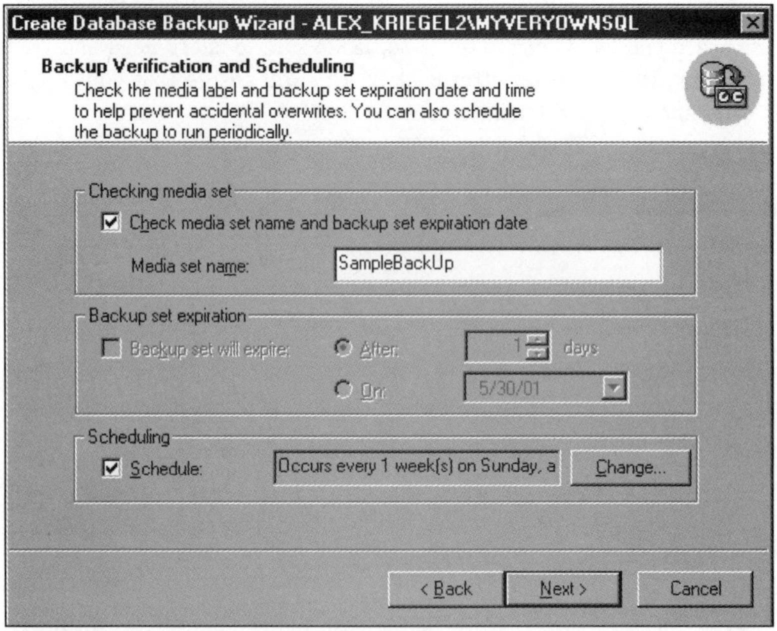

*Figure 18-3*
*Verifying and scheduling backup.*

6. The last screen will present you with a summary of the steps you took. Click Finish to start your backup. If you scheduled this backup it will be performed periodically and will appear under the Jobs node of SQL Server Agent in your Enterprise Management console.

The Backup Wizard does the job for you by creating Transact-SQL statements behind the scenes. If you feel adventurous you can examine these statements or perform a backup manually. The following code creates a logical device called Pubs_Backup on the disk (hard drive) and performs a full backup on it.

```
EXECUTE sp_addumpdevice 'disk', 'Pubs_BackUP', DISK ='C:\Program
Files\Microsoft SQL Server\MSSQL\BACKUP\PubsBackup.dat'
```

```
-- Back up the full Pubs database.
BACKUP DATABASE Pubs TO Pubs_BackUP'
```

The full syntax for creating and executing a backup can be quite intimidating if you specify all the options. Please refer to SQL Server Books Online for this information.

You also can perform a backup by selecting a database node in the Enterprise Manager console, and selecting All Tasks and then Backup from its right-click menu.

### Differential backup

A *differential backup* records all changes to the database since the last database backup. These are smaller and faster than full database backups and can therefore be run more frequently. You need to have performed at least one full backup before you can run a differential one. The steps for performing a differential backup with the Backup Wizard are essentially the same as those for performing a full backup: Just select the Differential database option on the screen shown in Figure 18-1.

### Transaction-log backup

A *transaction-log backup* contains a sequential record of all transactions since the last differential or database backup. These enable you to recover the database up to an exact point in time (that is, up to the last time you performed a transaction-log backup). These backups generally use fewer resources than the previous types of backups and should be run the most frequently.

You can run a transaction-log backup or schedule it to run by selecting Transaction log from the screen shown in Figure 18-1 during the process of creating a backup with the Backup Wizard.

By having different transaction-log and database backups you can recover to a specific point in time (that is, you can restore the database to its state a day, week, or year ago).

**20 Min. To Go**

## Selecting a Recovery Mode

The recovery model is a database property. It defines the method you wish to use when recovering your database; depending on the mode you select, different amounts of information will be preserved for each backup. When a database is created it follows the default simple-recovery model; the other two choices are full recovery and bulk-logged recovery.

### Simple recovery

This option restores a database to its state at the time of its most recent backup. Any changes made after the last full or differential backup are lost (no transaction-log backups are made). Simple recovery involves these two steps:

1. Restore the most recent full backup.
2. Restore the most recent differential backups, if any exist.

### Full recovery

This option restores a database to its state at the point of failure, and involves these steps:

1. Back up the currently active transaction log (if possible).
2. Restore the most recent database backup without recovery.
3. Restore the most recent differential backups.
4. Restore each transaction-log backup since the last restored backup.
5. Apply the log backup from Step 1.

### Bulk-logged recovery

This option enables bulk-logged operations, which means that certain database operations, such as SELECT INTO operations or BCP/Bulk Copy, will be logged minimally or not at all. The risk of data loss is higher than with the full-recovery model, as bulk-logged recovery does not provide point-in-time recovery.

## Restoring a Database

Restoring a database is a manual process. You cannot schedule it, as it is not a normal activity; you do it only when you have to.

Follow these steps to restore a database visually:

1. Highlight the Databases node of the Enterprise Manager. Then select the Restore Database option from the right-click menu.

   The resulting dialog box, shown in Figure 18-4, prompts you to select a database to restore. (With regard to the Restore as database combo box —

yes, you can restore a database under a different name, overwriting an existing database; see the discussion of the Option tab later in this session).

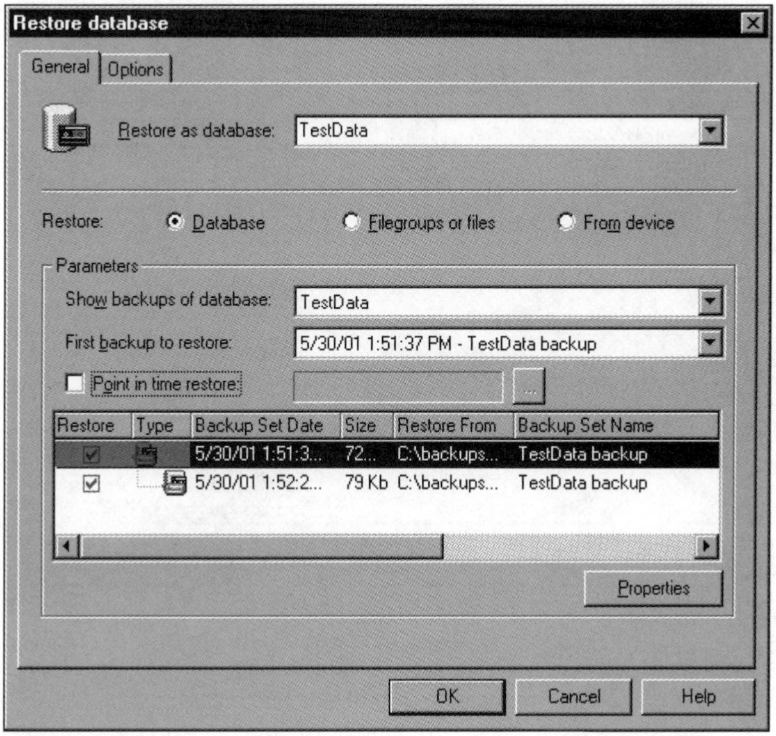

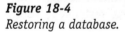

**Figure 18-4**
*Restoring a database.*

2. You now select where you are going to restore from (your backup files, devices, and so forth). If you have multiple backups, you also need to select the backup you wish to use. The Point-in-time restore option will record the time of your last transaction-log backup; selecting this option will apply a transaction-log restore after a database is restored.

3. On the Options tab (shown in Figure 18-5) of the Restore database dialog box (shown in Figure 18-4) you may specify additional settings prior to restoring the database. These settings include Force restore over existing database, which will cause your database in SQL server to be dropped and then recreated from the restore. If you are restoring differential backups you may want to be prompted before each backup is applied.

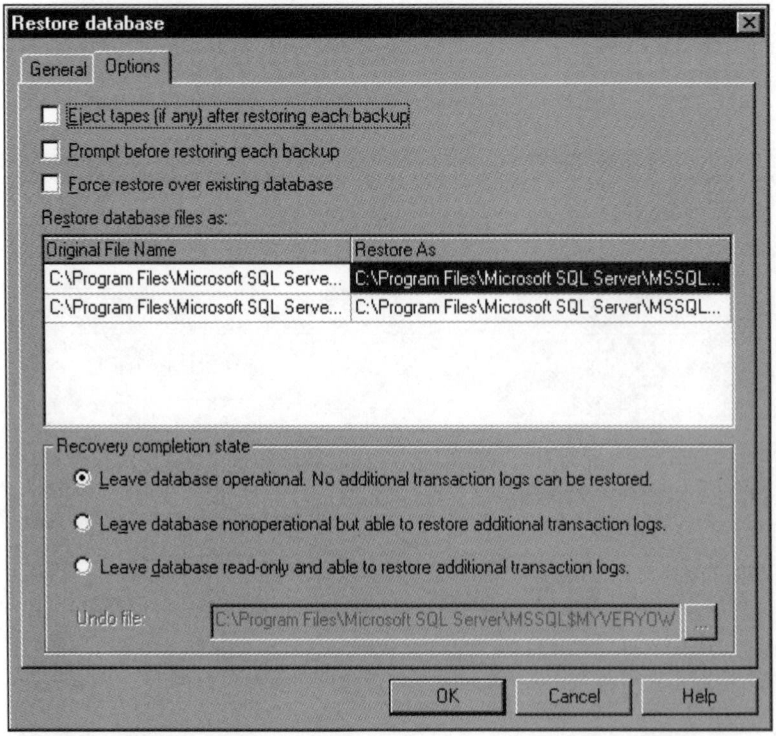

**Figure 18-5**
*Specifying restore-database options.*

After your database is restored you have several choices:

- Leaving the database operational, which means that the restored database and its log do not allow any additional restore operations; the database is ready for use.

- Making the database non-operational, if you intend to apply more transaction logs in the future.

- Creating a read-only database enabling the restoration of additional transaction logs; this selection also enables the undo file, which you will use to roll back any changes should the restoration of the transaction log be unsuccessful.

Click OK to run the restore operation.

**10 Min.
To Go**

## Managing Backups

Managing your database backups is a very important part of your backup strategy. You must be careful to ensure that you can restore your system when you need to. Each backup contains a description as well as expiration information. You can use this information to identify individual backups as well as to determine when it is safe to overwrite a backup. It is not necessary to keep all backups forever. In addition, the MSDB database contains a complete history of all backups and restore operations on the server.

**Use expiration dates on backups to prevent the overwriting of recent backups.**

Ensure that your backups are in a secure place, usually off-site. Keep old backups for a while so you'll have something even if the most recent backups are damaged or lost.

You can see a list of the database and transaction-log files contained in the backup set. Here you'll find the logical name, physical name, file type, file size (in bytes), maximum allowed file size, and other information.

If you performed a backup of a database to a device created on this system, you can view this information by examining Backup node members (you'll find them in the Enterprise Manager console's Management/Backup node); you can view backup performed to tape or file either by clicking the Properties button on the Restore Database screen (shown in Figure 18-4) or by clicking the Contents button of the Backup Database screen (an option of the database node right-click menu, All Tasks ⇨ Backup Database).

You can also retrieve information from the media header and the backup header for each backup. The backup header is recorded each time the backup is run and includes the backup devices used, the type of backup performed, and the start and stop time of the backup. The media header includes the media name and description, and the name of the software that created the media.

**Verifying a backup confirms that the backup is correctly written and readable. It does not, however, validate the structure of the data contained within the backup. To verify the structure of the data before creating a backup, perform database consistency checks (DBCC, discussed in more detail in Session 26).**

*Done!*

## REVIEW

- Database backup is essential for minimizing the risks of data loss; deciding what to back up and how frequently should be a part of your backup strategy.

- You can choose from four different types of backup: full, differential, transaction-log, and file-group. Select your database backup type based on your business requirements.

- Each database is assigned one of three recovery modes, which determines what information is preserved for backups. They are simple recovery, full recovery, and bulk-logged recovery.

- Each backup should be verified and stored in a safe place off site.

- Restoration is a manual process. You can restore any database under any name. It doesn't matter where the backup was created as long as you have a full set of restores.

## QUIZ YOURSELF

1. What is the difference between a full backup and a differential backup?
2. Why do you need to back up the transaction log?
3. Name the three recovery models. What is the default recovery model?
4. How do you restore your database to a specific point in time?
5. Why is it not a good idea to store your backups on the same drive on which you have your SQL Server installed?

# SQL Server Replication

## Session Checklist

✔ Reviewing SQL Server replication

✔ Selecting a replication model

✔ Preparing for replication

✔ Setting up replication

**30 Min.
To Go**

I n this session you will learn how to plan, set up, and administer a basic replication system in order to distribute data across multiple databases. You will acquire a basic understanding of the choices a replication presents, and learn how to configure the replication process through the Publishing and Distribution Wizard.

## Reviewing SQL Server Replication

*Replication* distributes data from the central database to one or more target databases, and merges changes from a target database into the central one. Both the source database and the destination database can be implemented as a SQL Server database or as any other data source, as long as an OLE DB provider is available to handle the nitty-gritty details of the particular data source you choose (such as ORACLE, Access, and so on).

The practical reasons to perform replication are to distribute workload and to synchronize data among remote databases that you want to keep in sync. By maintaining identical data sets across multiple databases you can provide better performance. Local users can connect to and use their own local databases, instead of connecting to a remote central server. Your mobile sales force will be able to send sales leads back to a central database. Or you can use replication to keep a standby server in sync so you can switch to it should your primary server fail.

The replication architecture is quite complex, as it was designed to meet a variety of needs. Here are the basic concepts you ought to understand before you set up and administer a replication process.

**Replication is tricky to configure and administer, and chances are that if you need to set it up you are not the only DBA on duty. I recommend getting all the help you can until you feel at home with replication.**

## Basic replication terminology

Replication consists of two major components:

- **Replication components** — SQL Server components used in replication: the Publisher, Distributor, and Subscriber.

- **Replication Agents** — Utility programs that assist in the replication process: the Snapshot Agent, Distribution Agent, Log Reader Agent, Queue Reader Agent, and Merge Agent.

The replicated data are organized into the following categories:

- **Publication** — A wrapper for distributed data; a collection of one or more articles scheduled for publication (replication).

- **Article** — A basic unit of replication. It can be a table, certain columns in the table, certain rows in the table, a view, or even a stored procedure. More than one article together comprises a publication.

- **Subscription** — A request to receive a publication. The two basic types of subscription are the Pull subscription (initiated by the Subscriber) and the Push subscription (initiated by the Publisher).

**In versions of SQL Server prior to version 7.0 it was possible to publish a single article. Now, the minimum amount you can publish or subscribe to is a publication that may contain only one article.**

Each server participating in the replication is assigned one or more of the following roles:

- **Publisher** — A source server for the distributed data. It maintains all the information about data specified for publishing.

- **Distributor** — An intermediary between the Publisher and the Subscriber; it can also be both Publisher and Subscriber. Its role varies according to the type of replication.

- **Subscriber** — The final destination of the distributed data. It is a recipient of the publications it has subscribed to; depending on the type of replication, it may also be able to propagate changes to its own set of data onto the Publisher.

**You cannot publish any of the system databases or any system tables in the Master database.**

SQL Server supports three different types of replication:

- **Snapshot replication** — This type of replication takes a snapshot of the data in the Publisher database and replaces it with the entire data set of one or more subscribers; subsequent replication again replaces the complete data set in the subscriber database(s). Though notable for being virtually foolproof in providing synchronous data sets, this type of replication increases network traffic and, as intervals increase, data sets become less synchronized.

- **Transactional replication** — This type of replication is all about changes. It propagates changes only to subscribers. It starts with an initial snapshot replication and then distributes selected transactions in the Publisher database transaction log (marked for replication) to the target servers. Snapshot replication is also regularly scheduled to ensure consistency of the data. Its major advantages are more timely updates and much lighter network traffic than you get with pure snapshot replication.

- **Merge replication** — This type of replication allows subscribers who make changes to their local copies of the data to merge these changes into the source database. Merge replication is not transactional and relies on conflict resolution to determine the precedence of the changes.

## Selecting a Replication Model

The term *model* refers to the physical structure of the replication process. As my favorite book says, the key to successful replication is proper planning. The following models of replication scenarios are designed to fit different needs:

- **Central publisher** — The most common replication model. It maintains Publisher and Distributor databases on the same server, with subscribers configured somewhere else.
- **Central publisher with remote distributor** — The Publisher database is on one server and the Distributor database on another; subscribers are by default placed on remote servers (you do not need to maintain a Subscriber on the same server as a Publisher).
- **Central subscriber** — One Subscriber collects data from several publishers; the data can then be republished, as nothing prevents the server from wearing several hats — it can be a Subscriber, a Publisher, and a Distributor at the same time.
- **Publishing subscriber** — Republishes received data to other Subscribers; see the preceding description of the central-subscriber model.

When selecting a replication model, keep in mind the main purpose of replication: reducing workload on the main server. The central-publisher model makes administration easier because both databases are on the same server; on the other hand, it puts an additional workload on the server for the same reason.

## Preparing for Replication

After you have selected your replication type and replication model you still need to perform a couple of preliminary tasks.

### Snapshot replication

For snapshot replication you need to consider space requirements, because the data will be moved as a whole, and timing, because replication is a strain on networking resources as well as on database resources. Also, you need to determine when replication should be performed — it makes no sense to distribute old data.

### Transactional replication

Since transactional replication is based on snapshot replication it should make you think of all the things relevant to snapshot replication and then a few more. With this type of replication transaction logs become very important: You might consider increasing transaction-log space and taking special measures to ensure that no transactions are purged from the publisher database until they have been successfully replicated.

**For transactional replication and merge replication, all published tables must have a primary key.**

### Merge replication

Merge replication is probably the most confusing type of replication. Since so much depends on conflict resolution, every distributed table must have a primary key; if any foreign key is specified, you must include the referenced table. Merge replication also places some restrictions on the data types allowed for publication.

**20 Min.
To Go**

### Setting up Replication

As you might expect, SQL Server 2000 provides you with wizards to guide you through the process of setting up and configuring replication. In fact, it provides you with five of them (from the Enterprise Manager console toolbar select Tools ⇨ Wizards). No doubt you are going to have hours and hours of fun exploring the available wizards, as replication is a subject complex enough to deserve a book of its own.

For the purpose of this session I am going to configure replication in one step, using the Configure Publishing and Distribution Wizard. You'll find this wizard in the Replication tab of the SQL Server Properties screen. If your SQL Server is not configured for replication Configure will be the only option available, as you can see from Figure 19-1.

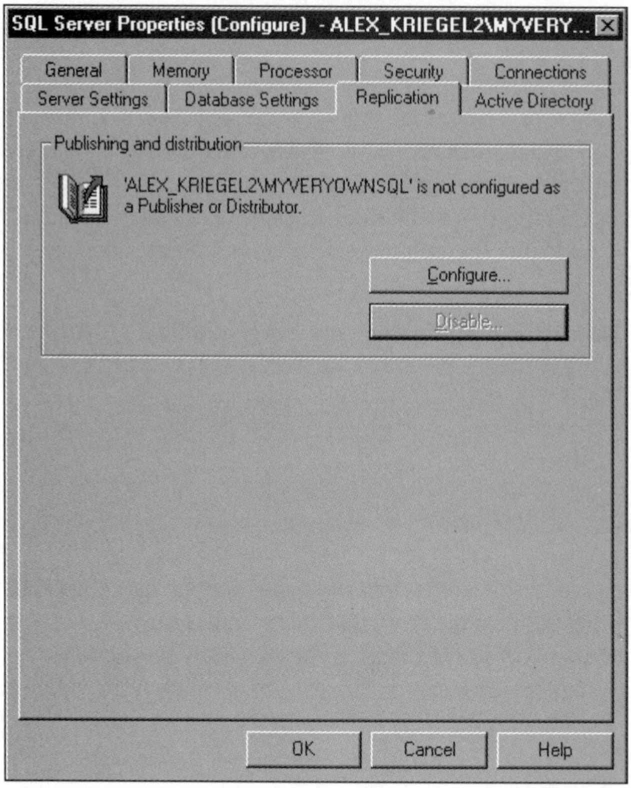

*Figure 19-1*
*Configuring replication*

Clicking Configure will invoke the Configure Publishing and Distribution Wizard, which will guide you through the following three-step procedure:

1. Configure a Distributor, as shown in Figure 19-2. Here you need to select the model of your replication, the default being central publisher.

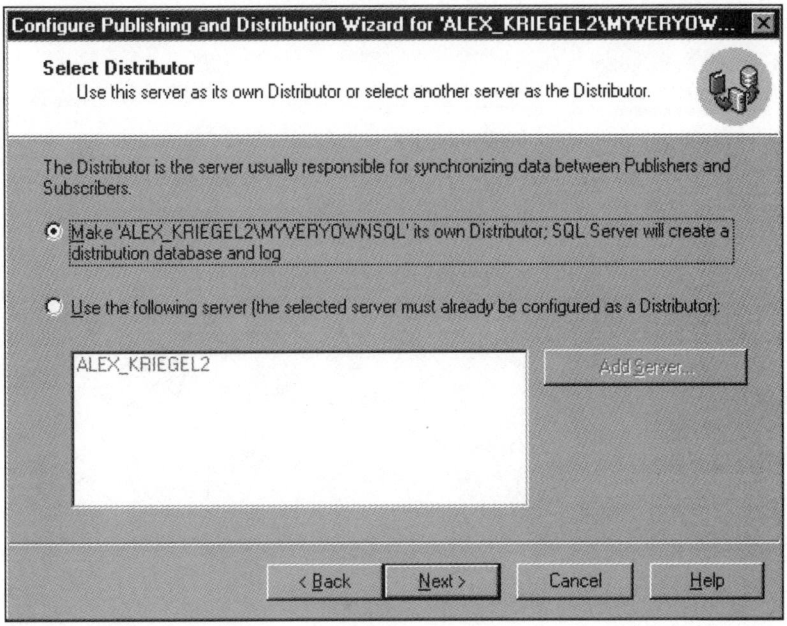

**Configure Publishing and Distribution Wizard for 'ALEX_KRIEGEL2\MYVERYOW...** ⊠

**Select Distributor**
Use this server as its own Distributor or select another server as the Distributor.

The Distributor is the server usually responsible for synchronizing data between Publishers and Subscribers.

◉ Make 'ALEX_KRIEGEL2\MYVERYOWNSQL' its own Distributor; SQL Server will create a distribution database and log

○ Use the following server (the selected server must already be configured as a Distributor):

ALEX_KRIEGEL2                                    [ Add Server... ]

[ < Back ] [ Next > ] [ Cancel ] [ Help ]

**Figure 19-2**
*Selecting a Distributor*

**Note**

**Since replication is a scheduled task, SQL Server Agent must be running. In addition, SQL Server Agent must use an account different from the system account.**

2. The next screen will prompt you for the startup options for SQL Server Agent. Unless you are going to manually administer your replication, I recommend choosing the default, Start Automatically.

   Snapshot data are the foundation of every replication. In the screen shown in Figure 19-3 you need to specify the folder where these data are going to be stored. You need to have full administrative privileges on your machine to use this folder, whether on a network or locally. Click Next.

3. The wizard prepares a summary of your choices. If you wish you can customize your configuration according to the needs of your organization; here I am accepting all defaults, meaning that I configure a central-publisher replication, with the Distributor residing on the same server as the Publisher. Click Next.

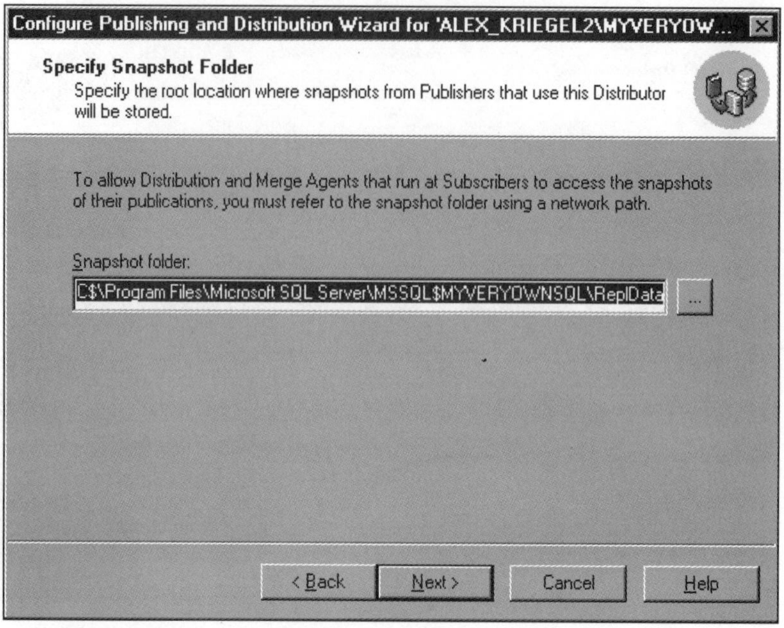

*Figure 19-3*
*Specifying a physical location for snapshot data*

SQL Server will implement all the options you've selected, creating the distribution database, configuring the Distributor, and enabling the Publishers, Subscribers, and Publication databases.

Once the replication is configured on your machine, the Replication tab on the SQL Server Properties screen (shown in Figure 19-1) acquires additional controls, enabling you to disable the replication and add a Replication Monitor Group to your Enterprise Manager console.

## Creating publications

Again, you are going to rely on the same wizard to do all the work in the following steps:

1. From the Replication node in the Enterprise Manager console, select the New Publication right-click menu option.

    After you go past the Welcome screen (be sure to click the Show Advanced Options check box at the bottom) the wizard presents you with all the databases on your Publisher server that are available for replication: These will be your custom databases, as system databases and TempDB cannot be replicated. Select the database you wish to replicate and click Next.

If you already have one publication defined for this database, the wizard will prompt you to use this publication as a template. Feel free to ignore this suggestion and create a new publication. Click Next.

2. On the next screen, Select Publication Type, select the type of publication, of course. (Refer to the section "Preparing for Replication" earlier in this session for help selecting an appropriate option.) Click Next.

3. The next screen, Updateable Subscriptions, offers you two choices regarding how the Subscriber will handle the replication — whether the changes will all be distributed immediately or whether they will be queued until they can be applied to the Publisher. (Refer to the section "Preparing for Replication" earlier in this session for help selecting an appropriate option.) Click Next.

4. The following screen is entitled Specify Subscriber Types.

   Your newly created publication has no subscribers as yet, but you should already know who's going to subscribe to this publication: SQL Server 2000 or 7.0, or some heterogeneous data source like ORACLE. Select the options appropriate to your needs and click Next.

5. You see the screen shown in Figure 19-4, which gives you the opportunity to specify your articles. Recall that an article can be almost any database object, though most often it is a table. You need to specify the objects you wish to publish.

   A publication must have at least one article to be valid; at the other extreme, you can publish the entire database. Depending on the selected table structure, the wizard might need to resolve some issues — by disallowing IDENTITY columns from being published, for example; if other types of objects are selected for publication the nature of the issues may be different. If any issues arise, the wizard will notify you with a very detailed explanation of the action the wizard took to resolve the issue. Click Next.

6. Name your subscription: You should also give it a short description to make it easier to maintain. Click Next.

7. You can either create your publication with all the options you've specified, leaving the rest to defaults, or you can apply filters to create subset data, allow anonymous subscriptions, and so on. I recommend leaving this screen to its own devices — for now. Click Next.

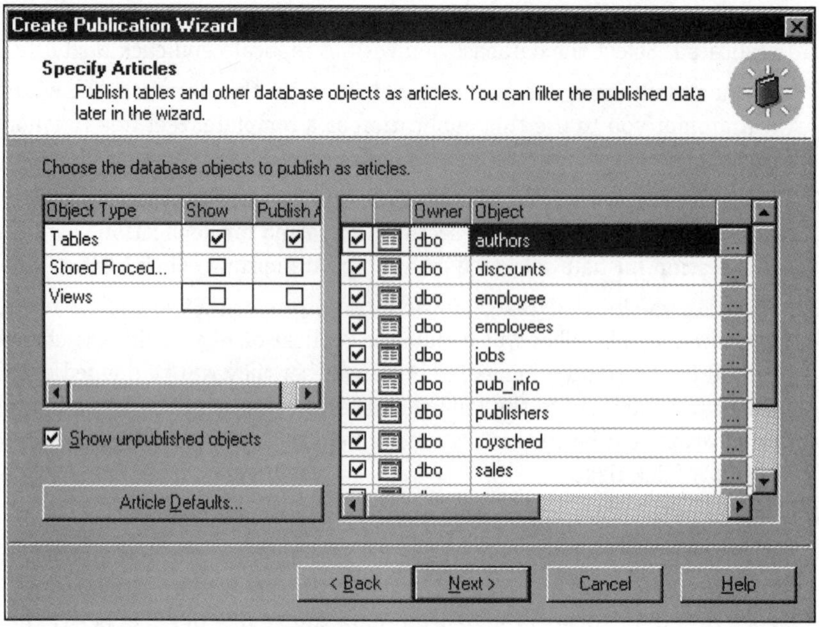

**Create Publication Wizard**  ☒

**Specify Articles**
Publish tables and other database objects as articles. You can filter the published data later in the wizard.

Choose the database objects to publish as articles.

| Object Type | Show | Publish |
|---|---|---|
| Tables | ☑ | ☑ |
| Stored Proced... | ☐ | ☐ |
| Views | ☐ | ☐ |

| | | Owner | Object | |
|---|---|---|---|---|
| ☑ | ▦ | dbo | authors | ... |
| ☑ | ▦ | dbo | discounts | ... |
| ☑ | ▦ | dbo | employee | ... |
| ☑ | ▦ | dbo | employees | ... |
| ☑ | ▦ | dbo | jobs | ... |
| ☑ | ▦ | dbo | pub_info | ... |
| ☑ | ▦ | dbo | publishers | ... |
| ☑ | ▦ | dbo | roysched | ... |
| ☑ | ▦ | dbo | sales | ... |

☑ *Show unpublished objects*

Article *Defaults*...

< *Back*   *Next* >   Cancel   *Help*

**Figure 19-4**
*Selecting articles for publication*

8. This is the last screen, which informs you that the design process is complete. Click Finish and observe the status report telling you that the publication was successfully created.

You can at any time modify or remove a publication from the Enterprise Manager console, Replication node, or Publications sub-node.

**10 Min.
To Go**

### *Managing subscriptions*

Once a publication is created you can push (send) it to subscribers. (Subscriber servers can also initiate a Pull (request) subscription on their own.) The Push Subscription Wizard guides you through the process.

1. From the Publications sub-node collection, select a publication you would like to push, and from its right-click menu select the Push New Subscription option.

2. The Push Subscription Wizard prompts you to select a Subscriber server from the list of available subscribers. Select one and click Next.

3. Select the recipient database. All replicated objects in the recipient database must have the same structure as the database of origin. Click Next.

4. Next, schedule your subscription: Either it will run continuously (usually not a good idea) or it is scheduled to occur every so often. The major considerations here are network load and the availability of data. Click Next.

5. If this is a new subscription, it has to be initialized. This means that the Snapshot Agent will create an initial snapshot of the data and the database schema for the subscriber. Click Next.

6. Subscription relies on certain services. The next screen, Start Required Services, will show you the status of these services and prompt you to start them if they're not running. Click Next and then Finish on the next screen to create a Push subscription.

Pull subscriptions are created in essentially the same way, only from the Subscriber side: Choose New Pull Subscription from the Publications sub-node collection to initiate a Pull subscription.

### Monitoring replication

Once the replication process is set in motion you need to monitor it. SQL Server provides you with the Replication Monitor, accessible through the Enterprise Manager console. To show the Replication Monitor in the console, go to the SQL Server Properties menu option (accessible from the right-click menu on the register SQL server node); then, from the Replication tab, select the Show Replication Monitor Group check box.

Through the Replication Monitor you can examine all current Publishers, publications, and subscriptions defined for the Distributor. It also enables you to view the status of replication agents and helps you troubleshoot the Distributors database.

**Done!**

## REVIEW

- Replication is a process of distributing data based on the Publisher/Subscriber paradigm.
- You can set up replication to include non-SQL Server components (such as ORACLE and DB2).
- The three different types of replication are Snapshot, Transactional, and Merge. Each type of replication serves a different business need.

- Each server participating in replication has to be assigned the role of Publisher, Distributor, and/or Subscriber. It is possible for a server to perform more than one role at a time.
- The two main types of subscription are Pull subscriptions and Push subscriptions. The first type is initiated by the Subscriber, the second by the Publisher.

## Quiz Yourself

1. What is the main purpose of replication?
2. Describe the roles of the Publisher, Distributor, and Subscriber.
3. What are the three different types of replication?
4. What are the advantages and disadvantages of using a central publisher with remote distributor replication model?
5. What is the difference between Pull subscriptions and Push subscriptions?
6. How do you monitor the replication process?

# *User Management*

## *Session Checklist*

✔ Setting up a user account

✔ Managing user permissions

✔ Managing a multiuser environment

**30 Min.
To Go**

I n this session you learn how to set up and administer user accounts and manage access permissions for the database object. I also introduce you to some of the considerations involved in setting up and administering multiuser environments.

## *Setting up a User Account*

Sooner or later you will have to allow someone other than yourself to connect to your SQL Server, and you have to make sure that he or she has just enough rights to do his or her job — no more, no less.

**I'll discuss security issues in depth in Session 28.**

## Roles

SQL Server uses *roles*. Two layers of access exist: access to the SQL Server and access to a database object within the server. Each can be configured separately. While I will discuss SQL Server roles in greater detail in Session 28, it will be beneficial for you to learn about some fixed database roles, namely these four:

- **Public** — Essentially anyone who has enough rights to connect to the database; the lowest role possible in terms of database permissions.

- **db_owner** — Someone who has full rights to this database, including the right to delete it altogether, create objects, and so on.

- **db_data_reader** — Someone who is allowed to read the data without any modifications, and who cannot create objects.

- **db_datawriter** — Someone who is allowed to read and write data, but who cannot create objects.

These roles are contained in every database, including system databases. Every user will belong to at least one of them.

## Logins

Each database has one or more users who have specific privileges for accessing data in this database. You can grant database access while creating a login or add a user to the database who would use an existing login. In any case you must create a login first and then add users and assign privileges. To do so, follow these steps:

1.  Start by creating a new login for your SQL Server. From the Enterprise Manager console, choose Tools ⇨ Wizards ⇨ Create Login Wizard. On the Welcome screen, click Next.

2.  The next screen (shown in Figure 20-1) prompts you to select an authentication mode. In general, you should connect to SQL Server using Windows account information (Windows Authentication) if you have a domain-based network, but in this case the user will be required to provide his or her credentials by logging in with a login ID and password. A SQL Server login is commonly used for dialup connections and peer-to-peer networks. Click Next.

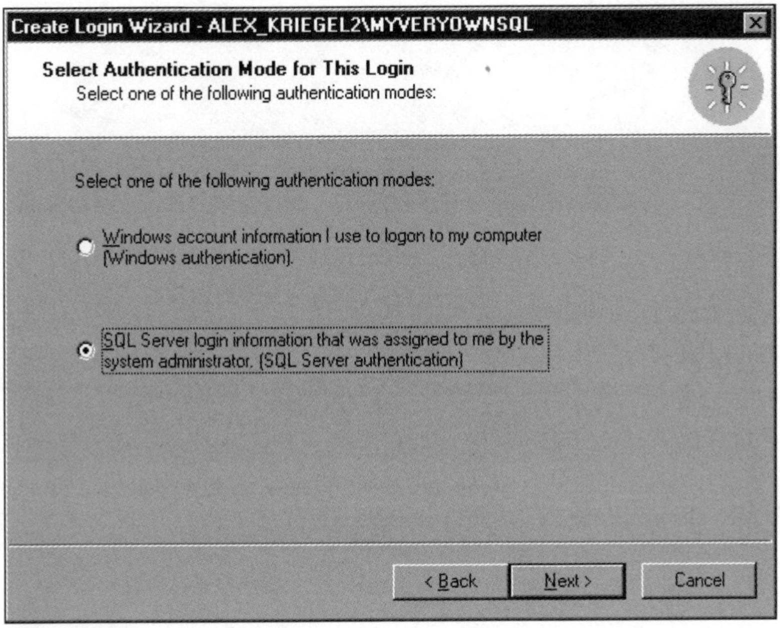

**Figure 20-1**
*Selecting the authentication mode*

3.  If you selected SQL Server Authentication you are prompted to enter a login ID and password, as shown in Figure 20-2. If you are using Windows Authentication you are asked for a valid Windows account on the network. Click Next.

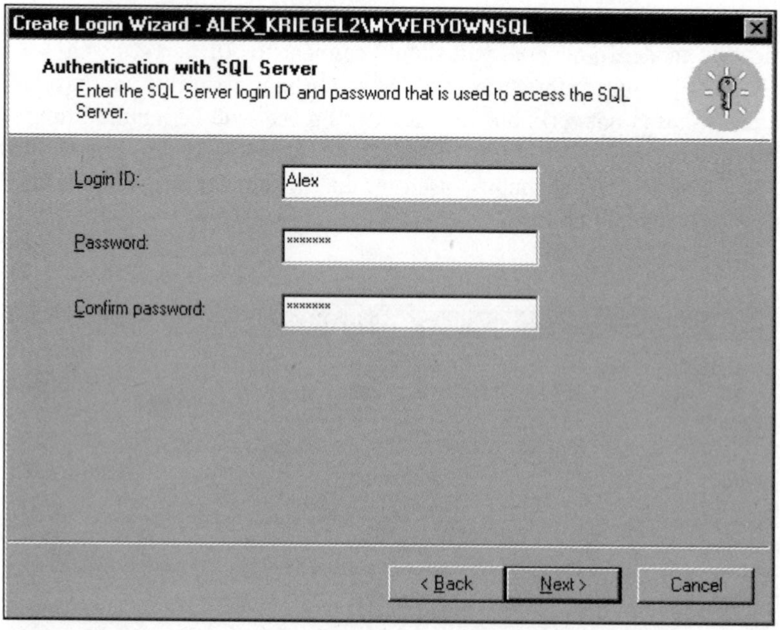

**Figure 20-2**
*Supplying a login ID and password for SQL Server authentication*

4. You may wish to grant access to security roles (see Session 28), though for the purpose of this session you should leave nothing selected on the screen shown in Figure 20-3. Click Next.

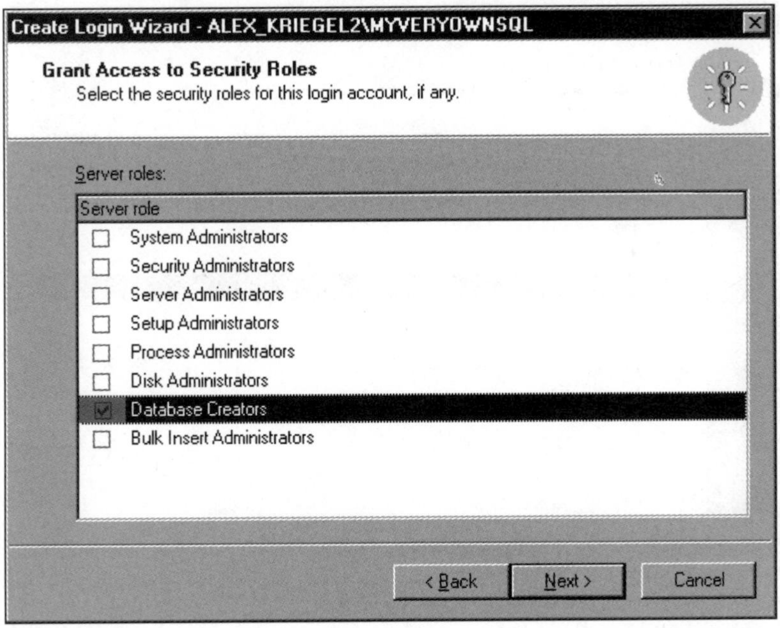

**Figure 20-3**
*Granting access to security roles*

5. The next screen (shown in Figure 20-4) enables you to set up database access permissions. This is what you are after: Select the databases you wish this login to access. Click Next.

6. The last screen will display a summary of what you've specified. Click Finish to create the login.

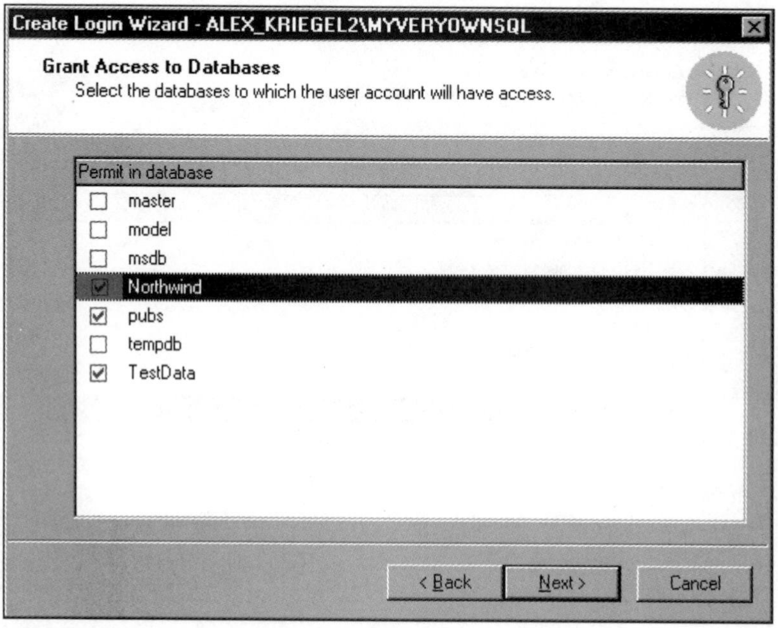

Create Login Wizard - ALEX_KRIEGEL2\MYVERYOWNSQL  ☒

**Grant Access to Databases**
Select the databases to which the user account will have access.

| Permit in database |
| --- |
| ☐ master |
| ☐ model |
| ☐ msdb |
| ☑ Northwind |
| ☑ pubs |
| ☐ tempdb |
| ☑ TestData |

< Back    Next >    Cancel

**Figure 20-4**
*Granting access to databases*

**20 Min.
To Go**

## Managing User Permissions

After the login is created, it is automatically entered into the Users collection of
every database it was assigned to. By default it is also assigned to the Public database role. You may revoke these default privileges either by modifying the properties of the login or by going to the Users collection for the database and deleting
any user you do not want accessing your data. If you assigned database privileges
for more than one database you will have to go to each of the databases to revoke
the privileges assigned.

To view and adjust properties, or to delete the user, expand the Databases node
in the Enterprise Manager and select the database you wish to examine. In the
Users sub-node for this database locate the user (login ID) and double-click it.

From the screen displayed in Figure 20-5 you can assign membership to different database roles such as db_owner and db_datawriter. The names of these roles
are descriptive enough that you can guess what kind of privileges they grant.

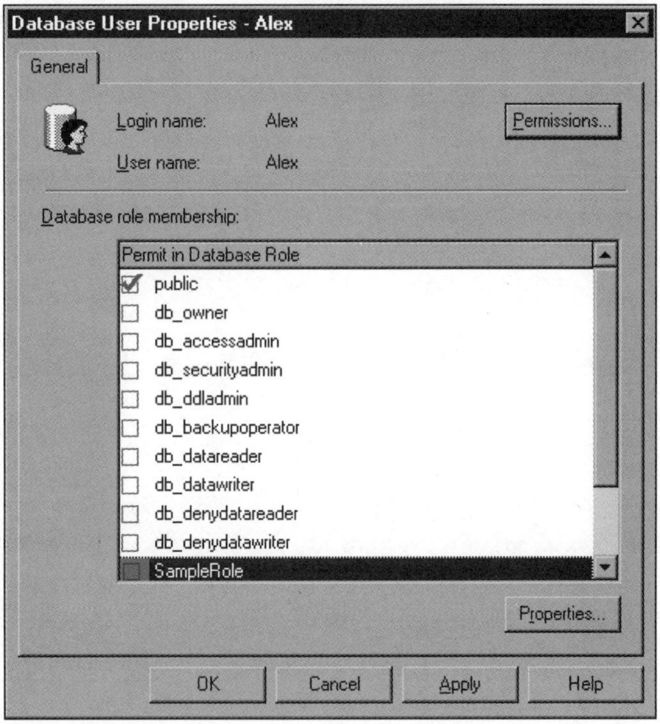

Database User Properties - Alex

General

Login name:      Alex                    Permissions...

User name:       Alex

Database role membership:

| Permit in Database Role |
|---|
| ☑ public |
| ☐ db_owner |
| ☐ db_accessadmin |
| ☐ db_securityadmin |
| ☐ db_ddladmin |
| ☐ db_backupoperator |
| ☐ db_datareader |
| ☐ db_datawriter |
| ☐ db_denydatareader |
| ☐ db_denydatawriter |
| SampleRole |

Properties...

OK      Cancel      Apply      Help

**Figure 20-5**
*Modifying database user properties*

SQL Server provides various levels of data-access granularity: You can restrict access to a particular view or table in the database, or even to a particular column within a table, and on the table you can grant permission to read data but not to update them (the same is true on the column level). You can also deny the right to execute a particular stored procedure (see Figure 20-6) for a particular user or group of users.

DRI stands for Declarative Referential Integrity. By checking this column's boxes you grant rights to execute these constraints. Double-clicking will prohibit execution; you will see a red cross in place of a green check mark.

**Note**

**The wealth of security choices is rather overwhelming and making the right choices requires meticulous planning. By granting more rights than necessary you compromise the security of your database, but by granting too few you hamper database performance and compromise maintainability.**

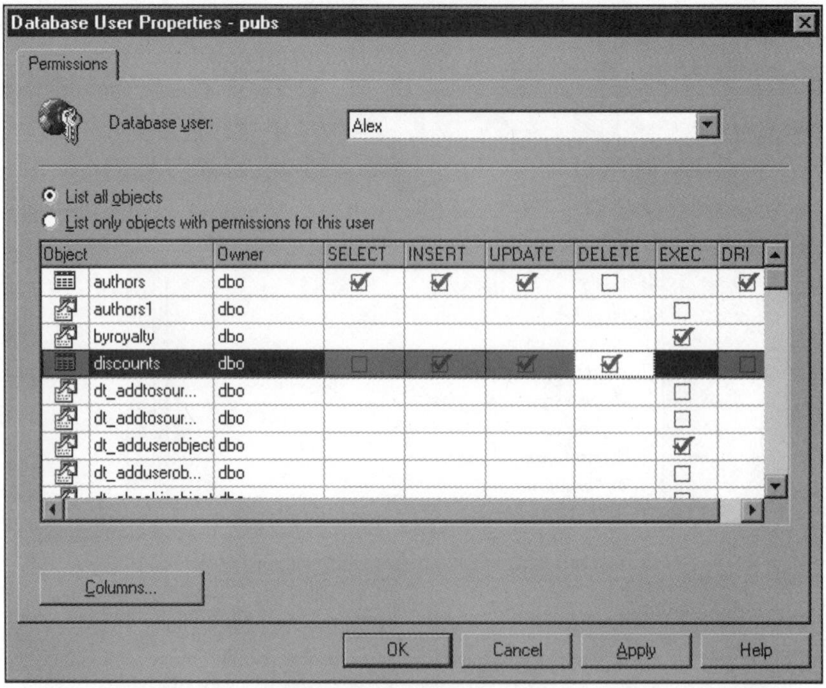

**Database User Properties - pubs**

Permissions

Database user: Alex

○ List all objects
○ List only objects with permissions for this user

| Object | Owner | SELECT | INSERT | UPDATE | DELETE | EXEC | DRI |
|--------|-------|--------|--------|--------|--------|------|-----|
| authors | dbo | ☑ | ☑ | ☑ | ☐ | | ☑ |
| authors1 | dbo | | | | | ☐ | |
| byroyalty | dbo | | | | | ☑ | |
| discounts | dbo | ☐ | ☑ | ☑ | ☑ | | ☐ |
| dt_addtosour... | dbo | | | | | ☐ | |
| dt_addtosour... | dbo | | | | | ☐ | |
| dt_adduserobject | dbo | | | | | ☑ | |
| dt_adduserob... | dbo | | | | | ☐ | |

Columns...

OK     Cancel     Apply     Help

*Figure 20-6*
*Granting privileges to database objects*

The Permissions button gives you access to the permissions assignment for the highlighted database role (see Figure 20-7). You can add or remove members of this particular role.

The fixed public role is the least flexible: You cannot add or drop members. For more on roles and database security please refer to Session 28.

**You can directly assign permissions to all objects in the database for the database role using the Permissions tab on the Database Properties screen.**

You may revoke permissions in exactly the same way that you grant them. Dropping a particular login will result in the removal from all databases of all users associated with that login; you may use this operation to disable the user account of an employee leaving your company, for example.

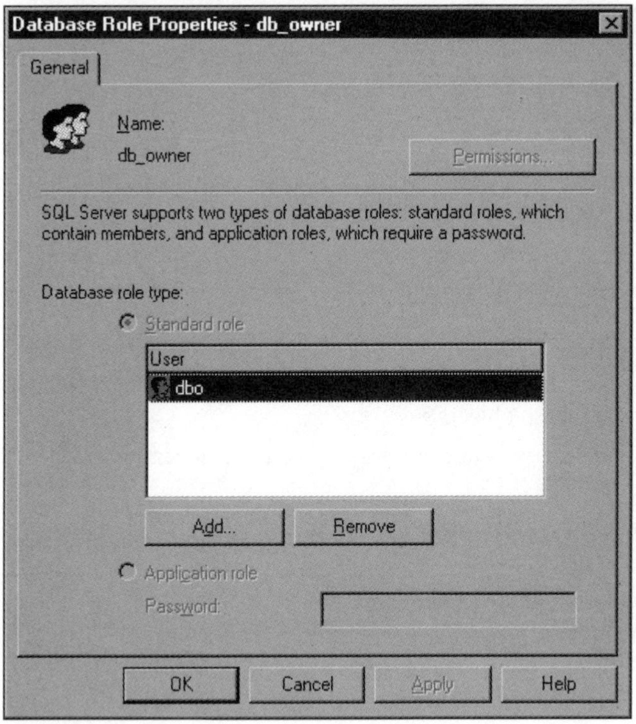

**Database Role Properties - db_owner**

General

Name:

db_owner

Permissions...

SQL Server supports two types of database roles: standard roles, which contain members, and application roles, which require a password.

Database role type:

⊙ Standard role

| User |
| --- |
| 🧑 dbo |

Add...    Remove

○ Application role

Password:

OK    Cancel    Apply    Help

**Figure 20-7**
*Adding members to fixed database roles*

## Managing a Multiuser Environment

**10 Min.
To Go**

Most likely, your SQL Server databases will operate in a multiuser environment, a database accessed by multiple users at the same time. Using such an environment increases the possibility of conflicts, as several users can access and modify the same data at the same time.

SQL Server provides you with several ways to reduce the probability of conflict. You can use locks, database design, referential integrity, and so on. The most important factor in preventing conflict, though, is managing the permissions assigned to users. It may make sense for you to assign different privileges to everyone in your organization. For example, you might give a salesperson permission to view data, a supervisor permission to remove or modify data, and a manager permission to insert new stuff into the database. You probably do not want your users to have privileges to drop and create objects; you probably also don't want everyone to have access to the company's sensitive data.

Though it adds to your maintenance burdens, administering user privileges in a multiuser environment will eventually pay off in the form of fewer headaches for you as DBA (no surprises or corrupted data) and for the management of your organization (no security breach involving sensitive data).

**Done!**

## REVIEW

- SQL Server 2000 provides several layers of access to the server, to the database, and to the database objects.
- Every user of the database is automatically given a membership in the public role.
- In order to access data, a user must be associated with a valid login.
- You can assign permission to access the database, and to view, modify, or delete the data. Finely granulated security enables you to restrict access at the column level and determine the type of operations users can perform in a given column.

## QUIZ YOURSELF

1. What type of access is controlled by database roles and server roles?
2. What are the considerations involved in selecting an authentication mode?
3. How can you add a user to every database at once?
4. What database role does not enable you to either add or remove members?

# PART

# IV

## Saturday Evening

1. What is the purpose of DTS?
2. What data sources can DTS connect to?
3. How do you transform data during the export/import procedure?
4. What tool can you use you use to design and modify DTS packages?
5. What is BCP?
6. What are the differences between BCP and the data transformation package?
7. What databases do you need to back up? Why?
8. What media can you back up to?
9. What is a backup device?
10. What are the two ways of creating a backup of a SQL Server database?
11. What is the purpose of a database transaction log?
12. What might cause a database transaction log to fill up?
13. How does full backup differ from differential backup?
14. Is it possible to create a differential backup for a transaction log?
15. What are the steps for restoring a database from a normal backup?
16. How does backup and restoration of the Master database differ from any other backup and restore operation?
17. What is the main purpose of a replication?

18. What are the three types of servers (components) in the replication model and what are their purposes?

19. What are the two types of subscription?

20. Name the replication agents.

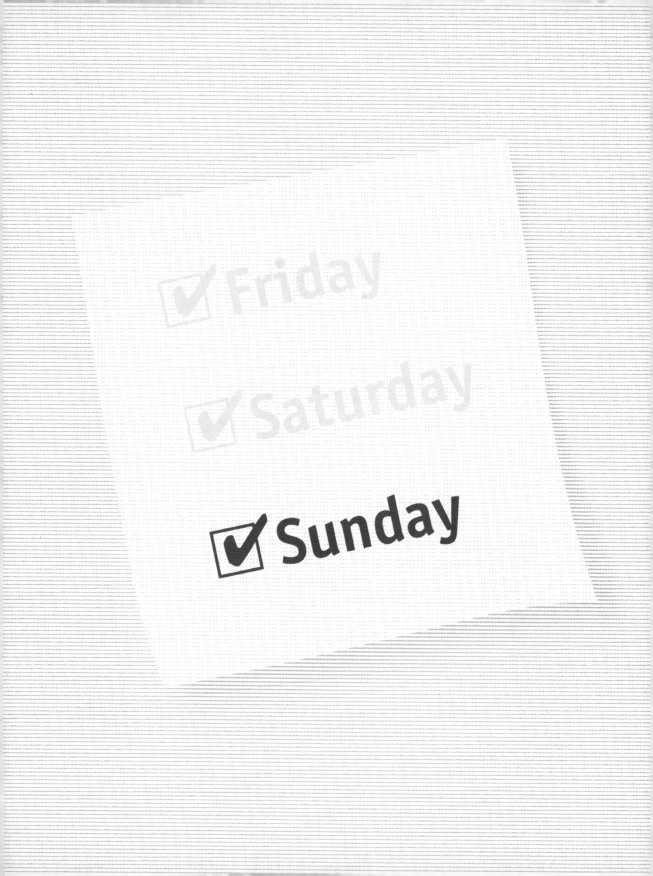

## Part V — Sunday Morning

## Part VI — Sunday Afternoon

# PART

# V

## Sunday Morning

# Managing Your Databases Visually

## Session Checklist

✔ Devising a database-maintenance plan

✔ Scripting and documenting your database

✔ Moving and copying database files

**30 Min.
To Go**

**T**his session shows you how to create, modify, and schedule your database-maintenance plan to ensure its optimal performance. It also introduces several database wizards that can help you perform various database-related tasks.

## Devising a Database-Maintenance Plan

Once created, a database has to be maintained. This goes double for the SQL Server system databases. Maintenance involves making sure your database is properly tuned for optimum performance, checking database integrity, and ensuring that you have the most recent backup of the database and its transaction log — just in case.

To do all this manually would be quite a task (which some hardcore DBAs still do). Fortunately, Microsoft supplies a Database Maintenance Plan Wizard to guide you through the process of creating such a plan and scheduling it.

**With the Enterprise Edition of the SQL Server you can even
schedule the transfer of transaction logs to a different server:
This is one way to keep data consistent across different servers.**

You can start up the Database Maintenance Plan Wizard from the Tools ➪ Wizards
menu (found under the Management node), or you can access it from the right-click
menu of the Database node by selecting All Tasks ➪ Maintenance Plan. Alternatively,
you may start the wizard from the right-click menu in the Database Maintenance
Plans node under the Management node in the Enterprise Manager console.

1. After skipping the Welcome screen of the wizard you get to the Select
   Database screen, shown in Figure 21-1.

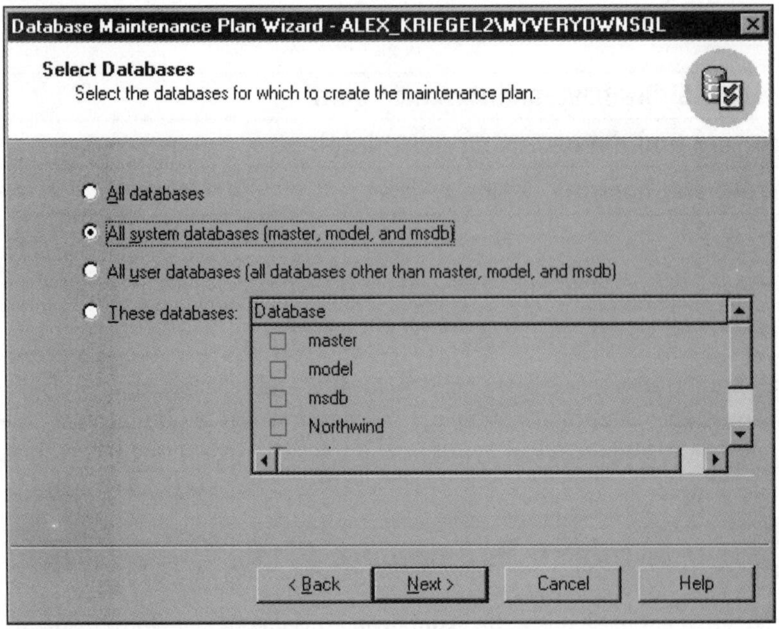

*Figure 21-1*
*Selecting databases for the maintenance plan*

From here you can select the database for which you are going to create
the plan. It is usually a very good idea to maintain all your system databases, especially your Master database. This example will create a maintenance plan for all system databases. Click Next to proceed to the next
screen, shown in Figure 21-2.

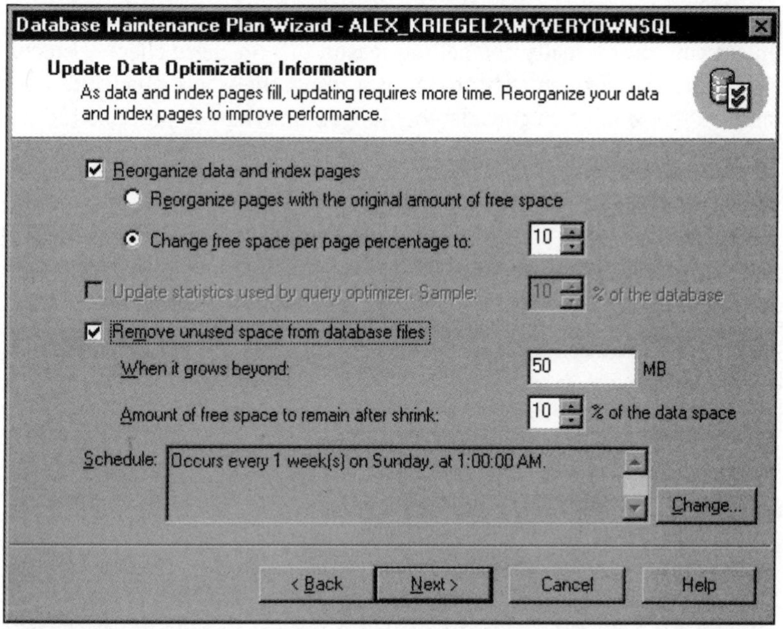

**Database Maintenance Plan Wizard - ALEX_KRIEGEL2\MYVERYOWNSQL** ☒

**Update Data Optimization Information**
As data and index pages fill, updating requires more time. Reorganize your data and index pages to improve performance.

☑ Reorganize data and index pages
  ○ Reorganize pages with the original amount of free space
  ◉ Change free space per page percentage to:   `10` ⏶

☐ Update statistics used by query optimizer. Sample:   `10` ⏶ % of the database

☑ Remove unused space from database files
  When it grows beyond:   `50`    MB
  Amount of free space to remain after shrink:   `10` ⏶ % of the data space

Schedule: Occurs every 1 week(s) on Sunday, at 1:00:00 AM.    ⏶
  ⏷   Change...

  < Back    Next >    Cancel    Help

**Figure 21-2**
*Specifying the tasks for your database-maintenance plan*

2.  You should select these options depending on your needs. Reclaiming unused space is usually a good idea if conserving disk space is of concern to you; reorganizing data and index pages makes sense in a database in which data changes frequently; you may choose to update statistics used by the SQL Query Optimizer. This option becomes enabled when you decide not to organize data and index pages, in order to speed up your queries. You can schedule all these tasks to be performed recurrently; if you do, keep in mind that this kind of operation is very resource-intensive and that the databases will not be functional until the procedure completes. Click Next.

**Statistics are created for each table automatically, unless you turn off the AUTO_CREATE_STATISTICS database option. This option, which pertains to the distribution of the values in the tables' indexed columns, is accessible from Auto Create Statistics on the Options tab of the Database Properties screen. The SQL Query Optimizer uses these statistics to determine which index to use for a particular query. Your choice of index has a significant impact on the efficiency of the query.**

**3.** The next screen (shown in Figure 21-3) deals with database integrity. Unless you have a really compelling reason to skip these checks, I recommend performing them every time. As a result the whole procedure might take longer, sometimes considerably longer, but there is no price too high for peace of mind. You may schedule this procedure as well. However, keep in mind that it is resource-intensive; if you schedule it to execute very often it may bog down your server because of the integrity checks. Click Next.

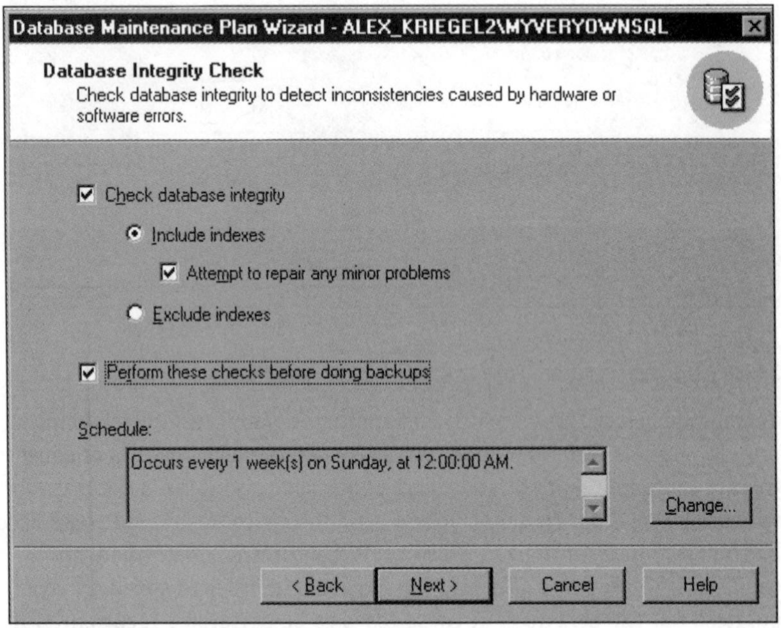

**Figure 21-3**
*Checking database integrity*

**3.** The next screen is fairly self-explanatory (that's why it is not shown here). It enables you to include a database backup as part of the maintenance plan. This is usually a good idea, if time, disk space, and tape availability permit it. Choosing to verify integrity upon completion will increase your down time but will also increase your peace of mind.

You also need to decide how long you wish to preserve your old backups. The answer usually comes from your company's policy for preserving data: Some companies are really paranoid and wish to keep every bit of information, while others have a more casual attitude. Click Next.

**5.** This screen is an exact replica of the one before it (which, again, is why I don't show it here). It deals with transaction logs. Everything I said about database backup also applies to transaction logs, which keep track of all changes and are very helpful in restoring the exact state of a database after the unmentionable — a server crash. Click Next.

**6.** The next screen (shown in Figure 21-4) enables you to set reporting options. After a maintenance cycle is completed a report is generated and stored in a file form; you may also choose to send e-mail notification to any of the operators on the list (Session 26 covers setting up the SQL Server Mail Agent and operators). Click Next.

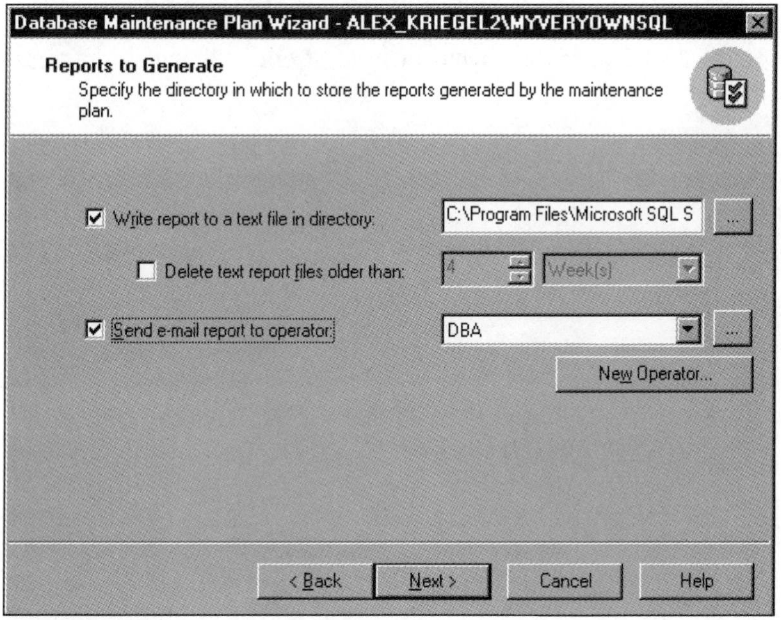

*Figure 21-4*
*Generating reports*

**7.** The next screen enables you to choose how many records of each occurrence of the maintenance-plan execution you wish to keep; 1,000 rows of buffer space seems reasonable to me.

Sometimes things do not go exactly as planned. You need to maintain a history of your maintenance-plan executions in order to find out where things went wrong and, if possible, to find out why. How much information you wish to preserve is up to you; the default setting limits the amount to 1,000 rows for this particular plan. Click Next.

8. The last screen presents you with a summary of the steps you took. Clicking Finish will store the newly created database-maintenance plan in the Maintenance Plans collection under Management ⇨ Database Maintenance Plans in the Enterprise Manager.

After the plan is created you can always modify its properties, or delete it altogether. Locate your maintenance plan under the Database Maintenance Plans node and choose Properties from the right-click menu on the plan you wish to modify or delete. Figure 21-5 depicts the screen you'll see after combining all the steps you've just been through.

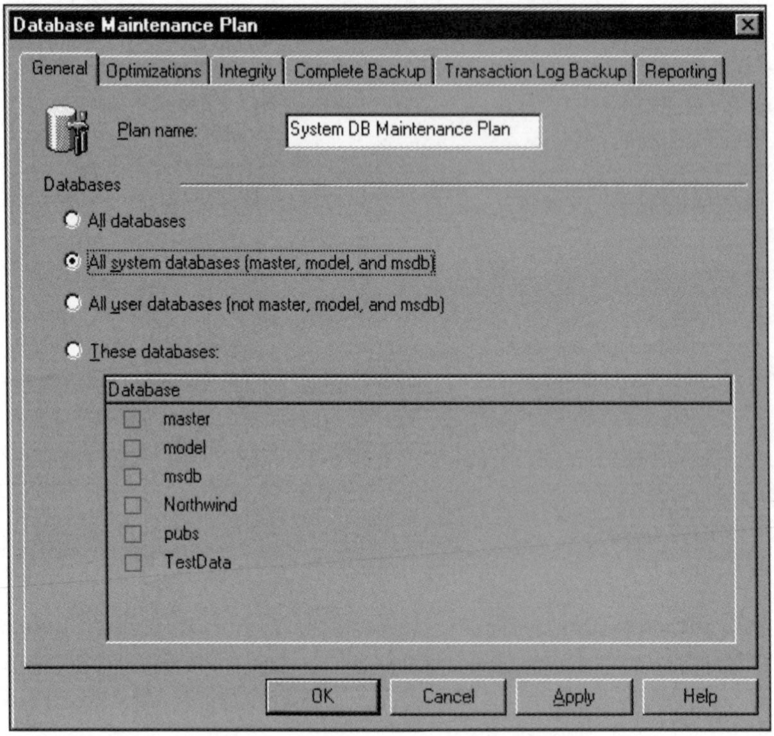

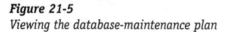

**Figure 21-5**
*Viewing the database-maintenance plan*

From the window shown in Figure 21-5 you can change the options you set when you created the plan, reschedule, apply this plan to another database, and so on.

## Scripting and Documenting Your Database

**20 Min.
To Go**

Your database is a living thing. It changes every so often, new tables come into existence, new rules replace old ones, and new stored procedures are created constantly. This analogy continues to the point when your database dies — either peacefully or not.

To be in control of the situation you need to know your database structure at any given point in time, or close to it, as database changes happen often. Start by scripting and documenting your database. SQL Server 2000 makes it easy for you: Select All Tasks ➪ Generate SQL Scripts from the right-click menu on the database you want to document. Figure 21-6 shows SQL objects to be scripted for the Pubs database (make sure you've clicked Show All, and then check Script All Objects).

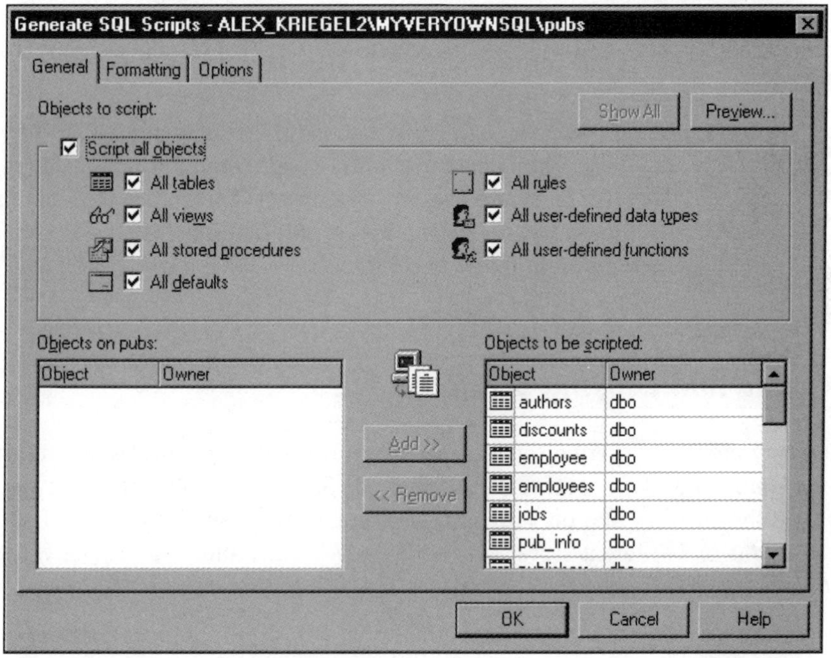

**Generate SQL Scripts - ALEX_KRIEGEL2\MYVERYOWNSQL\pubs**

General | Formatting | Options

Objects to script:                                    Show All    Preview...

☑ Script all objects
    ☑ All tables               ☐ ☑ All rules
    ☑ All views                 ☑ All user-defined data types
    ☑ All stored procedures     ☑ All user-defined functions
    ☑ All defaults

| Objects on pubs: | | | Objects to be scripted: | |
|---|---|---|---|---|
| Object | Owner | | Object | Owner |
| | | | authors | dbo |
| | | | discounts | dbo |
| | | Add >> | employee | dbo |
| | | << Remove | employees | dbo |
| | | | jobs | dbo |
| | | | pub_info | dbo |

OK    Cancel    Help

**Figure 21-6**
*Scripting the entire database*

Part V—Sunday Morning
Session 21

On the Formatting tab select the formatting options. The options you choose depend on the kind of objects you have in your database and on your business requirements. For example, including a DROP command for each object in the database will prevent an error that would occur when you try to create an object that already exists. Setting compatibility levels to 8.0 (SQL Server 2000) instructs SQL Server to use syntax that might be incompatible with previous releases.

The Options tab presents you with a variety of options:

- *Security options* — All your database users and roles, permissions and logins.
- *Table options* — Script indexes, full text indexes, triggers, and constraints.
- *File options* — Determines how the script file is formatted and saved. For example, saving a file as UNICODE will prevent the script from running on SQL Server 6.5 and earlier; you can also choose to have one file per object or all objects scripted in one big file.

For documenting purposes you probably want to include every option. Click OK to generate an .sql file: This is your database-structure snapshot. You may wish to open it to examine the resulting script, add your comments, and so on. Save it in a safe place. Of course, you will need to update it from time to time as your database changes.

**Using Generate Script you can script virtually any object in your database. Then you can run the script through the SQL Query Analyzer to create the scripted object. Remember that any data contained by an existing object will be lost: They are dropped before a new object is created.**

**10 Min. To Go**

## Moving and Copying Database Files

You may not do this very often but knowing how to move databases around will help you in your daily routine. Recall that SQL Server 7.0/2000 databases are physically stored as files on your system. If you copy these files with .mdf and .ldf extensions to a different server where SQL Server is installed, SQL Server will be totally unaware of them until you attach them to the server as a database.

**To ensure its integrity, always follow proper procedures when detaching and attaching a database; do not simply copy or move the files as you would any other file on your system.**

Follow these steps for detaching a database:

1.  Select the database you would like to move and choose All Tasks ⇨ Detach Database from the right-click menu. SQL Server determines whether there are any connections to this database and reports the status.

2.  If the database is ready to be detached, you may do so by clicking OK. However, you may want to consider updating the statistics first. You will see your chosen database disappear from the Enterprise Manager Console. Now you can copy the files to any location you want.

Once the files are copied to a new location you need to attach the database. To do so, right-click the All Tasks menu on the Databases node in the Enterprise Manager console. All you have to do is to specify the location of your main .mdf file; SQL Server will recognize the structure and display information about the database the file contains. Click OK to attach the file to the SQL Server. An attached database will immediately appear under the Databases node (if it does not, choose Refresh from the right-click menu of the Databases node).

**If you prefer doing things the hard way you can use the system stored procedures sp_attach_db and sp_detach_db to attach and detach databases, respectively.**

Detaching and re-attaching a database is a great way to move it around, but what if you just want to create a copy of the existing database on some other server? Meet the Copy Database Wizard. It enables you to copy a database between two servers and to copy the corresponding objects: logins, metadata, and so on.

1.  Start the Copy Database Wizard by selecting Databases ⇨ All Tasks ⇨ Copy Database Wizard.

2.  The first screen prompts you to select the source server. The default is your local server, but you can choose any server accessible to you from the network.

3.  Select the destination server(s) — yes, you can copy to several servers at once.

4.  Select the database(s) to be copied, as well as all the other objects you wish to copy. Click OK to start the process; once it is completed you will have an exact copy of your database on the destination server(s).

**You cannot copy any of the system databases using this wizard.**

SQL Server 2000 tries to make your life as a database administrator easier with a number of different wizards. But you should not think of these wizards as a substitute for knowledge of what is going on behind the scenes, of how things are *really* working.

**Done!**

## REVIEW

- You went through the process of creating a database-maintenance plan. It is very important to maintain a current maintenance plan and to execute it at regular intervals to ensure the integrity and optimum performance of your database.

- Scripting a database provides you with a documented schema for it, which you can use to recreate your database or to create an empty database copy on a different system.

- SQL Server 2000 provides you with a number of wizards with which to perform various administrative tasks. Detaching and attaching databases are two of these tasks.

- The other way to create a copy of your database is to use the Database Copy Wizard.

## QUIZ YOURSELF

1. Why do you need a database-maintenance plan?
2. What processes are included in your maintenance plan?
3. Where is a database-maintenance plan stored?
4. Why is it a good idea to script and document your databases?
5. How do you move databases around?
6. How do you create a copy of a database on a remote machine?

# Distributed Transaction Coordinator

## Session Checklist

✔ Using remote servers and linked servers

✔ Accessing external data sources

✔ Using Microsoft Distributed Transaction Coordinator (MSDTC)

**30 Min.
To Go**

I n this session you are going to learn about accessing external data sources from your SQL Server. You can do this in several different ways, including with linked or remote servers, or by using ad hoc queries. Microsoft Distributed Transaction Coordinator (MSDTC) handles distributed transactions that span more than one database and/or server.

## Using Remote Servers and Linked Servers

If you have one and only one SQL Server running in your organization and never intend to add more to your system, you may safely skip to the next session without feeling you missed something. Chances are, at some point in your DBA career you will need to use more than one RDBMS in general, and more than one SQL Server in particular. As systems become more and more distributed so do the data.

## Remote servers

SQL Server provides you with several tools to help you integrate various data sources with your SQL Server installation — tools like partitioned data, remote and linked servers, and replication. *Remote servers* enable you to execute stored procedures remotely; *linked servers* give you the same functionality as remote servers plus the ability to use distributed queries (explained later in this session). MSDTC manages transactions that span multiple databases on one or more servers. If any of these tools sounds like it might meet your current needs, read on.

The purpose of the remote server is to allow a client application connected to one server to use the services provided by another server (the remote one) without having to connect to it explicitly. With a remote server the client can call a remote stored procedure much as it would call a local one. Only SQL Servers can be set up for remote connection; heterogeneous data sources (such as ORACLE) are not allowed.

Remote servers are a thing of the past. SQL Server 2000 enables you to add a remote SQL Server only for backward compatibility, and you should avoid using them in new systems as they might not be supported in future releases. At the same time, they might be useful in legacy systems during the migration stage.

 **Remote servers are supported in newer versions of SQL Server for backward compatibility. The new feature introduced with version 7.0, linked servers, provides essentially the same functionality as remote servers. Use it instead of remote servers whenever possible.**

To set up a remote-server connection, follow these steps:

1. From the SQL Server Query Analyzer run the following commands:

```
EXEC sp_addlinkedserver <Server1>, 'SQL Server'
EXEC sp_addlinkedserver <Server2>
EXEC sp_configure 'remote access', 1
RECONFIGURE
GO
```

**2.** Stop and restart *<Server1>*

**3.** On the remote server (*<Server2>*), run the following T-SQL commands:

```
EXEC sp_addlinkedserver <Server2>, local
EXEC sp_addlinkedserver Server1
EXEC sp_configure 'remote access', 1
RECONFIGURE
GO
```

**4.** Add a login for the first server:

```
EXEC sp_addremotelogin <Server1>, <Server1 Login>,
<Server2 Login>
    GO
```

**5.** Stop and restart *<Server2>*.

Replace the names in angle brackets with the names of your local and remote servers, and make sure that you are using SQL Server Authentication Mode (with login and password). For the purpose of this example I assume that the passwords are the same for both servers. You also can use the stored procedure sp_addserver, which is still supported for backwards compatibility. To drop the remote server, use the sp_dropserver system stored procedure.

SQL Server also provides you with visual tools with which to set up a remote server. From the Enterprise Manager console select and expand the Security node, and then select the Remote Servers node. From the right-click menu select New Remote Server.

In the screen shown in Figure 22-1, supply the name of the remote server to be identified under the SQL Server console (you must supply a valid name of a SQL Server accessible from your network). Check the RPC box if you want to perform remote procedure calls, and provide login information.

To execute the stored procedure sp_StoredProc in the Pubs database of *<Server2>* from *<Server1>*, use the following syntax:

```
EXECUTE <Server2>.Pubs.. sp_StoredProc  <arg1>, <arg2>...
```

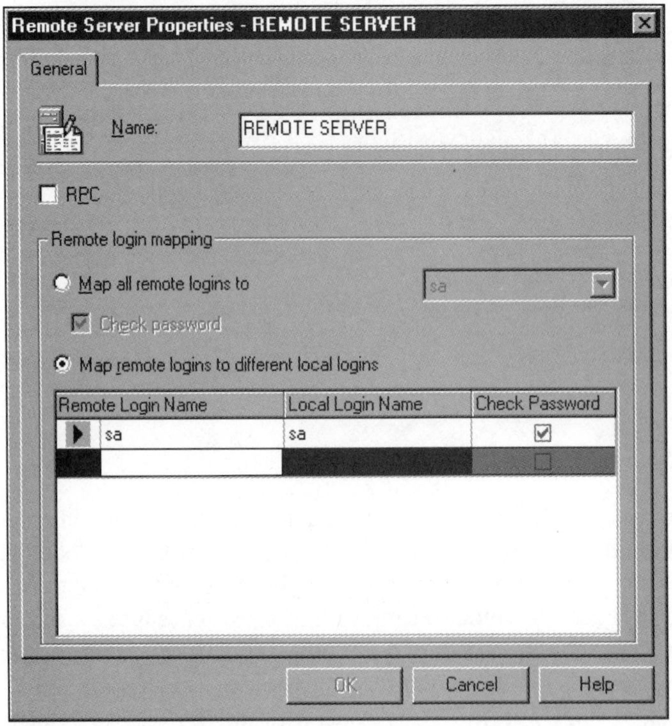

**Remote Server Properties - REMOTE SERVER**

General

Name: REMOTE SERVER

☐ R**P**C

Remote login mapping

○ **M**ap all remote logins to    sa

☑ Check password

⦿ Map **r**emote logins to different local logins

| Remote Login Name | Local Login Name | Check Password |
|---|---|---|
| ▶ sa | sa | ☑ |
| | | ☐ |

OK    Cancel    Help

*Figure 22-1*
*Adding a remote server.*

## Linked servers

Linked servers offer much more flexibility than remote servers do. First of all, they can be anything as long as an appropriate OLE DB provider can support the remote server's functionality. A remote server can only execute stored procedures. Linked servers support distributed transactions across multiple heterogeneous data sources, such as those between a database in ORACLE and a database in SQL Server 2000.

**An OLE DB provider (discussed in Session 29) is an interface that manages interactions with a particular data source. Think of it as a communication layer: On the data-source side it knows all the details of your specific data source, and exposes the consistent interface expected by the client on the other end.**

From the Enterprise Manager console select the Security node and expand it. Select the Linked Servers node, and from the right-click menu select New Linked Server.

As I mentioned before, the linked server can be anything; it doesn't have to be another SQL Server. To demonstrate this, I will add an Access database file as a linked server (see Figure 22-2). The file is named myDB.mdb, and it contains a single table named Customers. It is located in the C:\test\ directory. I created this file using Microsoft Access 2000; please substitute your data-source name and location. The name and structure are of no importance here; just make sure you have at least one table. Users of Microsoft Visual Studio 6.0 have the Nwind.mdb sample database installed, which is an Access version of the Northwind database supplied with SQL Server. (I assume that you have enough expertise to create an Access database. If not, send me an e-mail and I will send you a copy: You can find my contact information in the "Reach Out" section of the preface for this book.)

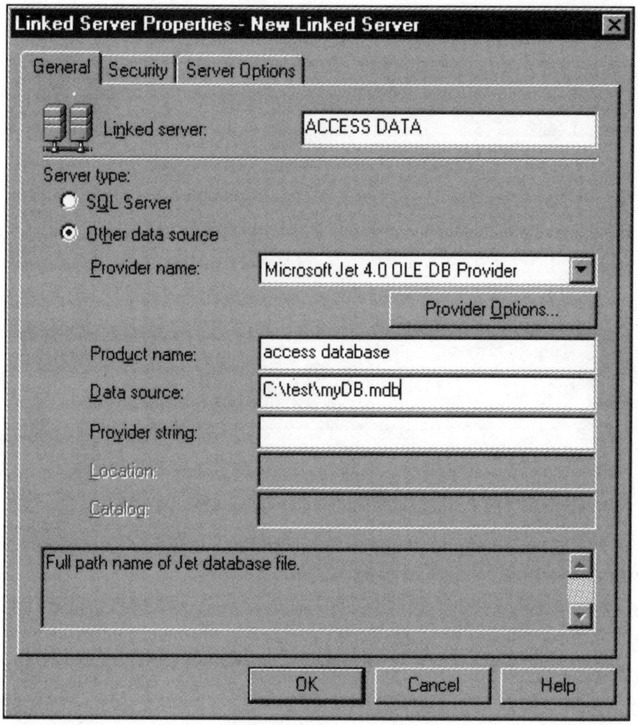

*Figure 22-2*
*Adding a linked server.*

As you fill in the various boxes on this screen, a brief description will appear in the lower pane. In Figure 22-2, the new linked server will be added as ACCESS DATA, and refers to the file myDB.mdb in the specified path. With the Provider Options button you can access the properties of this particular connection, as shown in Figure 22-3.

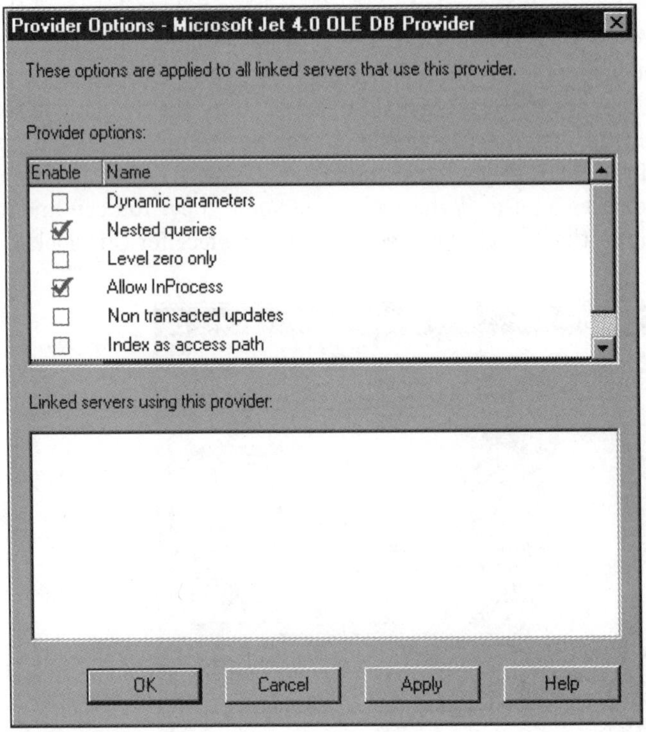

*Figure 22-3*
*Configuring OLE DB Provider properties.*

These options are provider-specific: You need to know the product (in my case Microsoft Access) in order to use them properly.

Next you need to set up security in the Security tab. Essentially, you must specify the login and password information required to access this server, and specify whether or not you wish to use the security context for each login that you did not specify. The default is No security context, which means that every process that tries to connect to this server has to supply a login/password combination to be forwarded to the server, which will then decide which privileges to assign.

The last tab on this screen (shown in Figure 22-4) deals with the linked-server properties such as collation order, data access, and connection timeout. RPC stands for remote procedure call: You need to decide whether you wish to allow the remote client to invoke procedures remotely on this server as well as allowing the server to call out.

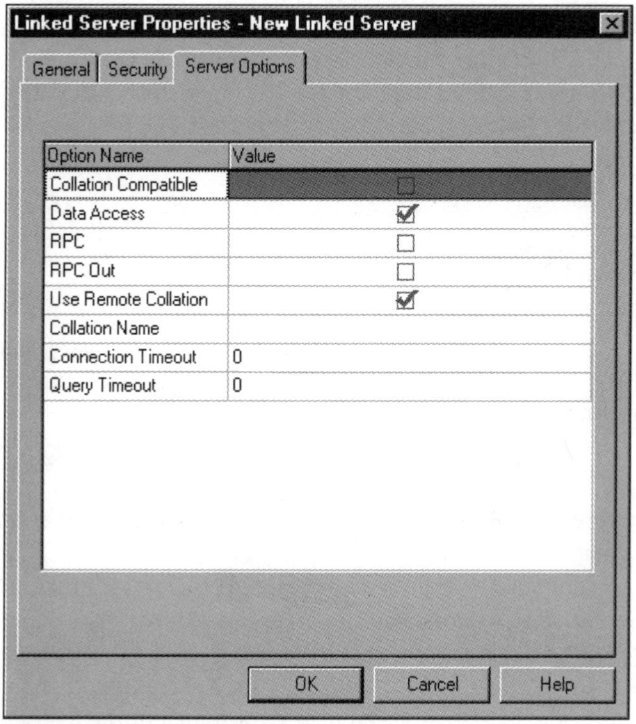

**Figure 22-4**
*Configuring linked-server properties.*

Once all the properties are set, click OK. If all the information supplied is correct, you now have access to the data contained in this database.

If you followed my example and linked to the Access database, myDB.mdb, you see the single table Companies in the myDB.mdb database (all Access system tables appear as well, but I ignore them because they are used internally by Access itself). Now you can query data directly from your SQL Query Analyzer and use data contained in the linked server in your distributed queries.

Using the Enterprise Manager interface you can remove your linked server as you would any other object from your SQL Server: by selecting an object's node and selecting Delete from a right-click pop-up menu. By deleting the linked server you do not delete the database itself, just its registration information within your SQL Server.

**Although in theory any OLE DB–compliant data source can be linked to SQL Server, Microsoft has only tested SQL Server against the OLE DB provider for SQL Server, Microsoft OLE DB provider for Jet, Microsoft OLE DB provider for Oracle, Microsoft OLE DB Provider for Indexing Service, and Microsoft OLE DB Provider for ODBC.**

## Accessing External Data Sources

**20 Min. To Go**

You use a different (from that of a standard T-SQL query) syntax to query linked servers' data tables. For example, to get all the information from the Companies table (from the preceding example), you run the following query:

```
SELECT * FROM OPENQUERY(ACCESS_DATA,'SELECT * FROM Companies')
```

Note the new keyword OPENQUERY, which you need to use in order to access data in the linked server.

SQL Server 2000 enables you to perform ad hoc queries against external heterogeneous (non-SQL Server) data sources. You can access an external data source without linking it to the SQL Server beforehand, though you need to supply more information. To query an external data source (such as my sample myDB.mdb database) without linking it, you must first specify the data source in the query, as shown here:

```
SELECT * FROM OPENDATASOURCE('Microsoft.Jet.OLEDB.4.0',
        'Data Source="C:\test\myDB.mdb"')...Companies
```

Another keyword you can use to access external data sources is OPENROWSET.

```
SELECT tblCompanies.*
FROM OPENROWSET('Microsoft.Jet.OLEDB.4.0',
    'C:\test\myDB.mdb';;,Companies)
    AS tblCompanies
```

You can think of a rowset as a virtual table, a data snapshot created from the external source. The preceding code snippet first creates tblCompanies and then performs the selection; tblCompanies was used to make the whole process more visual. You can rewrite this query as follows and get identical results:

```
SELECT *
FROM OPENROWSET('Microsoft.Jet.OLEDB.4.0',
   'C:\test\myDB.mdb';;,Companies)
```

If your data source requires that you provide a login and password, you must supply these in place of the blanks I left in the preceding query (right after the full path to the data file, <*data file*>;<*blank space*>;<*blank space*>). Please note that the login and password must be enclosed in single quotes (') when they are in the data-source path.

Using these techniques you can query any data source, provided there is an OLE DB Provider for it.

**With the distributed queries and transactions you cannot use any of the Data Definition Language (DDL) statements like CREATE and DROP. If you need to use these or similar statements you must create and call remote stored procedures.**

## Using Microsoft Distributed Transaction Coordinator (MSDTC)

**10 Min. To Go**

On the surface, distributed transactions are no different from local transactions, save for the fact that they span disparate data sources. Distributed transactions use either distributed queries or remote procedure calls.

An application can start a distributed transaction in two ways:

- *Explicitly*, by using the BEGIN DISTRIBUTED TRANSACTION keyword.
- *Implicitly*, by using a distributed query or calling a remote stored procedure within a local transaction.

I mentioned distributed transactions briefly in Session 16. In the same session I mentioned Microsoft Distributed Transaction Coordinator (MSDTC). Here we'll take a closer look (see Figure 22-5).

**Figure 22-5**
*Starting Microsoft Distributed Transaction Coordinator (MSDTC).*

MSDTC must be running on every server involved in the transaction. You start it or configure it for auto-start from the SQL Service Manager. Any given computer can have only one MSDTC service, regardless of the number of SQL Server instances running.

MSDTC goes through two phases in the commit process:

- In the *prepare phase*, it sends the prepare command to all resource managers involved. The resource managers tell MSDTC whether they succeeded or failed at the task.

- Once MSDTC has received these responses it initiates the *commit phase* by issuing the commit command, whereupon each of the resource managers attempts to commit the transaction. If all resource managers report success the transaction is marked as committed; otherwise it is considered suspect and must be resolved in order to continue. Unresolved transactions are rolled back. Previous versions of SQL Server had a visual interface with which to manage MSDTC; in SQL Server 2000 you have to take the vendor's word that it will work properly. The only way to troubleshoot distributed transactions is the SQL Server log, which can help you to pinpoint in-doubt transactions. If you see the following message in your SQL error log

```
<SQL Server detected a DTC in-doubt transaction for UOW
<UOW_ID>. Please resolve it following the guideline for
Troubleshooting DTC Transactions.>
```

you can kill the UOW (unit of work), either with a COMMIT or a ROLLBACK command, as follows:

KILL *UOW_ID* WITH { COMMIT | ROLLBACK }

You can use this KILL syntax only to resolve in-doubt transactions in the prepare phase.

## REVIEW

**Done!**

- You can access many data sources through SQL Server 2000 as long as they have appropriate OLE DB providers.
- You can access an external data source by linking it to the SQL Server or to an ad hoc query.
- SQL Server 2000 supports linked servers and remote servers. Remote servers must be other SQL Servers; linked servers can potentially access any data source.
- A transaction spanning one or more servers is called a distributed transaction. The Microsoft Distributed Transaction Coordinator (MSDTC) manages distributed transactions across multiple servers.
- Distributed transactions are committed in a two-phase process. (The two phases are the prepare phase and the commit phase.)

## QUIZ YOURSELF

1. What is the difference between a remote server and a linked server? Which should you use in a new system?
2. What types of data sources can you access through linked servers?
3. What additional keywords would you use when querying ad hoc external data sources?
4. What is a distributed transaction? How do you start one?
5. What is MSDTC?
6. How do you resolve in-doubt distributed transactions?

# Accessing SQL Server System Information

## Session Checklist

✔ Obtaining SQL Server system information

✔ Using information schema views

✔ Using system stored procedures

**T**his session introduces several ways to obtain information about SQL Server objects, and shows you how to manipulate these from outside the Enterprise Manager console.

**30 Min.
To Go**

## Obtaining SQL Server System Information

Sooner or later your client applications will need system information. How many tables are in the database? What are their names? What is the data type of the columns I am about to update? This information is vital to SQL Server itself. It is contained in system-catalog tables that contain metadata about all system objects.

**One of the ways to obtain this information would be by querying these tables directly. Don't. There is one point Microsoft is very specific about: The system tables are not for querying, as they will change in future releases.**

You have several legitimate ways to access system information in SQL Server 2000:

- **Information schema views** — An abstraction layer on top of system catalogs. They are independent of the catalog structure and thus any application using them is portable among SQL-92–compliant RDBMS(es).
- **ODBC catalog functions** — A set of ODBC API functions designed to retrieve information about underlying RDBMSes. It is implemented in ODBC drivers.
- **System stored procedures and functions** — A set of global stored procedures and functions installed with every SQL Server installation in the Master database.
- **OLE DB schema rowsets** — A programming interface exposed by OLE DB providers. It is independent of system catalogs, and applications using it should be portable (at least in theory).

INFORMATION_SCHEMA and system stored procedures are the two main means of getting information about your SQL Server system.

**Metadata is data that describes data; in the case of SQL Server the term is used to describe objects in the RDBMS.**

## Using Information Schema Views

The information schema views included in SQL Server conform to the SQL-92 Standard definition for INFORMATION_SCHEMA, though SQL Server uses different names. Table 23-1 maps SQL Server object names to their equivalents in the SQL-92 standard.

**Table 23-1**
*SQL Server Equivalents in the SQL-92 Standard*

| SQL Server | SQL-92 Standard |
| --- | --- |
| Database | catalog |
| Owner | schema |
| Object | object |
| User-defined data type | domain |

Use INFORMATION_SCHEMA as a prefix for the name of the object you would like to find information about. The basic syntax for using INFORMATION_SCHEMA is as follows:

```
SELECT * FROM INFORMATION_SCHEMA.TABLES
```

When run from the Query Analyzer, this query will produce the output shown in Figure 23-1.

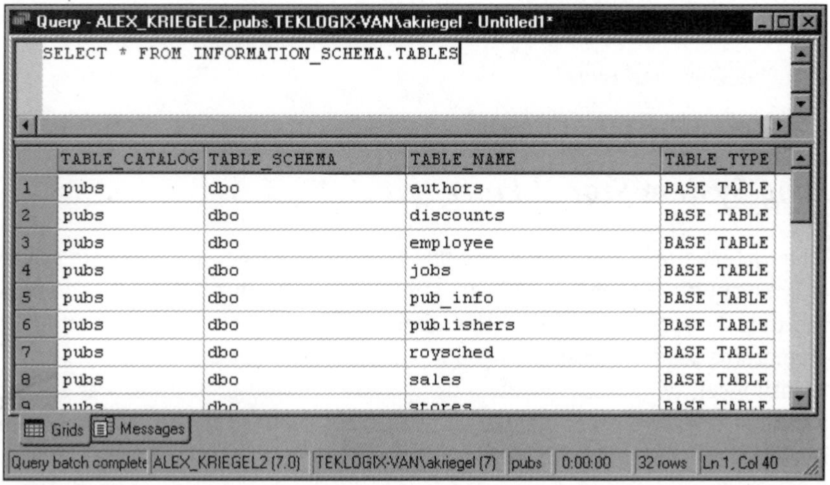

**Figure 23-1**
*Querying INFORMATION_SCHEMA tables' information*

Here are some samples of the more frequently used INFORMATION_SCHEMA objects — the names are very descriptive, though you should consult documentation (such as Books Online) to verify the view's columns you wish to query.

- Table information:

  ```
  VIEW_TABLE_USAGE
  TABLE_CONSTRAINTS
  TABLE_PRIVILEGES
  TABLES
  VIEWS
  ```

- Column information:
  COLUMNS
  VIEW_COLUMN_USAGE
  KEY_COLUMN_USAGE
- Constraint information:
  CHECK_CONSTRAINTS
  CONSTRAINT_COLUMN_USAGE
  CONSTRAINT_TABLE_USAGE
  REFERENTIAL_CONSTRAINTS

**20 Min.
To Go**

## Using System Stored Procedures

Using system stored procedures is a black art that can never be mastered in full. Yes, you can know them all by heart (all 930 of them plus 174 extended stored procedures) — only to find that the number has increased, and that names and parameter types have been changed in the newest release.

Until recently, no alternative to using system stored procedures was available. Even since the advent of INFORMATION_SCHEMA they remain the most comprehensive set of tools for your SQL Server system. You can use system stored procedures to administer SQL Server, to query it for information, and to create and drop database objects. In fact, SQL Server uses them itself, behind the scenes, in performing various administrative tasks. Unlike INFORMATION_SCHEMA, system stored procedures not only display information, but also modify it. Proceed with caution.

You can access most of the functionality offered by system stored procedures through the Enterprise Manager interface, but it's worth your while to familiarize yourself with the most common of them. To execute them directly you can use any of the access interfaces available: Query Analyzer, ISQL, OSQL, and so on.

The system stored procedures can be grouped into categories: Microsoft Books Online lists 10 of them. Here's a list of the ones you are most likely to use:

- General stored procedures
- Catalog stored procedures
- Security stored procedures
- SQL Server Agent stored procedures
- Extended stored procedures

I discuss these stored procedures in the following sections.

## General stored procedures

These procedures help you with basic system administration. General stored procedures, as the name implies, support general SQL Server activity. Table 23-2 lists some selected stored procedures.

**Table 23-2**
*Selected General Stored Procedures*

| Stored Procedure | Description |
| --- | --- |
| sp_help | Provides information about any object listed in the sysobjects table. |
| sp_helptext | Provides access to the text of a rule, default, unencrypted stored procedure, or user-defined function, trigger, or view. |
| sp_helpindex | Provides information about all indexes defined for a specific table or view. |
| sp_helpuser | Provides information about SQL server users, roles, and so on. |
| sp_who | Provides information about current users and processes. |
| sp_lock | Provides information about locks. |

## Catalog stored procedures

*Catalog stored procedures* return information about tables, columns, data types, privileges, and such. These procedures have been largely supplanted by INFORMATION_SCHEMA views. See Table 23-3 for a list of selected catalog stored procedures.

**Table 23-3**
*Selected Catalog Stored Procedures*

| Stored Procedure | Description |
| --- | --- |
| sp_databases | Provides a list of all accessible databases in a given instance of SQL Server. |
| sp_tables | Provides a list of all tables in a database. |

*Continued*

**Table 23-3** *Continued*

| Stored Procedure | Description |
| --- | --- |
| sp_columns | Provides column information for a table. |
| sp_server_info | Provides information about the SQL Server. |
| sp_stored_procedures | Provides a list of all stored procedures in a database. |

**Unless the documentation states otherwise, all system stored procedures are functions whose return value is 0 on success and an error-number value on failure.**

## Security stored procedures

These procedures are among those that modify system tables. Proceed with caution, and use the Enterprise Manager interface instead of these stored procedures whenever possible. Table 23-4 lists several security stored procedures.

**Table 23-4**
*Selected Security Stored Procedures*

| Stored Procedure | Description |
| --- | --- |
| sp_addrole | Creates a new role for a database. |
| sp_adduser | Adds a new security account. |
| sp_helpuser | Provides information about a particular user or database role. |
| sp_helplogins | Provides information about logins defined on the system. |
| sp_password | Adds or resets a user's password in SQL Server. |

**In examining a sysobjects system table (especially that of the Master database) you mzight find undocumented procedures. Refrain from using any of these, as it might lead to unpredictable results and non-portable systems.**

**10 Min.
To Go**

## SQL Server Agent stored procedures

These stored procedures are called behind the scenes to perform the tasks associated with SQL Server Agent — scheduling jobs, creating alerts, and so on. Unless you wish to create these objects programmatically, the SQL Server Agent interface should be your tool of choice. Table 23-5 lists some of the SQL Server Agent stored procedures.

**Table 23-5**
*Selected SQL Server Agent Stored Procedures*

| Stored Procedure | Description |
| --- | --- |
| sp_add_alert | Adds an alert to SQL Server Agent. |
| sp_add_job | Adds a job to SQL Server Agent. |
| sp_add_jobschedule | Creates a schedule for a given job. |
| sp_addtask | Creates a scheduled task. |
| sp_help_alert | Provides information about all alerts defined for the system. |

**Most "add" stored procedures have a corresponding "drop" procedure.**

## Extended stored procedures

*Extended stored procedures* are your window onto the operating system. They enable you to do things that would be difficult or impossible in T-SQL; at the same time they can open up potential security loopholes that provide access to your network through SQL Server. Extended stored procedures are usually, but not always, prefixed with xp_.

You create an extended stored procedure as an external Dynamic Linked Library (DLL), usually in C++, and link it into SQL Server. When an extended stored procedure is called, SQL Server actually loads a program (DLL), passes parameters to it, and retrieves the return values.

To execute an extended stored procedure you must have sufficient privileges. See Table 23-6 for a list of selected extended stored procedures.

**Table 23-6**
*Selected Extended Stored Procedures*

| Stored Procedure | Description |
| --- | --- |
| xp_cmdshell | Executes a command as you would from the command line, and returns text rows. |
| xp_logininfo | Provides details of the account and privileges for the login. |
| xp_sprintf | Formats values into an output string. |
| xp_sscanf | Reads formatted information from a string into the arguments' location. |
| xp_logevent | Logs event information into the Windows Event log as well as into the SQL Server log. |

**API system stored procedures are reserved exclusively for OLE DB providers, ODBC drivers, and DB-LIB functions. You should not call these procedures directly.**

## REVIEW

- SQL Server gives you several ways to access its system information.
- The recommended way to obtain information about SQL Server objects and their properties is to use INFORMATION_SCHEMA views. These hidden views are created for each database in SQL Server 2000.
- You can use system stored procedures to retrieve most of the information available through INFORMATION_SCHEMA; in addition, system stored procedures enable you to perform many administrative tasks.
- You should use the Enterprise Manager interface in place of system-stored procedures whenever possible, to ensure that the system stored procedures are used properly.

*Done!*

## QUIZ YOURSELF

1. What are the two primary methods of retrieving system information from SQL Server 2000?

2. What is an INFORMATION_SCHEMA?

3. Why is it not usually a good idea to query SQL server system tables directly?

4. What is the purpose of system stored procedures?

5. How does an extended stored procedure differ from a standard stored procedure?

# *Automating Administration Tasks with SQL Server Agent*

## *Session Checklist*

✔ Configuring and using SQL Server Agent

✔ Scheduling jobs

✔ Creating alerts

✔ Managing operators

✔ Administering multiple servers

*30 Min.
To Go*

**A**utomating some of the SQL Server administrative tasks will make your life easier. With SQL Server Agent, you can create and schedule various tasks, from database maintenance to data manipulations; you also can use alerts to keep in touch with your SQL Server via e-mail, Net Send pop-up messages, or even a pager.

## *Configuring and Using SQL Server Agent*

Behind every automated task executed in SQL Server 2000 stands SQL Server Agent (which I mentioned briefly in Session 4). Using it you can define, execute, and schedule for execution various database tasks. The system database MSDB drives it: When you modify its properties, schedule a new job, or add an alert, all the data are written into MSDB to be read by SQL Server Agent; there is no direct communication with the Agent.

**You should never attempt to modify MSDB tables directly: doing so could result in a corrupted system. Always use the interfaces provided by the SQL Server wizards.**

In order to run, SQL Server Agent requires that the SQL Server Agent Service be running. Usually you'll want the service to start when Windows starts: You can set it to do this in the SQL Server Service Manager. Running the service will ensure that any scheduled tasks are executed on time. You need to configure SQL Server Agent to run properly on your system.

### Configuration screen

You can access the configuration screen, shown in Figure 24-1, from the Enterprise Manager console ⇨ Management node ⇨ SQL Server Agent node ⇨ right-click menu Properties option. You will specify an account to use on startup; this account must have all the necessary permissions to execute tasks in SQL Server. If you wish to receive notifications from your SQL Server via e-mail or pager you will need to set a mail profile (I describe this process in detail in Session 25) corresponding to one on your e-mail server (which must be a MAPI-compliant application such as Microsoft Exchange). The Agent writes an error log for all its activities into a specific file, and if your system is on the network you can send the log to a net recipient by specifying the other computer's name.

### Properties

As you go through the tabs on the SQL Server Agent properties dialog you can instruct the Agent (on the Advanced tab) to restart SQL Server if it shuts down unexpectedly and even to restart itself. In a multi-server environment you may want to forward alerts and messages to some other server(s).

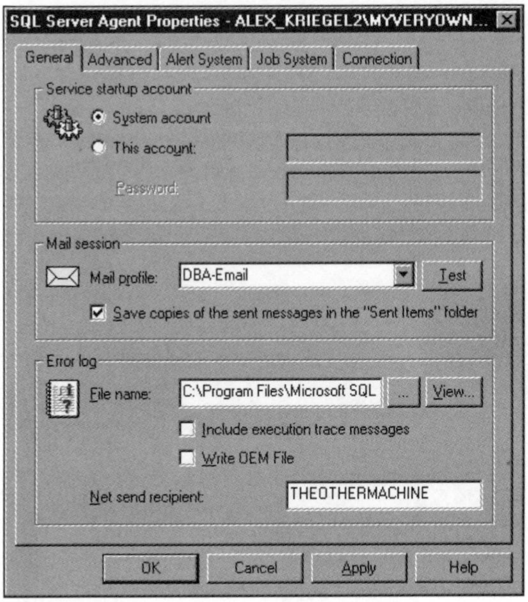

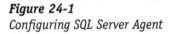

**Figure 24-1**
*Configuring SQL Server Agent*

### The Alert tab

The Alert tab enables you to specify the alert format as well as its recipients and a fail-safe operator (some poor guy to be awakened at 3:00 AM when something goes wrong) to be notified via e-mail or pager.

### The Jobs tab

The Jobs tab, as the name implies, deals with jobs — their scheduling, logging properties, job execution timeout, and such. I recommend leaving these to their defaults at this time.

### The Connection tab

The Connection tab enables you to set up the account the Agent will use to connect to SQL Server after it has started. This account may or may not be the same as the startup account. Make sure that it has all the necessary privileges.

## Scheduling Jobs

A *job* in SQL Server 2000 is a sequence of operations to be performed once, scheduled for execution, or run when a certain predefined condition occurs. The SQL Server Agent maintains a complete job history for every job, recording time, duration, and final result. You can access the Job Creation Wizard from the SQL Server Agent node: From the right-click menu choose New ➪ Job. Figure 24-2 shows the first screen you'll see.

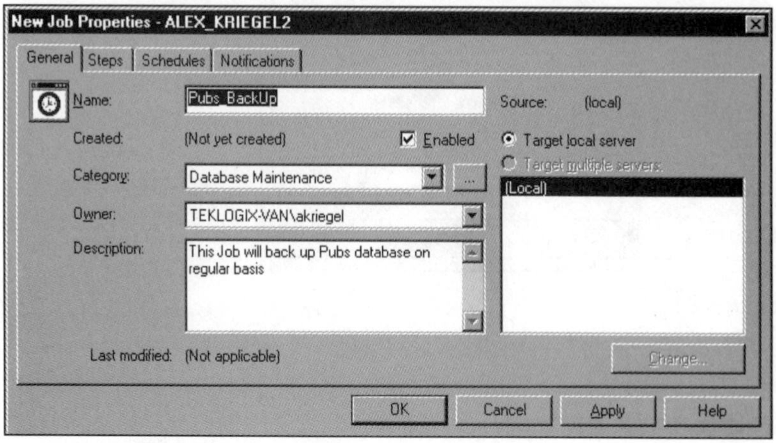

| New Job Properties - ALEX_KRIEGEL2 | ✕ |
| --- | --- |

General | Steps | Schedules | Notifications |

Name: `Pubs_BackUp`  Source:   (local)

Created:   (Not yet created)   ☑ Enabled   ⦿ Target local server

Category:   `Database Maintenance`   ▼ …   ○ Target multiple servers:

Owner:   `TEKLOGIX-VAN\akriegel`   ▼   [Local]

Description:   `This Job will back up Pubs database on regular basis`

Last modified:   (Not applicable)   Change...

OK   Cancel   Apply   Help

**Figure 24-2**
*Creating a new job, General tab*

A job can consist of one or more steps. In the following instructions you can specify a new step and edit or delete existing ones; you can insert the new step before or after an existing step.

1. On the Steps tab, click New to create a step. The screen shown in Figure 24-3 pops up; you need to add T-SQL statements to do the actual job. In this case I choose to schedule the backup of my Pubs database to disk in a backup file.

   On the Advanced tab you can specify the step that will be executed next, according to the success or failure of the previous step.

**You can reorder the steps or force the execution of the next step if any of the previous steps has a certain outcome. For example, if your scheduled backup fails and the next step is to drop the database, you obviously want to bypass that step.**

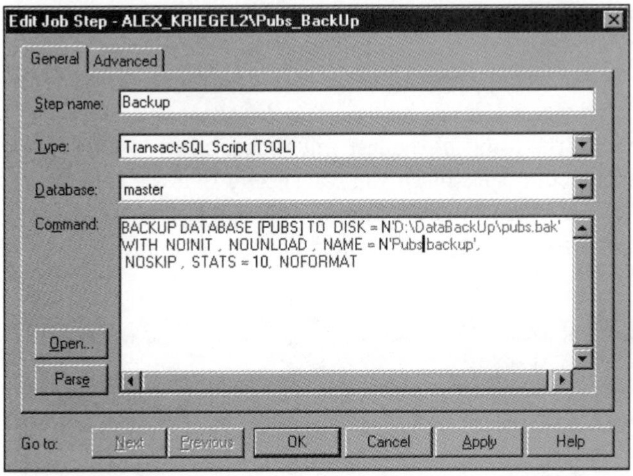

**Figure 24-3**
*Steps in creating a job*

**2.** The Schedules tab (shown in Figure 24-4) enables you to schedule the job, add a new schedule to it, and/or create an alert (covered later in this session). Scheduling a job is very similar to scheduling any other task: in fact, it uses the same interface.

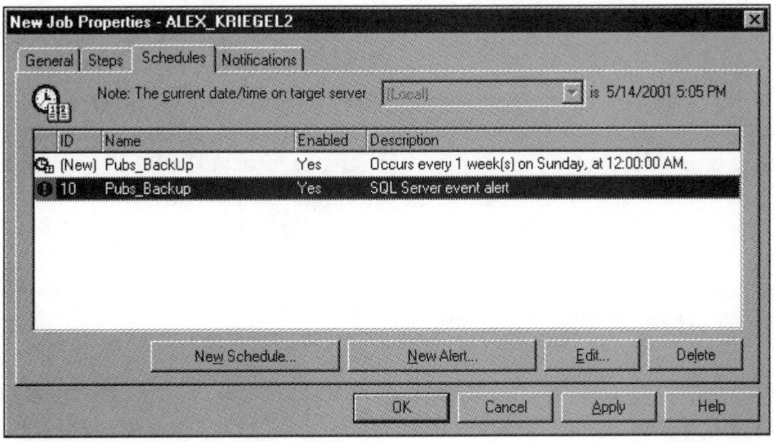

**Figure 24-4**
*Scheduling jobs and adding alerts*

3. The Notifications tab (shown in Figure 24-5) enables you to specify who is to be notified when certain events occur during the execution of the job. You can notify any of the operators (discussed later in this session) defined for the system, and also select the method of notification: e-mail, pager, or Net Send command (the result of the last will appear as a pop-up message on the network computer specified). You can specify that the results be written into a log file for future examination. You can also automatically delete a job if you have executed it once and don't need it anymore.

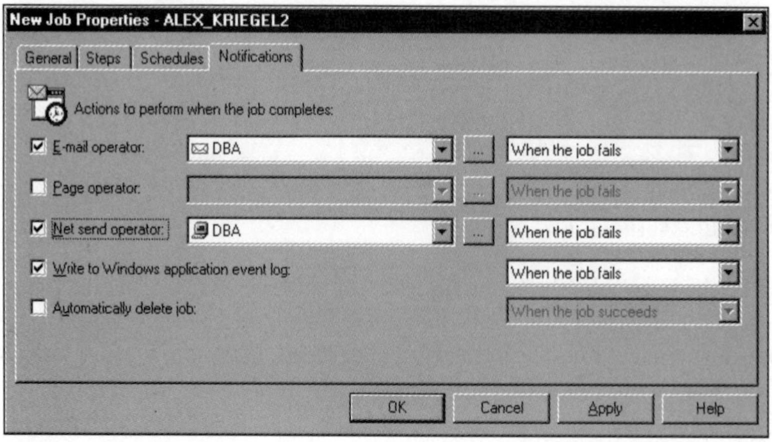

![New Job Properties dialog showing the Notifications tab with options for E-mail operator, Page operator, Net send operator, Write to Windows application event log, and Automatically delete job.]

**Figure 24-5**
*Sending notifications*

All jobs created for the system are maintained under the SQL Server Agent node in the Jobs collection. Once the job is created it appears in the Details pane of the Jobs node. You can edit, delete, or disable the job at any time: To do so, choose Properties from the job's right-click menu option.

## Creating Alerts

**20 Min.
To Go**

*Alerts* enable your system to take an action in response to some event on the system. The SQL Server Agent monitors the Event Log of your machine, and if it encounters an event for which you created an alert it responds by taking an action: by invoking a job, sending a message (via e-mail or to a pager), or (in a multi-server environment) passing the alert to other SQL Servers to process.

**The Event Log is a system log wherein Windows reports all events that occur on the system. You can view it with the Event Viewer (Start ⇨ Program Files ⇨ Administrative Tools ⇨ Event Viewer).**

You can specify an alert during job creation or independently, as shown in Figure 24-6. If you specify an alert during job creation the alert will refer to an event that may occur during the execution of the job.

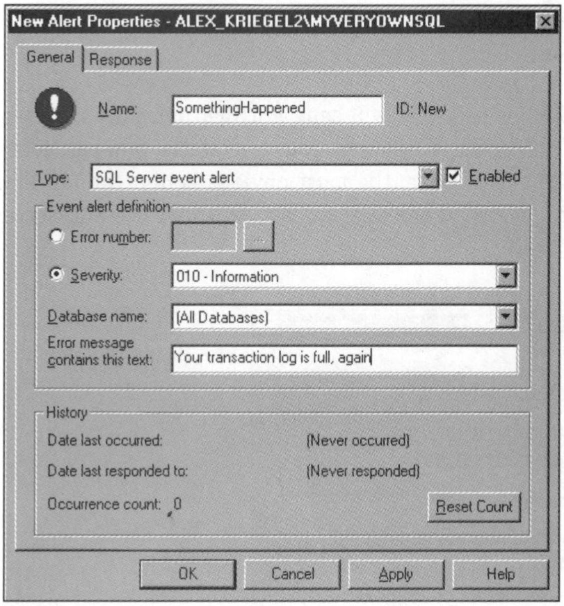

**Figure 24-6**
*Setting new alert properties*

You specify type, specific error number or severity (how serious the event is), the scope (all databases or just one), and the text of the message: This text will be entered into the Event Log and sent to you via e-mail or the Net Send feature.

Next you must specify the response — the course of action to be taken when the event occurs. You may choose to execute some canned job, or, if the event requires human intervention, to send a message to an operator (which I'll discuss in the next session).

> **Alerts also are integrated with various performance counters, enabling SQL Server Agent to take an action whenever a certain threshold is crossed (for example, when memory usage climbs above a preset limit).**

Once saved, an alert joins the alerts collection under the SQL Server Agent node; you can view, modify, or delete it at any time through a properties window accessible from its Properties menu option.

## Managing Operators

An *operator* is a contact to whom an alert will send notification. (You can specify e-mail, pager, or Net Send notification.) As with jobs and alerts, you can access the operator's properties in a variety of ways, the most obvious being through New Operator from the right-click menu of the Operators node under the SQL Server Agent (as shown in Figure 24-7).

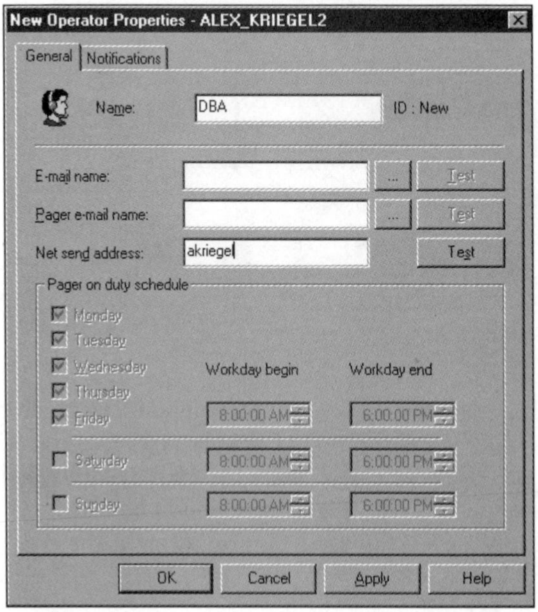

*Figure 24-7*
*Creating a new operator, General tab*

You also can set up the times an operator can be reached via a pager. You should test every method of notification (use the Test button on the right) to make sure that the intended person can be reached.

**In order to notify an operator via e-mail you have to configure a SQL Server Mail Agent (explained in Session 25).**

Next, from the Notifications tab, select the type of notification (alerts or jobs) for this particular operator. If you select alerts, all alerts defined for the system will be displayed. If you select jobs, all jobs this operator is assigned to will be displayed. You cannot assign a job to an operator; you assign an operator to a job from the Jobs menu.

## Administering Multiple Servers

**10 Min.
To Go**

SQL Server 7.0 enables you to use SQL Server Agent in multi-server administration. When administering multiple servers you need to set up one server as a master that manages jobs for the target servers and processes alerts from these target servers by means of *event forwarding*. This feature pertains to networks with multiple SQL Server installations, and it can be a great time-saver. For example, by forwarding events to a central server, you avoid having to configure alerts for each and every server on your network. The same goes for jobs: By configuring a job to run on a remote server you avoid having to physically access your target servers whenever you want to modify the job. You make your modifications once, on your Master server.

You can configure event forwarding on the Advanced tab of the SQL Server Agent Properties screen (shown in Figure 24-1).

You configure your servers through MSX and TSX wizards, available from the Multi- Server Administration option on the right-click menu on the SQL Server Agent node; MSX refers to the Master server and TSX to the target server.

These are advanced features that you certainly need to learn more about — once you are through with this book.

**Done!**

---

## REVIEW

- You can automate various database tasks using SQL Server Agent. An automated task is called a job and can be scheduled to execute recurrently.

- SQL Server Agent enables you to send notifications and alerts to designated operators using e-mail, pager, or the Net Send feature.

- Every alert is entered into the system Event Log as an event, the severity level of which determines its status: notification, error, and so on. In response to an alert you can set your system to notify an operator or to execute a job defined on the system.

- You can run jobs on multiple servers by setting one server up as the Master server and all others as target servers; the alerts can be forwarded from the target to the Master for an appropriate response.

---

## QUIZ YOURSELF

1. Where does the SQL Server Agent find information about the jobs it is supposed to execute?

2. What service must you configure in order to receive notifications via e-mail?

3. If a job takes more than one step to be executed, how do you specify the next step?

4. Can a job raise an alert?

5. How do alerts relate to system events logged in the Event Log?

6. What is an operator?

7. How do you automate tasks on multiple servers?

# Configuring SQL Server Mail

## Session Checklist

✔ Setting up your mail profile

✔ Configuring SQL Mail and SQL Server Agent Mail

✔ Sending mail through extended stored procedures

✔ Troubleshooting

**T**he ability to communicate via e-mail is one of the useful features of SQL Server 2000. In this session you are going to learn how to set up and configure a mail account for SQL Server Agent and SQL Mail.

**30 Min.
To Go**

## Setting up Your Mail Profile

SQL Server 2000 enables you to communicate with it via e-mail. To help you do this, SQL Server provides two services: SQL Mail and SQL Server Agent Mail. Collectively, these two services are referred to as SQL Server mail services. You use the first service, SQL Mail, to execute stored procedures remotely and return results by e-mail. You use the second service, SQL Server Agent Mail, for e-mail and pager notifications.

SQL Server uses your existing infrastructure, which means you need to have a MAPI-compliant e-mail server and a compatible mail client (such as Microsoft Outlook). You need a MAPI-compliant client because it will supply components — MAPI extensions — used by both SQL Server mail services.

*MAPI* **stands for Messaging Application Programming Interface. It is an industry standard that enables Windows-based applications to communicate with many other messaging services, such as the Internet, Microsoft Exchange, CompuServe, and so on.**

I assume for the purpose of this discussion that you are running Microsoft Exchange, which is the de facto standard for Windows servers. Follow these steps to set up your mail profile:

1. Create a distinct mailbox for both SQL Server mail services. You can use your existing ones, though it is usually not a good idea as things can get mixed up very easily. It makes more sense to set up a separate mailbox for each service. You create the mailbox on the Exchange Server machine; you will probably need assistance from your network administrator to use this feature.

**SQL Server Mail runs in the security context of MSSQLService, and you therefore have to configure its Exchange mailbox for a domain account with sufficient privileges to run MSSQLService. SQL Server Agent Mail runs in the context of the SQL Server Agent service, and you must configure the mailbox for this service for a domain account with sufficient privileges to run it.**

2. Create a valid mail profile using the Mail control panel on the machine on which SQL Server is installed, as shown in Figure 25-1.

3. Click Show Profiles. This will display all the existing profiles and enable you to add a new one, as shown in Figure 25-2.

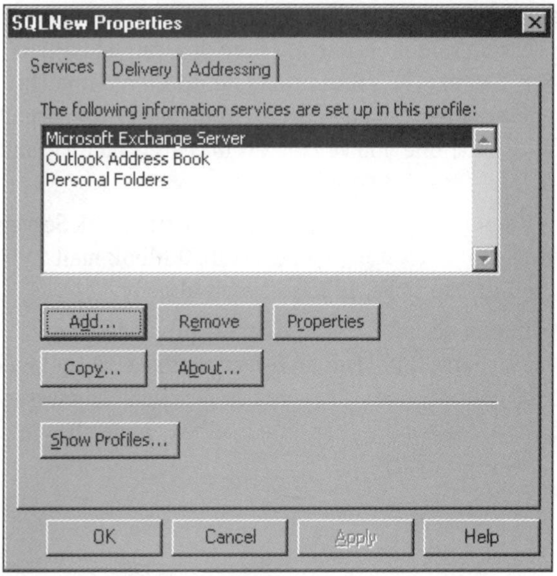

**Figure 25-1**
*Examining mail-profile properties*

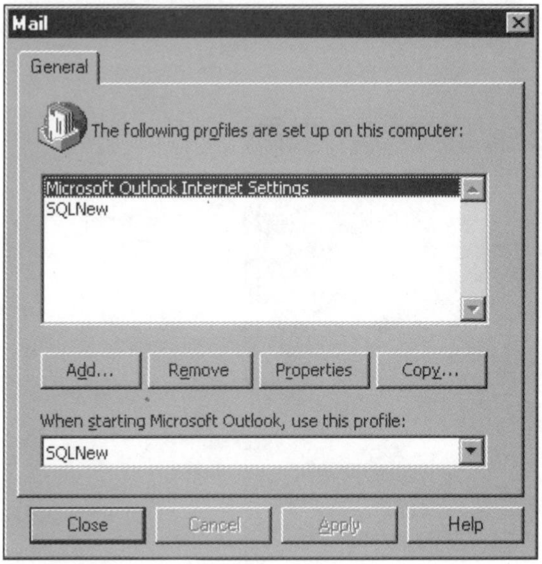

**Figure 25-2**
*Creating a new profile*

Since you have already installed a mail client program (such as Microsoft Outlook) you will see at least one profile. From here you can add a new profile to be used by SQL Server. The procedure is no different from the one you use to set up any regular e-mail account: You specify the e-mail server to use, the mailbox (the one you've created for this account), and the profile name. Click Apply to save your settings.

4. Test your mail profile. When configuring my profile I instruct SQL Server to use this newly created profile to start my Microsoft Outlook mail client; I suggest that you do the same, if you haven't already.

5. Log onto the system using an account with sufficient privileges for SQL Server, start up your mail client, and send an e-mail message to the mailbox assigned to either of your services. Once you've received the message, consider the job done (if you use more than one mailbox, remember to test them all).

**20 Min.
To Go**

## Configuring SQL Mail and SQL Server Agent Mail

You configure SQL Mail from the Enterprise Manager console. To do so, select Support Services node ⇨ SQL Mail sub-node ⇨ choose Properties from the right-click menu. From the drop-down box shown in Figure 25-3, select the profile you are going to use.

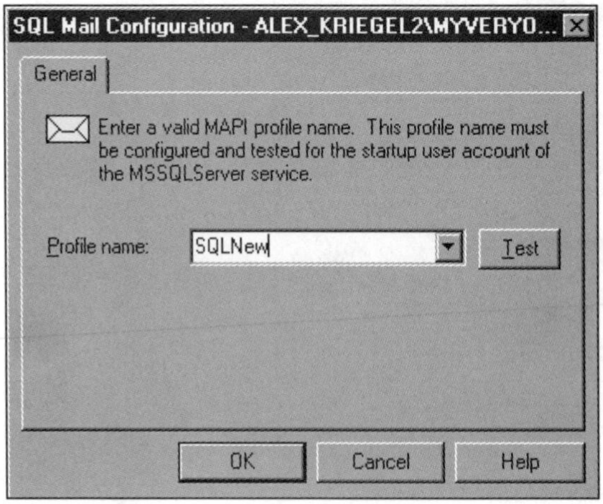

```
SQL Mail Configuration - ALEX_KRIEGEL2\MYVERYO...  ☒

 General

      ✉  Enter a valid MAPI profile name.  This profile name must
         be configured and tested for the startup user account of
         the MSSQLServer service.

   Profile name:    SQLNew              ▼     Test


              OK          Cancel          Help
```

*Figure 25-3*
*Configuring SQL Mail*

Test the profile by clicking Test. If the test is passed, you are ready to use your new mail capabilities; otherwise, refer to the "Troubleshooting" section later in this session.

The procedure for configuring SQL Server Agent is essentially the same: Choose Properties from the right-click menu of the SQL Server Agent (under the Management node) and specify a mail session (see Figure 25-4). You can use the same profile you've just tested or specify a different one. It is a good idea to test the profile before you click OK.

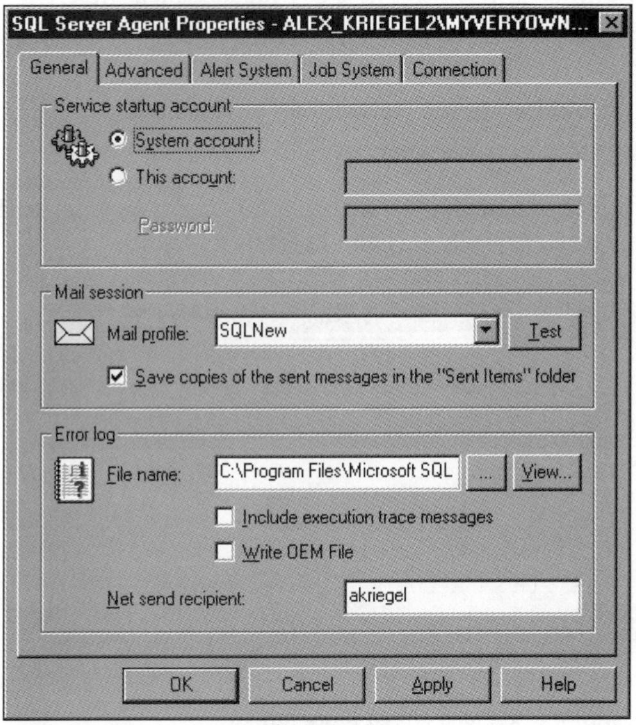

**Figure 25-4**
*Configuring SQL Server Agent Mail*

You should configure both SQL Mail and SQL Server Agent to start up automatically once the SQL Server starts, in order to provide constant e-mail access.

## Sending Mail through Extended Stored Procedures

Once you have your mail configured properly you can use your SQL Server Query analyzer to send e-mails. To do this, you use the following extended stored procedures:

- xp_startmail, to start a MAPI session.
- xp_stopmail, to stop a MAPI session.
- xp_sendmail, to send an e-mail message to any valid e-mail address.
- xp_readmail, to read the message from your mailbox into the SQL Server Query Analyzer.
- xp_processmail, to retrieve the full message, not just headers.
- xp_deletemail, to purge your messages.

For example, the stored procedure executed inside SQL Query Analyzer sends an e-mail to an outside e-mail recipient, as shown in Figure 25-5.

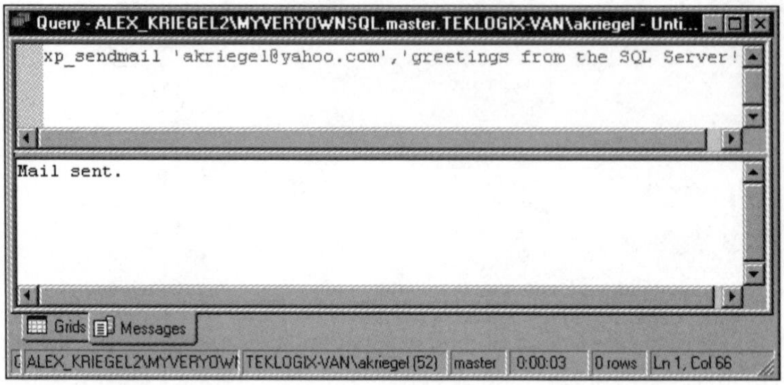

**Figure 25-5**
*Sending e-mail with an extended stored procedure*

Because my SQL Mail is configured to auto-start, I do not need to use xp_startmail.

**Of course, you can call these extended stored procedures in your own stored procedures like this: exec xp_sendmail 'somebody@somewhere.com','greetings from the SQL Server!'**

## Troubleshooting

If things go well everything will be up and running in no time; if they do not — well — then it won't. This section deals with the problems you are most likely to encounter while setting and configuring your mail services.

The simple fact that you can send and receive mail through your mail application does not guarantee that SQL Mail and SQL Server Agent Mail will run.

Most problems with configuring the mail capabilities come from account-security settings. If you find that you are unable to set up your mail, check the following:

- Is your mail client running on the same account as your SQL Server Service? It should be. You can verify this or set it up from Control Panel ➪ Services in Windows NT, or Administrative Tools ➪ Services in Windows 2000.

- Is SQL Server running under the same account for which you've set up your mailbox?

- Is your mail messaging service installed? You can set this in your Mail control panel.

In order for SQL Server Mail to function properly in the network environment you have to log onto your machine as the domain account under which your SQL Server Service is running. From the Services menu you can view and modify the properties of the accounts under which these services are running. The screen shown in Figure 25-6 shows you how to change these properties on Windows NT/2000; clicking Browse will present you with all the accounts accessible from the machine you're using.

Note that you must supply your domain password in order to use this service.

**If none of these tips helps, try Internet links on the CD supplied with this book. If you decide to join some SQL Server mailing list, be warned — you may get what you ask for and more (I am getting about 150 mail messages a day).**

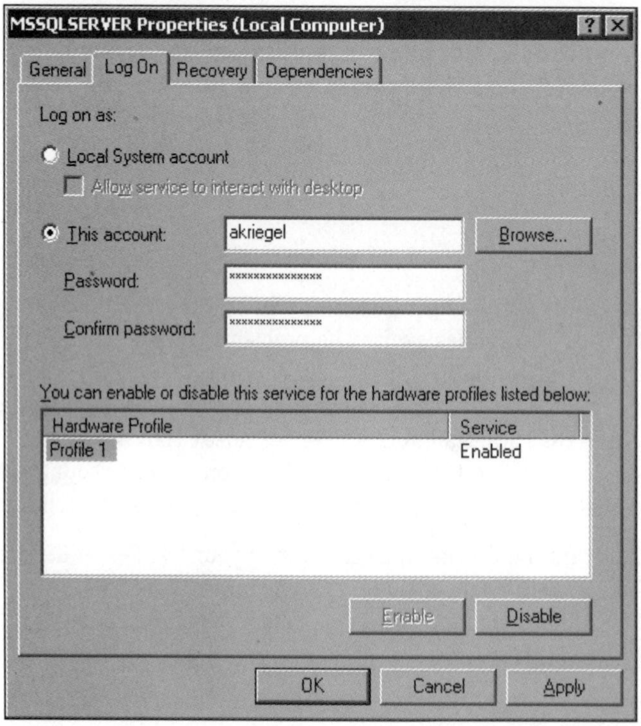

**MSSQLSERVER Properties (Local Computer)**                    ? ×

| General | Log On | Recovery | Dependencies |

Log on as:

○ Local System account
   ☐ Allow service to interact with desktop

◉ This account:      akriegel                    Browse...

Password:          ***************

Confirm password:  ***************

You can enable or disable this service for the hardware profiles listed below:

| Hardware Profile | Service |
| --- | --- |
| Profile 1 | Enabled |

[Enable]  [Disable]

[OK]  [Cancel]  [Apply]

*Figure 25-6*
*Configuring SQL Server Service for a domain account*

**Done!**

## REVIEW

- In order to use SQL Server Mail and SQL Server Agent Mail you need a MAPI-compliant mail client configured to connect to your e-mail server.

- You need to set up mailboxes for these services and add to the profiles on your computer a valid MAPI profile that points to them.

- Though you configure SQL Mail and SQL Server Agent Mail separately, the procedures you use are essentially the same. You can use one MAPI profile for both services.

- You must configure your SQL Server Service and your SQL Server Agent Service to start on the same account as your Exchange service.

## QUIZ YOURSELF

1. What is the difference between SQL Mail and SQL Server Agent Mail?

2. What is MAPI? What is a MAPI profile?

3. Does SQL Server have mail-server capabilities, or does it need an external mail server to receive and send e-mail messages?

4. On what domain account should you start SQL Server if you want to communicate with a MAPI-compliant mail server?

# *Performance Tuning and Optimization*

## Session Checklist

✔ Monitoring and profiling

✔ Tuning SQL queries

✔ Using the Index Tuning Wizard

✔ Optimizing TempDB and the Transaction Log

✔ Using Database Consistency Check (DBCC)

**0 Min.
To Go**

**T**his session introduces tools and techniques you can use to achieve and maintain high SQL Server system performance, from monitoring and profiling SQL Server to the Index Tuning Wizard to Database Consistency Check statements.

## *Monitoring and Profiling*

To get the most out of your SQL Server you need to tune it for the tasks it is running. Microsoft includes a graphical tool, SQL Profiler, that you can use to trace the performance of hundreds of events happening in your server. You can search the results for potential bottlenecks and other problems.

Follow these steps to set up monitoring and profiling:

1. Start SQL Profiler from the Tools menu in the Enterprise Manager console.

2. Click New Trace on the toolbar to design a new trace or to use one of the canned templates. A *trace* is a record of the process execution wherein you specify what events you want to monitor. Templates describe standard traces, the ones that fit most common scenarios: Whenever possible, save time by choosing one of these.

3. Set up the trace properties from the Trace Properties screen, shown in Figure 26-1. Several predefined trace templates are installed with SQL Server: I recommend using them until you acquire more experience in running traces.

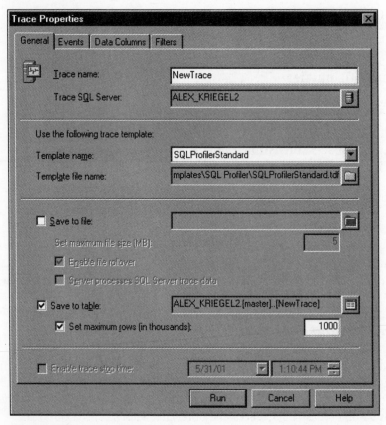

**Figure 26-1**
*Specifying general trace properties*

You can save the results of a trace to a file or to a table within a database. Unless you really wish to sift through the tons of information generated by SQL Profiler you probably want to limit the number of rows in the trace table. If you're sending output to a file, set a maximum size in megabytes. You also can specify both a file and a table for your trace-output results.

4. Select the events you wish to monitor by displaying the Events tab, shown in Figure 26-2. Start with a vague idea of what might need improvement on your database. You might want to determine if the cursors are slowing down your servers, or it might be that locking issues keep you up at night, or simply that you would like to monitor the performance of your database. Use your common sense in selecting what to monitor, in addition to using the general recommendations from this book and SQL Server Books Online.

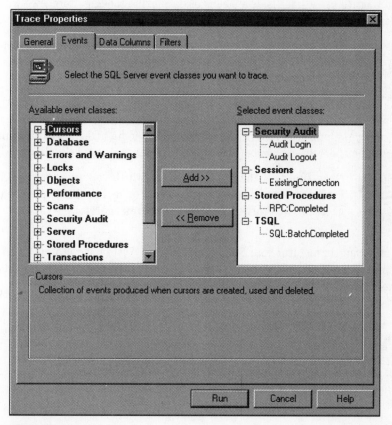

*Figure 26-2*
*Selecting events to trace.*

5. Select the data you would like to capture for these events. You do this from the Data Columns tab. Again, common sense will substitute for experience: If it is performance you are after, select data relevant to performance — such as reads, CPU usage, and so on; if it's security, select security-related columns.

6. Finally, apply a filter from the Filters tab. You might want to filter out some events that you deem unnecessary for your trace (like accumulating data on SQL Profiler itself while running the trace). Click Run.

You can use the accumulated data to monitor the performance of your SQL Server, and to identify bottlenecks (like slow queries) and potential problems (such as memory or CPU usage). You can also use it when debugging stored procedures, as it enables you to view each step involved in the execution. One of the most common ways to use a trace is as a means of optimizing index performance with the Index Tuning Wizard.

**You can record a trace on your live production server and then replay it on your test machine to identify problems without shutting down the production environment.**

One way to use SQL Profiler is during auditing, as it enables you to use SQL Server to record a number of events for a client, from login attempts to attempts to access various database objects (tables, stored procedures, and the like).

**Make sure that the user account on which you are running SQL Profiler has sufficient privileges to connect to SQL Server and execute SQL Profiler–related stored procedures.**

You may want to monitor your SQL Server with the System Monitor or third-party tools: This will give you some information about how SQL Server interacts with the system, and how it affects or is affected by it.

## Tuning SQL Queries

In order to tune a query you have to understand what is involved in query execution. One of the features of SQL Query Analyzer I haven't discussed yet is the *execution plan.* Viewing how SQL Server executes a particular query, the properties and cost of each step, and the indexes used, can be invaluable when you're optimizing SQL queries.

Consider a simple query performed in the Pubs database:

```
SELECT * FROM authors
```

To view this query's Execution Plan, select Query Analyzer ⇨ Query ⇨ Display Estimated Execution Plan (Figure 26-3).

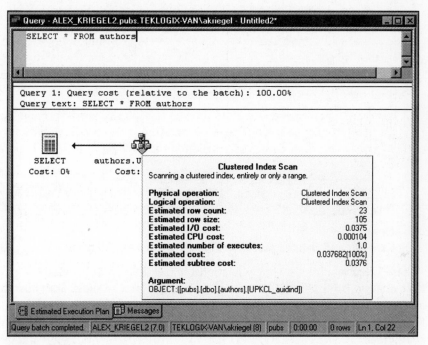

**Figure 26-3**
*Viewing the Estimated Execution Plan for a simple SQL query*

To execute this query, SQL Server performs a clustered index scan at a cost of 100 percent (meaning that the whole operation takes 100 percent of the allocated time). Place your cursor onto the node in the Query Execution Plan and you'll see a pop-up screen showing you the details of the operation. There is nothing you can optimize here.

More complex queries yield somewhat different results, as shown in Figure 26-4.

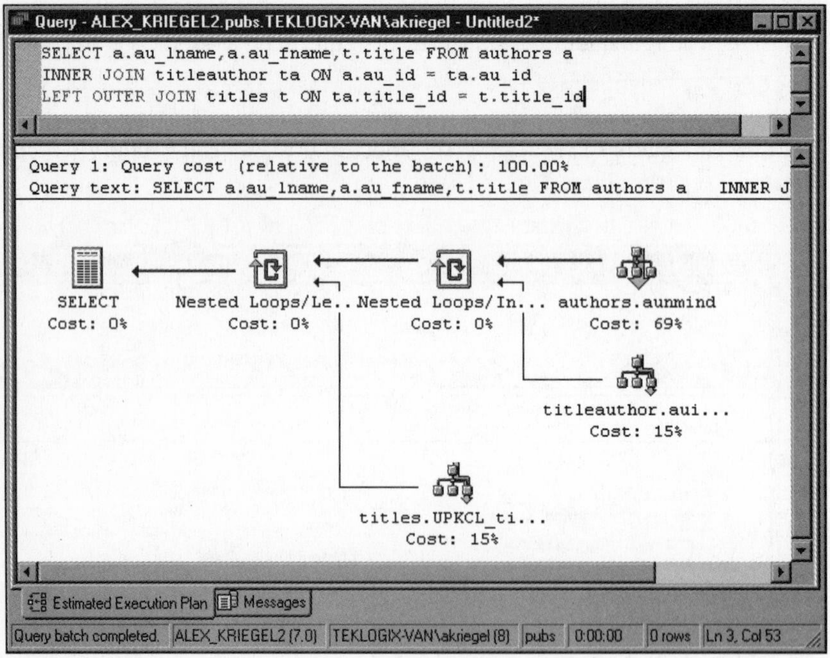

**Figure 26-4**
*Viewing the Estimated Execution Plan for a complex SQL query*

Here I resolve a many-to-many relationship (see Session 6) between the Authors table and the Titles table. SQL Server chooses to perform an Index Scan operation on the table Authors and an Index Seek on the Titles and Title_Author tables. Running a trace on this query might provide some useful suggestions for index strategy.

> **Some queries just cannot be optimized beyond a certain point because of their inherent complexity and database limitations. You can get around this problem by adding more memory, revising your business logic, or rewriting the query altogether.**

In general, you can optimize queries by reducing your use of cursors, eliminating nested loops with GROUP BY or CASE statements, and using subqueries.

**You can speed up query execution on a multi-processor machine by implementing parallel processing, the details of which are quite complex and beyond the scope of this book. If you need more information, refer to Books Online or some more advanced books on SQL Server.**

With SQL Server 2000 you can create statistics on the values distribution in the column in the table. These statistics are used by the SQL Server Query Optimizer to determine the best path of the execution for a particular query. This information is created automatically whenever an index is created for a table, and in addition, you may maintain statistics on non-indexed columns frequently used in queries. Over time, as data in the index columns are changed, these statistics may become obsolete, resulting in less-than-optimal Execution Path decisions.

SQL Server automatically updates statistics, unless you instruct it not to. The frequency of updates depends on the size of the table and the relative number of rows that change. Statistics can become out of date on very large tables in which few rows (say, fewer than 10 percent of the total) are changed over time. You can manually update statistics by issuing a T-SQL command, like this:

```
UPDATE STATISTICS authors
```

This ensures that the Authors table has up-to-date statistics for use with the Query Optimizer.

**20 Min. To Go**

## Using the Index Tuning Wizard

The Index Tuning Wizard helps you analyze queries and improve performance. To use the Index Tuning Wizard you need workload data, which are represented by a SQL script or SQL Server Profiler trace file (see "Monitoring and Profiling" earlier in this session).

Follow these steps to run this wizard:

1. Start the wizard from the Enterprise Manager console by selecting Tools ➪ Wizards, or from SQL Profiler's Tools menu.

2. Click Next on the Welcome screen and select the database you wish to optimize (see Figure 26-5). Also, if you can afford (in terms of time and server resources) the Thorough Tuning mode, go for it; do not use it on a live production server, however. Click Next.

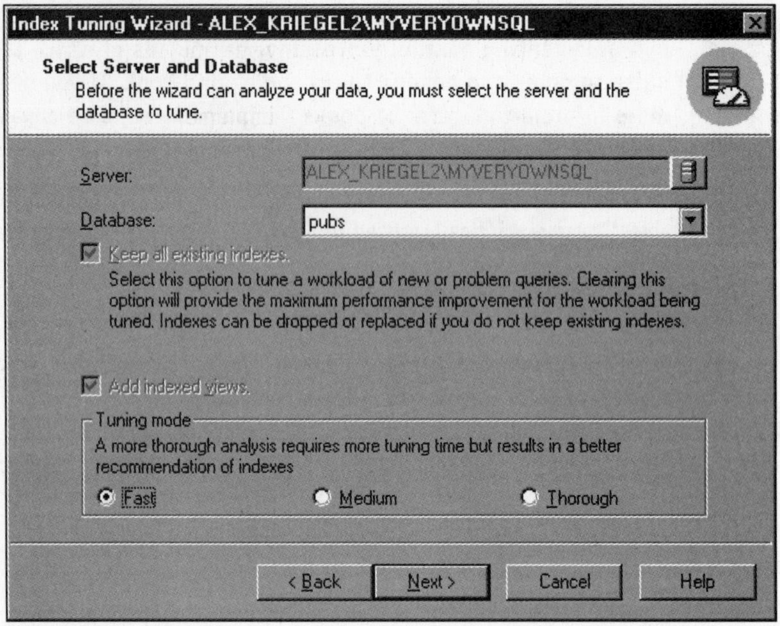

*Figure 26-5*
*Selecting a database for optimization with the Index Tuning Wizard*

3. On the next screen, Specify Workload, choose a workload file or trace. (Refer to "Monitoring and Profiling," earlier in this session, to learn how to create a trace.) On the same screen you can set Advanced Options to limit the number of queries, restrict the maximum size of recommended indexes, and so on. Click Next.

4. On the next screen, Select Tables to Tune, choose the tables you wish to optimize. Click Next.

   The wizard examines the data to determine if any good would come of applying indexes. It returns to you a number of suggested indexes on the tables for which you created the workload data, along with an estimate of how much improvement implementing these indexes would produce. It will also show you the 100 queries that would benefit the most from the recommended indexes.

5. Click the Analysis button on the preceding screen, Index Recommendations, to see how the Index Wizard came to its conclusions.

You can make your workload data as big as you wish, within physical limits; make sure that you are selecting meaningful and diverse queries to represent the whole spectrum of queries used in your database.

The wizard will also ask you if you would like to implement these improvements right away. If you are in a production environment I strongly advise against that; click OK only if you are using a test server.

It is possible to analyze a single query by using the Index Tuning Wizard in the SQL Query Analyzer. Type the query into the Query Analyzer window and select the Index Tuning Wizard from the Query menu. Instead of a workload or trace table the input for the wizard will now be the SQL query.

Take the Index Tuning Wizard's suggestions with a grain of salt. It does have the very best intentions but only you know what is best for your database. Remember that while an index can speed up some operations it can also slow down others (such as INSERT, UPDATE, and DELETE, because of the need for SQL Server to update the indexes at the same time).

**10 Min.
To Go**

## Optimizing TempDB and the Transaction Log

TempDB is a system database that may affect the performance of every other database on the system; therefore, it should be optimized for maximum performance. The Transaction Log is a major database component that you should keep in mind when optimizing general database performance.

### Optimizing TempDB performance

TempDB is a whiteboard for everything that is happening on the server (which I discuss in detail in Session 6). Make sure that its initial size is such that no resources will be wasted expanding it to fit your needs. Because TempDB is recreated on every SQL Server startup, save the size, growth rate, and other settings to the model database.

Also, when increasing the size of TempDB, make a sufficient allowance for growth so that it won't be too small nor require frequent resizing. Placing TempDB separately on a subsystem with good input/output time may further improve performance.

According to Microsoft, it doesn't matter which file system you choose (FAT or NTFS). Keep in mind, though, that the FAT file system is more prone to fragmentation (and thus to slower performance) than NTFS.

## Optimizing Transaction Log performance

The Transaction Log is a very busy component. After all, it keeps track of virtually everything that happens in SQL Server. SQL Server 2000 does shrink and expand files automatically. If you need the last drop of performance, you are better off doing the shrinking yourself, rather than waiting for the SQL Server (see Session 7). Do not try this on a busy server, though, as the process will slow it down.

You can improve the performance of SQL Server processes on your Windows NT or Windows 2000 machine by configuring virtual memory and server tasking (priority). This is a rather advanced setting, so you may need to refer to Windows OS Help.

# Using Database Consistency Check (DBCC)

Maintaining your database integrity is an important part of your duties as an administrator. Microsoft supplies you with a set of commands that you can run on your system just as you would run a SQL query. These commands fall into four broad categories, listed in Table 26-1.

**Table 26-1**
*DBCC Commands Categories*

| Category | Purpose |
|---|---|
| Maintenance | Performs general maintenance of a database, index, or filegroup. |
| Status Report | Reports on the status of a specific object. |
| Validation | Performs validation operations on the database and database objects. |
| Miscellaneous | Does everything else. |

Usually you run these commands whenever you suspect a problem with your database. About 30 DBCC commands exist and mastering them will take some time. The SQL Server 2000 DBCC statements can repair some minor problems.

Here is a sampling of the commands you are likely to use most often:

- DBCC DBREINDEX — Rebuilds one or more indexes for a particular table.
- DBCC DBREPAIR — The name is quite misleading, as this command drops a damaged database; it is supported for backwards compatibility only.
- DBCC INDEXDEFRAG — Defragments indexes of a table or view.
- DBCC SHRINKDATABASE — Shrinks the size of the data files in the database.
- DBCC UPDATEUSAGE — Reports and corrects inconsistencies in the sysindexes table.
- DBCC SQLPERF — Provides statistics about the use of Transaction Log space for all databases.
- DBCC SHOW_STATISTICS — Displays the current distribution statistics.
- DBCC CHECKDB — Checks the allocation and structural integrity of all the objects in the database.
- DBCC CHECKTABLE — Checks the integrity of the data and index as well as the pages of the specified table or indexed view.

SQL Server performance optimization is a vast topic that deserves a book of its own. In this three-day course I can only cover some basics and point to what is available. SQL Server Books Online provides a wealth of information on the subject, and numerous books also address it.

## Service Packs

Once in a while, Microsoft releases a Service Pack for its products (SQL Server included). "Service Pack" is a euphemism for "bug fix," and normally you should apply one as soon as it's available. Be cautious when using Service Packs because they can introduce new bugs even while fixing the old ones. Read the description of every new Service Pack and determine whether you use the buggy features that it is supposed to fix. Keep in mind the old saying: If it ain't broke, don't fix it. At the time of this book printing, Microsoft has released Service Pack 1 for SQL Server 2000. It's available for download from Microsoft's Web site.

**Done!**

## REVIEW

- It is vitally important to monitor and profile your SQL Server system in order to maintain optimum performance.
- Inside the SQL Server you can use a trace to maintain top performance. Outside, you can use third-party tools or the System Monitor.
- To tune indexes for your database tables you use the Index Tuning Wizard. This wizard takes as its input trace data produced by SQL Profiler.
- You can use an Execution Plan to fine-tune your SQL queries.
- Optimizing the Transaction Log and TempDB helps you achieve maximum performance.
- DBCC provides you with tools for checking and maintaining database integrity.

## QUIZ YOURSELF

1. What is the purpose of using SQL Profiler?
2. What is the purpose of filters in a SQL Profiler trace?
4. What do you use an Execution Plan for?
3. Where do you access the Estimated Execution Plan?
5. What does the Index Tuning Wizard use as input data?
6. What is the main function of DBCC?

# PART

# V

## *Sunday Morning*

1. What is a database maintenance plan and why do you need one?
2. Why it is usually a good idea to maintain a script of your database?
3. How do you detach and attach a database?
4. What databases cannot be attached or detached?
5. What is the difference between a linked server and a remote server?
6. What data sources besides SQL Server can you link to SQL Server 2000?
7. How do you start a distributed transaction in SQL Server 2000?
8. What is the two-phase commit procedure?
9. What are the two main legitimate ways to gain access to SQL Server 2000 system information?
10. What is an INFORMATION_SCHEMA?
11. How do you execute a system stored procedure?
12. What are catalog system stored procedures?
13. What is an extended stored procedure in SQL Server 2000?
14. What is the purpose of SQL Server Agent?
15. Where does SQL Server Agent store and pick up information about tasks scheduled for the system?
16. What is an Operator in SQL Server? ?
17. What is event forwarding?
18. What is one example of a MAPI-compliant server?

19. What is the difference between SQL Server Mail and SQL Server Mail Agent?

20. What is the security context of SQL Server Mail Agent?

21. How do you send ad hoc e-mail messages?

22. What is the SQL Server Profiler and what can you do with it?

23. How do you view an estimated execution plan for a query?

24. How do you create statistics for a table? Who uses statistics?

25. What would you use as input data for the Index Tuning Wizard?

26. How can you optimize transaction-log performance?

27. What is DBCC?

# PART

# VI

## Sunday
## Afternoon

# Disaster Recovery

## Session Checklist

✔ Planning for disaster

✔ Identifying basic disaster scenarios

✔ Creating standby servers

✔ Managing the disaster

**30 Min.
To Go**

**D**isaster can happen to your system at any time. It might be a hardware failure, a software failure, or both; it might be a problem with your power supply; it might be one of thousands of other things. You need to be prepared to recover from any of these disasters. This session deals with the most common disaster scenarios and the ways to recover from them.

## Planning for Disaster

No matter how well-tuned your system, or how well-behaved your client applications, sooner or later it is going to happen: You are going to get a call at 3:00 AM telling you that your server is down, nobody can connect to the database, and your presence is required *immediately*. If I had only enough time to give you one piece of advice, it would be this: Don't panic. Fortunately, I have more time and space to elaborate on the subject.

The basis of disaster recovery is planning. Recovery is really easy — in theory: All you need to do is plan ahead for a disaster and then, when it happens, implement your plan — step by step. Later in this session I discuss the most common disaster scenarios. You will need a separate plan for each one of them, and then for every additional one you can think of. However, for practical reasons, you probably won't create more than a dozen plans.

Every SQL Server RDBMS system consists of at least three components:

- Operating system
- SQL Server
- Client applications that connect to SQL Server

Any of these components can malfunction. While you probably won't have to fix the OS or client-application problems, you should have enough information on hand that other professionals will be able to do so.

Start with the assumption that your data are of paramount importance and must be protected. Next, ask yourself: What could go wrong? Blackout, faulty hard drive, computer virus, hacker's attack, earthquake, alien invasion ... to mention just a few.

You need to have a valid up-to-date recovery plan; moreover this plan has to be tested, and the amount of testing should be proportional to the importance of your data. While you are at it, make sure that you are not the only person capable of performing the recovery, because you might be away just when you are needed the most.

To sum it up:

- Disasters happen
- You need multiple recovery plans, one for each possible scenario
- You need to test your plans and keep them up to date
- Don't panic

## Identifying Basic Disaster Scenarios

So you've got your server up and running: Your cleverly written custom applications pump tons of data into your properly designed databases, and get them back when necessary. What could possibly go wrong?

## Physical destruction

Chances are that you have one or two computers in your system (it's mightily diffi-cult to run RDBMS without them, you know). The only way to recover from physical destruction of one of these computers is to replace your system with an identical or compatible (and tested!) hardware configuration. So that you'll be able to do this if the need should arise, you need to maintain a detailed hardware-configuration list for your system.

**Your hardware is your first line of defense: Take proper care of it. You need UPS — uninterruptible power supply — so that your com-puters can shut down gracefully in the event of a power failure. If you can afford it, I recommend an air conditioner to keep your computer lab at a constant temperature. Computers do produce heat, and they can operate only within a fairly narrow range of temperatures.**

## Failed operating system

Computers cannot run without operating systems, and SQL Server requires Windows NT or Windows 2000 Server. The purpose of configuration management is to maintain a fully restorable configuration: You need to know, in addition to the OS that is in use, the Service Pack that is required, what other software has been installed on the server, and the sequence in which that software was installed. You need ready access to all the software you need to install from scratch and you need step-by-step instructions for installing it.

**Though not foolproof, one technique is to create and archive (possibly Zip) an image of your fully functional system. You will be able to restore this image in much less time than it would take you to perform a step-by-step installation of all the neces-sary stuff; of course, the image must be up to date to be useful.**

## Database corruption

On a typical system you will have one or more SQL Server instances, each contain-ing one or more custom databases, plus the master, model, MSDB, and TempDB databases. Any of these can become corrupted. Corruption can occur on various levels — from compromised data integrity to physical corruption of the data files and Windows Registry.

## Back Up and Restore!

When it comes to restoring data and databases nothing beats backups. I discuss backing up databases and transaction logs in Session 18; I hope I've convinced you of the paramount importance of timely backups. Once you've got your OS, SQL Server, and all the applicable Service Packs installed, restore the master database from your backup.

Restoring your master database from a backup is not the same as rebuilding it. Restoring it from backup brings the old master database back to life, with all the old changes and preferences; rebuilding gives you a new master database with all the default settings of a newborn SQL Server.

You need to have a full up-to-date backup of every important database in your SQL Server installation (you can restore Northwind and Pubs databases from SQL scripts, however; see Session 6 for details). Moreover, you must store these backups safely so that they will not perish with your RDBMS system. You must maintain proper records of the basic configuration of your SQL Server: passwords, network libraries used, collation order — all the choices you made when installing and configuring your SQL Server.

### Verifying functionality

Once you've restored your working configuration you need to verify that all the functionality is there. You need to do this yourself; you cannot rely on the users to tell you. This means that you need a testing program (preferably a script you can run from the command line) that will test the base functionality of the restored system.

You need a disaster-recovery plan for each of the scenarios I've mentioned so far. Your plan must be up-to-date and it must be tested — you'll have no time for tune-up operations while recovering a system.

## Creating Standby Servers

When you're dealing with disaster recovery time is always in short supply. Your database is supposed to be operational five minutes ago; it was not supposed to be down in the first place.

**20 Min.
To Go**

While you are trying your patience restoring your primary server, you can switch a standby server into operation to supply all the data services.

To create a standby server, follow these steps:

1. Install an identical copy of SQL Server on identical or compatible hardware. Make sure that the configuration of both servers is identical (identical passwords, collation order, code page, and so on).

2. Copy all the databases from the primary server to the standby server. You can do this in a variety of ways: by restoring backups of the primary server to the standby; by copying databases through DTS; by running SQL scripts, and so on.

3. Periodically synchronize data between the primary server and the standby server.

When your primary server fails, bring your standby server online. Before doing this you need to restore the most recent backup and apply all the transaction logs from the primary server.

 **Any changes you make to your standby server you must also make to your primary server after bringing it back to life.**

It is important to remember that all the current users of a primary server must log onto this standby server once it is brought online; none of the user processes will be switched to the standby server.

## Managing the Disaster

**10 Min. To Go**

It has happened. You have all this expensive hardware junk in front of you and you need to bring it back to life — *now*. But you aren't panicking — you are prepared!

If you are using standby servers, bring one online immediately (do not forget to apply the most recent backups). Ask users to save whatever work they might be in the middle of, log off, and log on again. This will give you time to concentrate on the task at hand: restoring your primary server.

Evaluate the type of disaster and characterize it as one of the following:

- Hardware failure
- OS failure
- SQL Server failure
- Some combination of the above

Once you've determined the type, you need to determine your course of action, based on the plans you prepared and tested for a case like this. (Though recovery from hardware failure and OS malfunction in general is a fascinating topic, here I will discuss SQL Server recovery only, being constrained by the topic of the book.)

You might only have a corrupted database (although this hardly qualifies as a disaster): In this case you can restore the database from a backup, verify its functionality, and bring the server back online.

Things will get much hairier if you cannot start SQL Server. The simplest thing is to reboot the system. If SQL Server comes back normally, analyze the logs for a possible cause and run a series of tests before bringing it back online; if it does not, try starting from the command line. The *<instance name>* in the following code refers to your SQL Server name. Drop it if you are starting the default SQL Server instance. Also make sure that you are in the directory in which the SQL Server executable is installed.

```
sqlservr.exe -c - m -s <instance name>
```

Starting SQL Server in single-user mode ensures that nobody else can interfere with recovery. If this operation succeeds you may continue restoring your master database and then proceed with the rest of your plan.

If your attempt to start SQL Server fails you can try rebuilding the Registry with a SQL Server installation. This procedure falls a little short of reinstalling SQL Server: It fixes any Registry settings for your SQL Server installation that might have been corrupted, but it will not fix a corrupted master database. If you included the Registry rebuild in your recovery plan, make sure you perform it correctly by following these steps:

1. Repeat all the steps you went through in Session 1 when installing SQL Server for the first time. Make sure that you select all the options you installed SQL Server with originally.

2. Select Advanced from the Installation Selection Screen (shown in Figure 27-1).

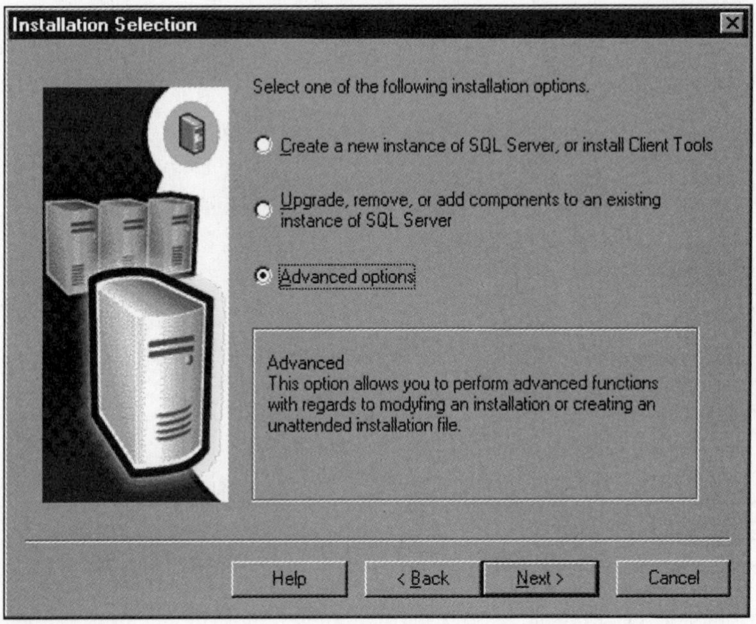

**Figure 27-1**
*Selecting the Advanced installation option*

3. Select Registry Rebuild from the screen shown in Figure 27-2. SQL Server warns you about the importance of specifying all the same options you specified in the original installation; if you are not sure which options you specified, you are better off reinstalling the server.

If after rebuilding the Registry you still cannot start SQL Server, you have one more option before choosing to reinstall: rebuilding the master database. SQL Server comes with a utility, Rebuildm.exe, that does this. This utility is located in the directory Microsoft SQL Server\80\Tools\Binn. Unlike many command-line commands, this one actually offers a visual interface. Click Browse to specify the location of your data files, and — once you have made your selections — click Rebuild.

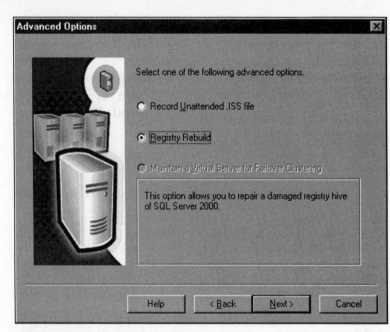

**Figure 27-2**
*Rebuilding the registry from SQL Server*

Once your master database is rebuilt you should apply the backups you made of the previous master database so you won't lose your information.

**Rebuilding the master database is only slightly less drastic than reinstalling SQL Server from scratch, because doing so will cause you to lose all the information about your custom databases and you will have to restore them from backups. The other use of the Rebuildm.exe utility is to change the collation order for your SQL Server: The same warning applies.**

If rebuilding the master database does not enable you to start SQL Server, your last option is to reinstall SQL Server from scratch. Follow the guidelines in Session 1 for SQL Server installation. Please make sure that you follow the guidelines exactly and that you select exactly the same options you selected when installing SQL Server the first time.

Once you have installed SQL Server, first apply the most recent full backup, and then perform the Transaction Log backup. Run scripts to confirm the basic functionality of your system.

If you were running a standby server while repairing the primary one, you need to apply the most recent active Transaction Log backup to the primary server before bringing it back online.

**Once your primary server is up and running you have time to examine the SQL Server log and OS Event Log for clues as to what happened and what you can do to prevent similar disasters in the future.**

As you gain more experience with SQL Server you may forget all the advice I've given you in this session and find better ways of doing things, but trust me on this one: Don't panic.

**Done!**

## REVIEW

- You need recovery plans for different disaster scenarios.
- You must have backups for every database in your SQL Server, especially the master database.
- Using a standby server might be a bit expensive but it is a viable option if your database needs a lot of up time.
- Though this is simple common sense, it is often overlooked: When recovering from a disaster, move sequentially from a simple fix to a full restore (if necessary). Try the solution that is least expensive — in terms of time and complexity — first.

## QUIZ YOURSELF

1. Why do you need a disaster-recovery plan?
2. What is a disaster scenario? How many disaster scenarios do you need to go through for your system?
3. What is a standby server and why might you need one?
4. How do you rebuild the Registry?
5. How do you rebuild the master database?
6. How do you verify the base functionality of your SQL Server?

# SQL Server Security

## Session Checklist

✔ Planning for security

✔ Understanding SQL Server Authentication Modes

✔ Configuring SQL Server roles

✔ Using views as a security mechanism

✔ Understanding SQL Server file permissions

✔ Auditing SQL Server

**30 Min.
To Go**

**T**his session will give you an overview and some hands-on examples of setting up and administering your SQL Server security on various levels, from connection authentication mode through adding members to the Server Fixed roles through setting up custom database roles.

## Planning for Security

Your company relies on the data contained in your SQL Server database. The database might contain sensitive information that could compromise your company's position on the market if discovered by competitors, or your employees might be less than thrilled to find out that they are in the lowest-paid category in the company — you can add your own examples and concerns.

Your data are sacred and must be secured. SQL Server provides multi-layered fine-grained security and all you need to do is use it. Each user in your company hierarchy should be assigned just enough rights to perform his or her job efficiently.

You need to formulate a security plan according to your company's business practices. The plan must be tightly integrated with your network security, because SQL Server Service usually runs in a high-privileges security context and can be used to penetrate your network.

## Introducing SQL Server Authentication Modes

SQL Server 2000 supports two modes of authentication:

- Windows Authentication Mode
- Mixed Mode for Windows Authentication and SQL Server Authentication

Windows Authentication Mode is very similar to the authentication mode you use to log onto the network computer. Your network administrator creates a user account and assigns certain privileges for accessing network resources. SQL Server is such a resource because it revalidates the account name and password either by calling Windows back (in the case of a user with an account on the machine running SQL server) or by using the Windows domain controller. The actual built-in Windows security is much more complex than this, but as a DBA-in-training you can afford to have this simplistic view.

SQL Server authentication handles non-trusted connections. A user who requests connection is validated against a SQL Server–maintained login, and once validated has all the privileges and permissions assigned to this login. If validation fails, the user receives the SQL Server error message "Login failed."

Follow these steps to set up your authentication mode from the Enterprise Manager console:

1. Click on the Properties option and select the Security tab from the screen shown in Figure 28-1.

2. From this tab select either Windows Authentication (Windows only) or Mixed Authentication Mode (SQL Server and Windows).

   Optionally, you may want to set the Audit level (which I'll discuss later in this session), which will keep track of all login attempts, either successful, unsuccessful, or both, depending on the option you select.

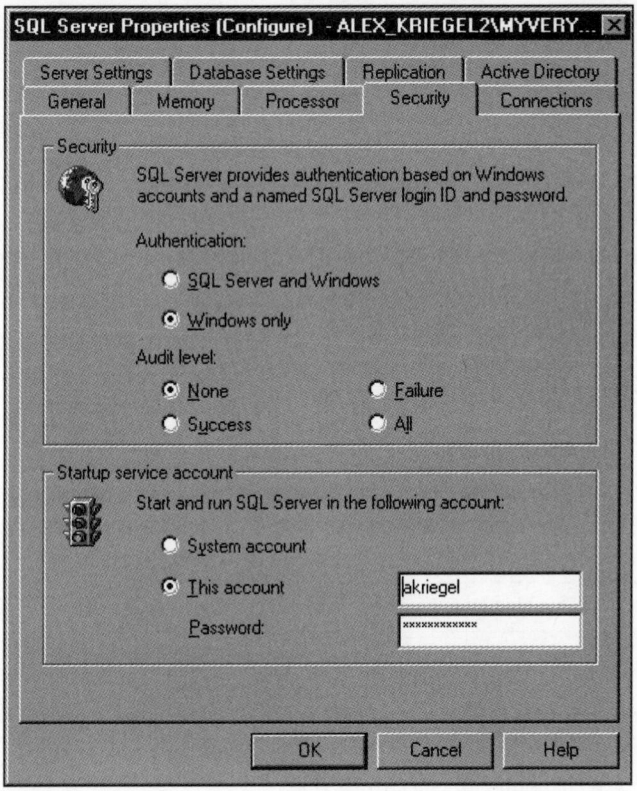

**Figure 28-1**
*Setting Authentication Mode for SQL Server 2000*

> **SQL Server Authentication is provided for compatibility with previous versions (version 7.0 and earlier) as well as for SQL Server instances running on Windows 98.**

## Configuring SQL Server Roles

*Roles* in SQL Server 2000 are modeled after Windows groups and make it easier to assign or revoke permissions and privileges to a group of users at once. SQL Server supports two groups of roles:

- **Fixed server roles** — Applied and administered at the SQL Server level.
- **Database roles** — Applied and administered at the database level.

## Fixed server roles

Server roles are predefined (fixed). You cannot add a new role on the server level, although you can add users to these roles. Table 28-1 lists the fixed server roles adapted from Microsoft SQL Server Books Online.

**Table 28-1**
*SQL Server 2000 Fixed Server Roles*

| Fixed Server Role | Description |
| --- | --- |
| sysadmin | Grants you the highest security privileges possible. Overlaps any other role (fixed or not); enables you to perform any task possible in SQL Server. |
| serveradmin | Enables you to configure server-wide settings. |
| setupadmin | Enables you to add and remove linked servers, and to execute some system stored procedures. |
| dbcreator | Creates and alters databases. |
| diskadmin | Manages physical disk files. |
| securityadmin | Manages server logins. |
| processadmin | Manages processes running in an instance of SQL Server. |
| bulkadmin | Executes the BULK INSERT statement. |

## Adding a member to a fixed server role

Follow these steps to add a member to a fixed server role:

1. From the Enterprise Manager console, expand the Security node and select the Server Roles node: Fixed security roles appear in the right-hand pane.

2. Select an appropriate role and from the right-click menu choose Properties. From the Server Role Properties screen (shown in Figure 28-2) you can add any valid login defined on the SQL Server.

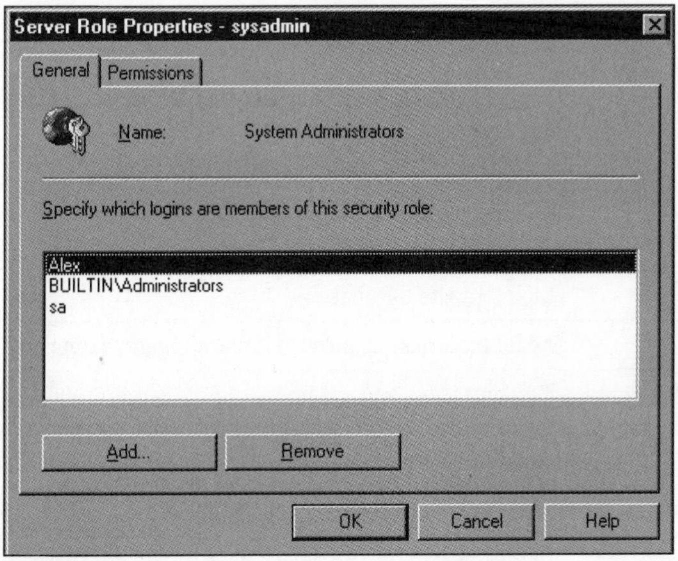

**Figure 28-2**
*Adding a member to a fixed server role*

3. From the Permissions tab you can view the privileges this role has; you cannot change this list.

**Any Windows (NT or 2000) users belonging to the BUILTIN\ Administrators group are automatically members of the SQL Server sysadmin fixed server role.**

**20 Min. To Go**

## Database roles

Database roles are more flexible than fixed server roles in that they include fixed roles to which you can add new members as well as custom roles you can create for your own use. You learned a bit about fixed database roles in Session 20 when you learned how to set up a new SQL Server user. The list of predefined roles for the database is presented in Table 28-2.

**Table 28-2**
*Fixed Database Roles*

| Fixed Database Role | Description |
| --- | --- |
| db_owner | The highest possible permission level for the database; overlaps any other database role. |
| db_accessadmin | Enables you to control access and set up or remove user accounts. |
| db_datareader | Enables you to read (see) all the data in the entire database. |
| db_datawriter | Enables you to add, change, or delete data in all user tables in the database. |
| db_ddladmin | Adds, modifies, or drops database objects (runs all DDLs). |
| db_securityadmin | Manages roles and members of SQL Server 2000 database roles, and manages statement and object permissions in the database. |
| db_backupoperator | Enables you to back up the database. |
| db_denydatareader | Denies permission to select data in the database. |
| db_denydatawriter | Denies permission to change data in the database. |

## Adding a member to a database role

Adding a user to a database role is no different from adding a user to a fixed server role. A user must exist before he or she can be added to the role, and the user can belong to more than one role in the same database.

If you ever need to create a custom database role, you can do it, though the fact that you can create a database role does not necessarily mean you should. Microsoft suggests creating new database roles only if there is no existing Windows group that satisfies your criteria, or you simply do not have the rights to administer Windows accounts.

**Adding a Windows (NT or 2000) login to a database role when there is no corresponding user account in the database results in SQL Server creating the user account automatically.**

Once you've decided that you need a new database role, follow these steps:

1. From the Enterprise Manager console, select the database for which you wish to create the role.

2. Expand the database node and select Roles from the database nodes.

3. Finally, choose the New Database Role right-click menu option. On the Database Role Properties screen (shown in Figure 28-3), type in the name of your new role and add users.

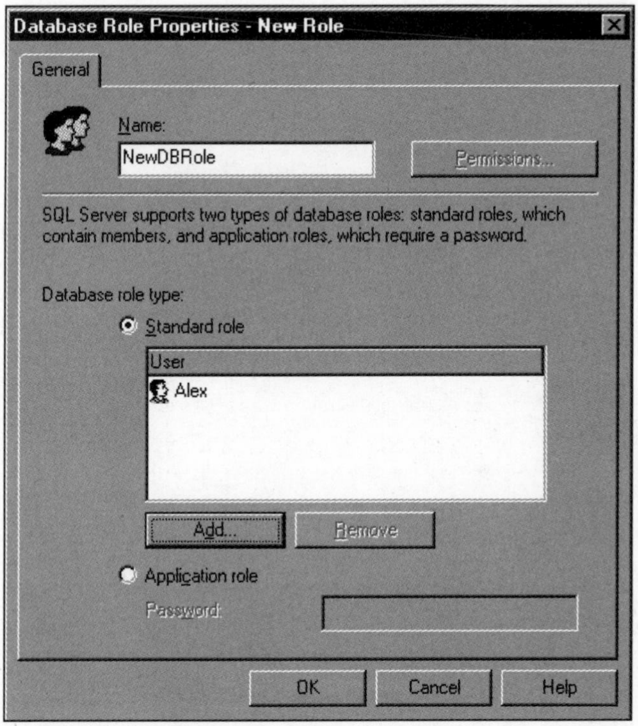

**Figure 28-3**
*Creating a new database role*

> **If you have more than one custom database role created for your database, you will be able to add these roles as members of the newly created role. Doing this will establish a hierarchy of rights and privileges. Avoid deep nesting of roles, as it will have a negative impact on your database performance.**

## Application roles

You may also restrict database users' access by specifying an application role. Users assigned to an application role can access the database through a specific application only. Application roles differ from other types of roles in that they have no members, must be activated, and once activated bypass all standard permissions.

Essentially, using an application role tells SQL Server that an application, rather than SQL Server itself, is going to manage security. You can create an application role much as you would create an ordinary database role, through the Enterprise Manager (as shown in Figure 28-4).

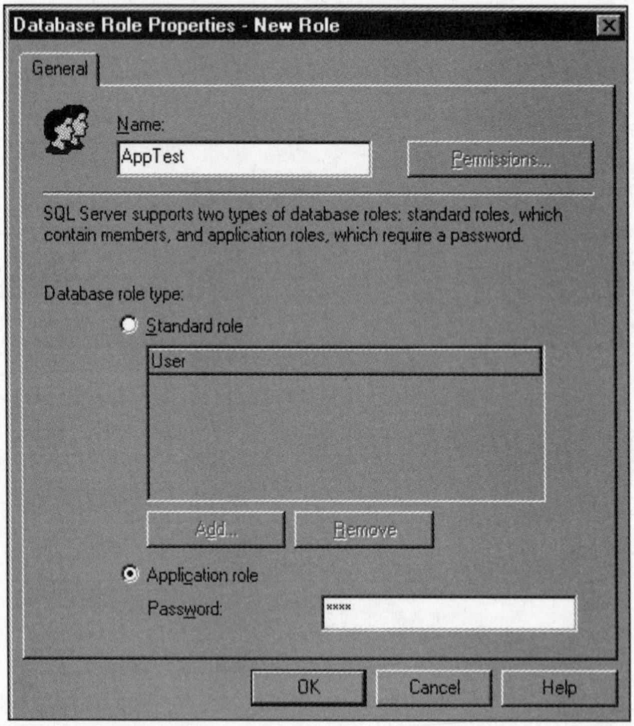

**Figure 28-4**
*Creating a new application role*

Instead of Standard role, select Application role and provide a password. This password is the only means by which the SQL Server can authenticate the application.

In order to use this role you must activate it through a system-stored procedure, sp_setapprole.

```
EXEC sp_setapprole 'AppTest', 'Test'
```

Once the role is activated, all previous user privileges are dropped.

**It might be a good idea to encrypt the password before sending it over the network to the SQL Server. You can use ODBC encryption: EXEC sp_setapprole 'AppTest', {Encrypt N 'Test'}, 'odbc'.**

**10 Min. To Go**

## Using Views as a Security Mechanism

Using views you can access data from one or more underlying tables. A *view* is a database object that behaves very much like a standard table in SQL Server, except that it is based on the T-SQL query.

Views are created, altered, and dropped in the same way that SQL Server tables are. SQL Server 2000 also gives you the ability to index views. Views are in general not updateable, though SQL Server 2000 enables you to create an INSTEAD OF trigger on a view to update it.

Here is the sample syntax for creating a view. Say that you decide to give the Fishing Committee access to some information about your employees. The committee does not need to know anything about the employees except their names, phone numbers, and the fact that they indicated fishing as a primary hobby on their résumés.

```
CREATE VIEW Employees_Hobbies
AS
SELECT FirstName, LastName, Phone WHERE hobby = 'Fishing'
FROM emloyees e LEFT OUTER JOIN hobbies h ON e.emp_id = h.emp_id
```

Once the view is created you can access it just as you would a regular table.

Views are provided primarily for convenience, speed, and security. The view restricts the data available to the user, and you can assign separate permissions for different views. The view usually operates on a data subset, hiding the rest of the columns from the users (even if they have full permissions to see the view, they will see only the columns listed in the T-SQL statement underlying it).

## Understanding SQL Server File Permissions

Almost all database objects in SQL Server 2000 are stored as physical files on your hard drive. This being the case, SQL Server must maintain some security context for accessing these files. This context is set up by a security account; which account is used depends on how SQL Server was started in the first place.

If you start SQL Server from the Service Control Manager it will use the SQL Server Service security account; if you start it at the command prompt it will use the security account of the logged user. Adjust the security of these accounts accordingly to prevent unauthorized file access.

**Windows 98 does not support Windows services. Though these services will be simulated, there is no need to create user accounts for them.**

## Auditing SQL Server

Audit logs are maintained for security reasons, in case you need to analyze who was connected to the server, how long a connection lasted, and so forth. You set the audit level from the Server Properties screen (shown in Figure 28-1). The records of clients' activities are accumulated in audit logs.

The maximum size for an audit log is 200MB; when this limit is reached a new file is created. Once you've run out of space on your hard drive, SQL Server will stop.

You can configure SQL Server 2000 to perform C2 auditing, which is an advanced security feature that has more to do with standard guidelines than with SQL Server itself. Use it only if your system is C2 certified by U.S. government standards.

**Done!**

### REVIEW

- SQL Server 2000 supports two modes of user authentication: Windows Authentication Mode and Mixed Mode (both Windows and SQL Server authentication).

- You set the authentication mode on the server level; it applies to all SQL Server objects.

- You can assign users in SQL Server to roles, which are modeled after Windows user groups.
- Two types of roles exist: server roles and database roles. Server roles are fixed and cannot be custom-created; database roles include both fixed and custom roles.
- You can use views as a security mechanism by restricting data access.
- SQL Server supports auditing, which is set up at the server level. The audit logs contain information about all attempts to connect to the server.

## Quiz Yourself

1. What are the two Authentication Modes supported by SQL Server 2000?
2. How are server roles different from database roles?
3. Which role are members of the Windows account BUILTIN\Administrators automatically assigned in SQL Server?
4. How does a view differ from a table?
5. What is the maximum size of an audit-log file?

# Database Connectivity

## Session Checklist

✔ Understanding DBLIB, ODBC and OLE DB

✔ Configuring the ODBC data source

✔ Learning about DAO, RDO, and ADO

✔ Interoperability with non-Windows machines and the Internet

**30 Min.
To Go**

S QL Server serves as the foundation (*back end*, in programming jargon) for client applications that connect to it to request or change data. The interfaces DBLIB, ODBC, and OLE DB provide you with connectivity. You can use network libraries to connect to SQL Server from virtually any non-Windows platform. Coupled with Internet Information Server (IIS), SQL Server can be accessed via Internet standard Hypertext Transfer Protocol (HTTP). This session covers these topics, and more.

## Introducing DBLIB, ODBC, and OLE DB

Every single application designed to use SQL Server services must first establish a connection. Establishing a connection enables a client to send requests and receive responses. Client applications can be running on the same machine, across the network, or over the Internet. SQL Server 2000 provides a number of interfaces you can use to establish a connection.

## DBLIB

The oldest interface still supported is DBLIB. This is a call-level interface (CLI) to the SQL Server libraries. It is adapted for use with the C/C++ programming language and is sometimes used to squeeze the last drop of performance from client/server communications. It is a relatively complex interface that requires considerable expertise in programming. Though this interface is still supported for backwards compatibility, Microsoft increasingly discourages users from accessing SQL Server with DBLIB by providing new, more user-friendly interfaces.

**The main reason for not using DBLIB is that it is a vendor-specific interface: If you change your data source to a different RDBMS vendor, you will have to revise and recompile your application.**

## Open Database Connectivity (ODBC)

By and large, the most popular connectivity mechanism is ODBC. It is an application-programming interface (API) that supports access to virtually any data source for which an ODBC driver is available. It is also a non-proprietary open standard supported by American National Standards Institute (ANSI) and International Organization for Standardization (ISO) standards. You can easily switch a client that uses ODBC from one data source to another (for example, from Oracle to SQL Server), simply by reconfiguring Data Source Name entries (covered later in this session in the section "Configuring ODBC Data Sources").

## OLE DB

This is the latest interface from Microsoft. It is a COM/OLE/ActiveX-based interface designed for COM-compliant clients. (For non-OLE–compliant clients OLE DB Provider for ODBC is available.) Unlike ODBC, OLE DB has no externally configurable components; you specify the OLE DB provider right in your application inside a connection string.

## Configuring ODBC Data Sources

In order to use an ODBC data source you must create it on the machine on which the client is going to be installed. ODBC DSN (Data Source Name) is nothing more than a number of entries in the Windows Registry. You can set it up manually or programmatically, or use a visual interface provided by Microsoft in the Windows control panel.

To create a DSN on your machine, follow these steps:

1.  Select Start ⇨ Settings ⇨ Control Panel and then double-click the Data Sources (ODBC) icon (ODBC32 on Windows 9x machines).

    As DSN can be configured for every data source for which there is an ODBC driver, you are likely to see several of these drivers on your machine (such as Microsoft Access Driver, SQL Server Driver, and so on). Because you are creating DSN for SQL Server, select ODBC Driver for SQL Server.

    You can select System DSN, User DSN, or File DSN. The main difference among these is scope: A User DSN is local and can be accessed only by the current user for whom it was created; a System DSN is also local, but accessible to every user on the machine; and a File DSN is represented by a physical file and can be placed either on a local machine or on the network.

2.  The Drivers tab lists all currently available ODBC drivers on your computer. To add a new driver, use that drive's install program.

3.  The Tracing tab enables you to configure traces to monitor drivers' usage. This information is stored as a log file.

*Connection pooling* contributes to a more rational use of resources as it allows several applications to use one open connection; when the connection is released by one client it can be given to another without the need for more connections. Connection pooling also lets you enable the Performance Monitor (Perf Mon) in order to accumulate statistics for optimization analysis.

The last tab on the screen shown in Figure 29-1, the About tab, will provide you with information about which libraries serve which ODBC components.

Now I'll walk you through the process of configuring System DSN for SQL Server:

1. Start the ODBC Data Source Administrator (in Windows NT go to the Control Paneland double-click the Data Sources (ODBC) icon; in Windows 2000 select Programs ➪ Administrative Tools ➪ Data Sources (ODBC)) and select the System DSN tab. Click Add.

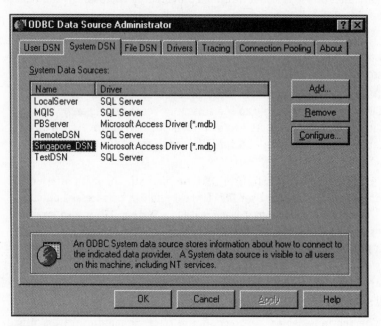

**Figure 29-1**
*Adding DSN for a local SQL Server*

2. Select the appropriate driver to use with your DSN from the screen shown in Figure 29-2. Click Finish. Now the wizard takes you through the process of creating the DSN.

3. On the screen shown in Figure 29-3, enter the name of your DSN (your client application will use this name to connect to SQL Server), a description, and the SQL Server instance you wish to connect to. The drop-down combo box will contain a list of all SQL Servers visible from your machine. Click Next.

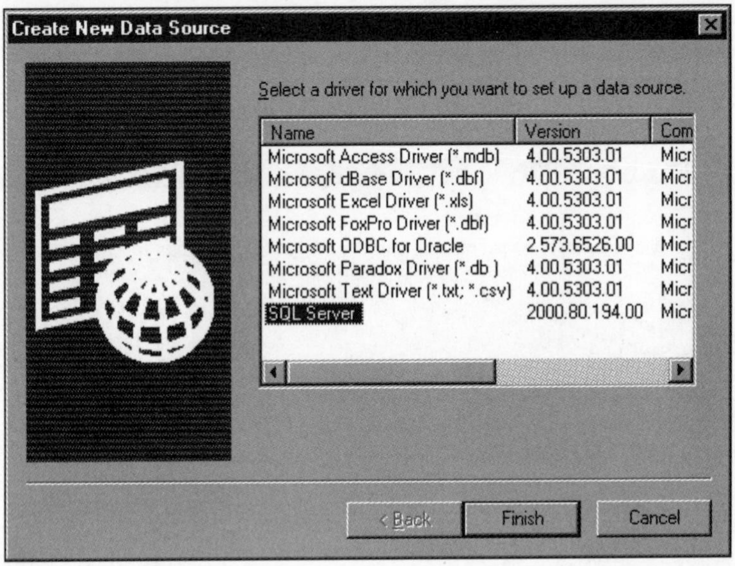

**Create New Data Source**

Select a driver for which you want to set up a data source.

| Name | Version | Com |
|------|---------|-----|
| Microsoft Access Driver (*.mdb) | 4.00.5303.01 | Micr |
| Microsoft dBase Driver (*.dbf) | 4.00.5303.01 | Micr |
| Microsoft Excel Driver (*.xls) | 4.00.5303.01 | Micr |
| Microsoft FoxPro Driver (*.dbf) | 4.00.5303.01 | Micr |
| Microsoft ODBC for Oracle | 2.573.6526.00 | Micr |
| Microsoft Paradox Driver (*.db ) | 4.00.5303.01 | Micr |
| Microsoft Text Driver (*.txt; *.csv) | 4.00.5303.01 | Micr |
| SQL Server | 2000.80.194.00 | Micr |

< Back    Finish    Cancel

**Figure 29-2**
*Selecting the ODBC driver for SQL Server*

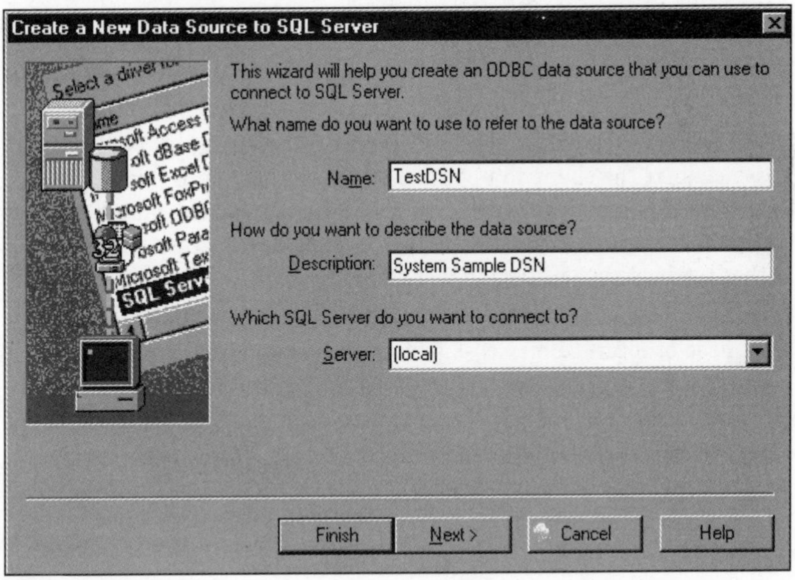

**Create a New Data Source to SQL Server**

This wizard will help you create an ODBC data source that you can use to connect to SQL Server.

What name do you want to use to refer to the data source?

Name: TestDSN

How do you want to describe the data source?

Description: System Sample DSN

Which SQL Server do you want to connect to?

Server: (local)

Finish    Next >    Cancel    Help

**Figure 29-3**
*Specifying properties and the destination data source*

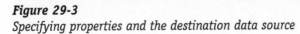

Part VI—Sunday Afternoon
Session 29

**4.** On the next screen (shown in Figure 29-4), select the authentication mode for the client; you should generally use Windows Authentication on the trusted network and SQL Server authentication in other cases. Click Next.

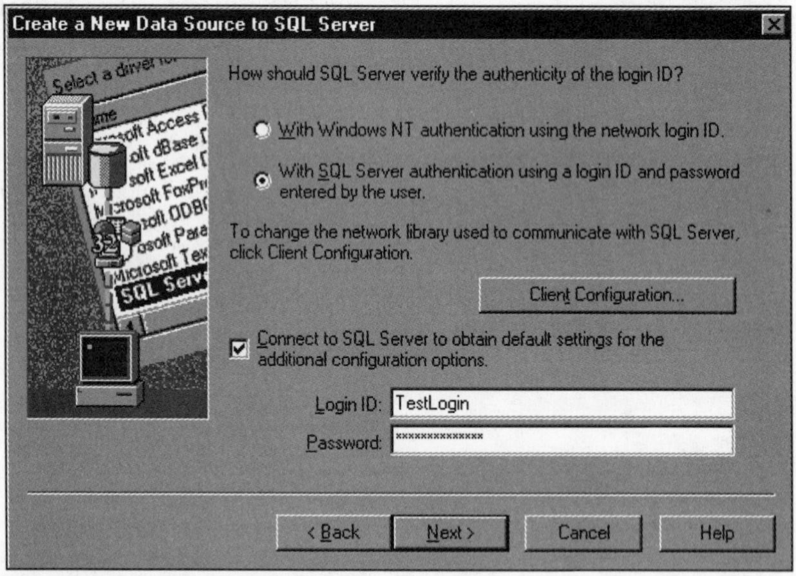

**Figure 29-4**
*Choosing an authentication mode*

**5.** The next screen prompts you for default database settings (which database context the client will be in once the connection is open). For example, if you are configuring your DSN for the Pubs database you may want to change the database context to Pubs; in this case you leave all other settings at their defaults. Click Next.

**6.** The next screen enables you to set some advanced settings, such as the language of returned messages (the default is English), where to save statistics, and what to do with the queries that take too long to complete. Optionally you can set up data encryption and instruct the driver to format output into local settings. Click Finish.

7. The last screen to appear is the summary of the ODBC DSN you just created. Click OK to finish the process.

**The last screen will also contain the Test Data Source button with which you can test your new DSN. Click it and make sure that you see the message "Tests Completed Successfully"; otherwise, act on the information in your error message. The most common problem is an invalid login or password.**

Now your client can use your newly created ODBC DSN to connect to your SQL Server. You can always reconfigure the properties of your DSN from the same ODBC Data Source Administrator.

## *Presenting DAO, RDO, and ADO*

**20 Min. To Go**

To provide access for its database products Microsoft went through several iterations, and as a result application developers have a wealth of components to work with: ODBC API (call-level interface), DAO (Data Access Objects), RDO (Remote Data Objects), and ADO (Active Data Objects).

As the story has it: In the beginning there was DAO and Microsoft saw that DAO was good and took it through several iterations to version 3.6 and stopped there. Then Microsoft introduced RDO and RDO lived long enough to give birth to ADO, and ADO grew and grew and became the data-access component of choice, as it remains today.

All these three-letter acronyms represent object models on top of data-access layers, such as ODBC drivers or OLE DB providers; to ensure backwards compatibility Microsoft created MSDASQL, the OLE DB Provider for ODBC, with which your ODBC applications can continue to work while using the new OLE DB interface.

The relationships between data-access components such as ADO and the ODBC-OLE DB layer are represented on the diagram shown in Figure 29-5.

In order to use any of these data-access objects an application must either be COM-compliant or use ODBC API and DBLIB. The exact syntax for opening a connection will depend on the programming language of choice for the application making use of the SQL Server database.

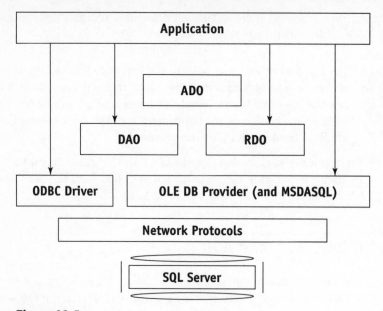

**Figure 29-5**
*Visualizing the data-access components relationship*

Table 29-1 lists the OLE DB providers tested with SQL Server; it's adapted from Microsoft SQL Server 2000 Books Online.

**Table 29-1**
*List of OLE DB Providers for SQL Server 2000*

| Data Source | Provider Name |
| --- | --- |
| SQL Server 6.5 or later | Microsoft OLE DB Provider for SQL Server |
| ODBC Data Sources | Microsoft OLE DB Provider for ODBC |
| Microsoft Access (Jet) databases | Microsoft OLE DB Provider for Jet version 4.00 |
| Microsoft Excel spreadsheets | Microsoft OLE DB Provider for Jet version 4.00 |
| Data Transformation Service Package Data Source Object | Microsoft OLE DB Provider for DTS Packages |
| Oracle databases | Microsoft OLE DB Provider for Oracle version 2.6 |

| Data Source | Provider Name |
| --- | --- |
| Local file system (through Indexing Services) | Microsoft OLE DB Provider for Microsoft Indexing Service (requires Microsoft Windows NT 4.0 Service Pack 4 or later) |
| IBM DB2 databases | Microsoft OLE DB Provider for DB2 |

You do not need to configure OLE DB providers; it remains the responsibility of the clients to connect to them programmatically.

## Interoperability with Non-Windows Machines and the Internet

**10 Min. To Go**

Microsoft has tightly integrated its Internet Information Server (IIS) with SQL Server 2000. There is nothing mysterious about that, but some assembly is required.

A client can submit POST and GET commands via HTTP, or even execute a SQL query. The standard Internet addressing syntax is supported. An HTTP request directed to SQL Server is then redirected to the ISAPI filter and submitted to SQL Server. The results are returned to the client as an XML document, as shown here:

```
http://<IISServer>/Pubs?sql=SELECT+*+FROM+Authors+FOR+XML+AUTO&roo
t=root
```

It is the responsibility of the client application to parse the XML document, and before queries can be specified using HTTP, you must create a virtual root using the IIS Virtual Directory Management for SQL Server. This requires some familiarity with IIS, which is beyond the scope of this book.

You can run clients accessing SQL Server from the following platforms:

- Windows NT Workstation
- Windows 2000 Professional
- Windows 9x
- Apple Macintosh
- UNIX
- OS/2

The actual connection is supported via one of the network libraries, such as TCP/IP, AppleTalk, Banyan VINES, Named Pipes, and so forth. These hide the complexity of the communication, wrapping it in familiar interfaces that can be accessed by clients running on heterogeneous platforms.

**While creating DSN on the screen where you specify authentication mode, you can specify that the client use one of these network libraries. To do so, click Configure Client on the screen.**

*Done!*

## REVIEW

- You have several choices regarding how the client application will connect to the SQL Server: namely, you can use DBLIB, ODBC, or OLE DB.
- ODBC Data Sources provide information for the client applications accessing a particular instance of SQL Server. You can configure ODBC to point to any data source for which an ODBC driver exists.
- OLE DB is the latest data-access interface provided by Microsoft. It is COM/ActiveX-based and supports ODBC (through the OLE DB provider for ODBC) for backwards compatibility.
- You can access SQL Server through HTTP over the Internet; to do this you will need Internet Information Server (IIS).
- You can access SQL Server from any non-Windows machine as long as the appropriate network libraries are installed to support it.

## QUIZ YOURSELF

1. In what sequence were the data-access interfaces (DBLIB, ODBC, and OLE DB) introduced?

2. What does DSN stand for? What are the differences among User DSN, System DSN, and File DSN?

3. What components did Microsoft provide to enable you to program data access to its data sources?

4. What is the prerequisite for accessing SQL Server via HTTP?

5. From which platforms can you connect to SQL Server?

# Advanced Features of
# SQL Server 2000

## Session Checklist

✔ Using English Query

✔ Performing full-text searches

✔ Using SQL Server 2000 Analytical Services

✔ Running the Web Assistant Wizard

✔ Getting SQL Server XML support

**30 Min.
To Go**

This session introduces you to some advanced features of SQL Server. English Query enables you to query SQL Server data in plain English. You'll learn how to conduct searches within text data without splitting information into columns first. You'll also learn how to use SQL Server to support complex business decisions. Finally, I'll show you how to connect SQL Server to the Web with standard HTML (Hypertext Markup Language), and how to use HTML's superset eXtensible Markup Language (XML).

## Using English Query

The language you use to query SQL Server — Transact SQL — is a powerful and versatile programming language. As such it serves very well anyone who took the time to learn it, which probably does not apply to the majority of the people on this planet. The rest of humanity (the rest of whatever percentage of humanity uses SQL Server, anyway) has two choices: abstain from ad hoc SQL Server queries, or learn English and use Microsoft English Query.

English Query does not enable you to query SQL Server in English, make no mistake about that. It only provides you with the means to build an application capable of translating English into Transact SQL.

English Query is not a part of the standard SQL Server installation; you must install it separately. To install it, repeat the steps you went through in Session 1 when installing SQL Server 2000. From the Welcome screen select SQL Server 2000 components; on the next screen select Install English Query. Now, the English Query installation comes in two flavors: Full Installation (which enables you to develop English Query applications), and Run Time (which only supports the deployment of an English Query application).

If you choose Full Installation you will be able to develop an English Query application. Microsoft provides two wizards to assist you with this task: the SQL Project Wizard and the OLAP (On Line Analytical Processing) Project Wizard. I'll discuss OLAP in more detail later in this session, in the section "Using SQL Server 2000 Analytical Services."

After the wizard creates a basic model consisting of entities and relationships (see Session 5) you can refine the model by testing it with your business requirements until it satisfies all your criteria. Then you can build, compile, and deploy your application.

You can deploy an English Query application in two ways:

- As a stand-alone Visual Basic or Visual C++ application (or any ActiveX supporting technology, for that matter).

- As part of a Web page running on the Microsoft Internet Information Server (IIS). In this case your English Query application runs as part of ASP (Active Server Pages).

**ActiveX is a Microsoft programming technology that helps ActiveX-compliant Windows applications provide services to each other. Active Server Pages is a technology for generating dynamic Web pages on Microsoft Internet Information Server; it uses a mix of VBScript (or JavaScript) and HTML/XML.**

Along the way, you will encounter numerous wizards that will assist you in deploying your English Query applications; please refer to the English Query Books Online (supplied with the English Query installation) for more information about these wizards.

## Performing Full-Text Searches

Transact SQL (and now English Query) enables you to conduct searches wherein selection criteria are values in different columns; it will not help you find a phrase in the text. The main requirement for running the Relational Database Systems is that the data be structured. Structuring the data brings them closer to the machine and thus requires a computer language (T-SQL) to manipulate them. But the world around us is chock-full of unstructured data we would love to query: Structuring them is not always feasible, and sometimes it's downright impossible. Full-text indexing solves this problem — to some extent.

 **See Session 6 for a discussion of the first normal form.**

The full-text search engine (Microsoft Search Service) is installed by default with a typical installation of any edition of Microsoft SQL Server 2000, but to use it you need to enable and configure it. You can start and stop the Microsoft Search Service from the SQL Server Service Manager console.

Each database must be enabled to allow full-search indexing, and the tables you are going to use in full-text searches must be enabled as well. The easiest way to index them is to use the Full-Text Indexing Wizard, which will guide you through the process of selecting indexes and columns for the search string and saving all the information in a full-text search catalog. These catalogs are distinctive objects in the database, viewable under their own node, Full-Text Catalogs, in the Enterprise Manager console.

Once the full-text catalog is created you can issue queries against indexed columns. Unlike a regular-pattern search with the LIKE predicate, the full-text search operates on words and phrases.

You issue queries on full-text search columns in much the same way that you issue standard queries. Transact-SQL introduces the new predicates CONTAINS and FREETEXT for use in full-text queries.

Here are a couple of examples to help you visualize what full-text queries are all about. Let's say you are in the habit of scanning your employees' résumés, and instead of bothering with structuring the information they contain into a bunch of tables, you dump it as text into a single column Résumé of the Employees table — not that you would normally do that!

Now say you need to find an employee whose résumé lists "salmon fishing" as a favorite activity, because you need a companion for your fishing trip. You would issue this query against your Employee database:

```
SELECT resume FROM employees WHERE CONTAINS (resume, '"salmon
fishing"')
```

You can see that your standard LIKE search would not help you with unstructured data, because the Résumé column contains much more than employees' recreational activities.

You also can use the FREETEXT predicate, as follows:

```
SELECT resume FROM employees WHERE FREETEXT (resume,'"salmon
fishing"')
```

The difference is that with CONTAINS the search engine looks for the exact phrase "salmon fishing," whereas with FREETEXT you are likely to find employees who also fish for halibut or swordfish, as well as those whose favorite dish is salmon soufflé.

**Using full-text search predicates you can conduct searches on the Image data-type columns. SQL Server provides support for many other types of documents you can store in databases, such as Microsoft Word documents, Excel documents, ASCII text files, and HTML files.**

Take into consideration that full-text searches are usually less precise than regular searches, which is a reflection of their "human" nature.

**No support exists for the full-text search function over SQL Server–linked servers.**

Recall that you need to create and maintain full-text indexes in order to conduct full-text searches. Regular and full-text indexes are significantly different. Table 30-1, from Microsoft Books Online, lists these differences.

**Table 30-1**

*Differences and Similarities between Regular SQL Indexes and Full-Text Indexes*

| Regular SQL Indexes | Full-Text Indexes |
| --- | --- |
| Stored under the control of the database in which they are defined. | Stored in the file system, but administered through the database. |
| Several regular indexes are allowed per table. | Only one full-text index is allowed per table. |
| Updated automatically when the data upon which they are based are inserted, updated, or deleted. | You can request the addition of data to full-text indexes, which is called population, through either a schedule or a specific request, or you can set it to occur automatically with the addition of new data. |
| Not grouped. | Grouped within the same database into one or more full-text catalogs. |
| Created and dropped with SQL Server Enterprise Manager, wizards, or Transact-SQL statements. | Created, managed, and dropped with SQL Server Enterprise Manager, wizards, or stored procedures. |

Since full-text indexes are not stored in the SQL Server database, you cannot back them up and recover them with the standard BACKUP and RECOVERY procedures; you need to manage them manually.

**Using the Microsoft Indexing Service along with the Microsoft Search Service you can conduct full-text searches against data in regular system files. The Indexing Service is included as part of the Windows 2000 OS, and you can install it on Windows NT with the Windows NT 4.0 Option Pack.**

## Using SQL Server 2000 Analytical Services

**20 Min.
To Go**

SQL Server 2000 Analytical Services are new to this version of SQL Server. In version 7.0 they were called OLAP, and lower versions did not mention them at all. Whether you are using these built-in services or decide on third-party components (such as Business Intelligence Platform by Cognos), one thing is sure: You need to know what you are doing.

## Linking OLAP and Business Logic

Using OLAP services requires a deep understanding of the business logic of your company and what kind of analysis is required. Consider the following sample scenario.

You are the manager of a successful fast-food chain. Your accounting department just warned you that your profits are down in spite of the advertising campaign for a line of new super-burgers: The campaign costs you an arm and a leg and you need to know what's wrong. Your database contains all the information you need: sales figures for various regions, population, age distribution, number of customers per day, economic activity, and much more.

You decide to compare sales of this new super-burger with sales of your mega-burger, which was introduced a year ago and has met with a huge success. You create two groups of sales figures and create a ratio between these two groups, and then you track this ratio by location and customer group.

You can see that in some regions sales of your super-burger far exceed sales of your other burgers, and that in some regions sales are lagging. Comparing historical data with your current data you see that in some regions sales of the super-burger took off much more slowly than in others; but the same thing happened before with your mega-burger. Are the lackluster sales the result of inadequate promotion? Or a recent anti-fast-food campaign in the region? You dig up the data and see that the regions lagging in sales are in the Bible Belt; the historical data also show that these regions are in general suspicious of your flashy new "welcome to the future" ads.

Now, combine all this information into one simple OLAP query so that your OLAP software will visualize it for you in charts, Gantt-Charts, histograms and such, and report to upper management or make a decision.

This is a simple example, but it offers you a glimpse into the potential OLAP offers.

Online Analytical Processing (OLAP) Services and the Multidimensional Expressions (MDX) they use are by far the most complex and advanced SQL Server components. Companies are using OLAP more and more as they try to make sense of their tons of accumulated data. OLAP is used in the mysterious field called "data analysis," and many books are dedicated to this use. This session will only briefly mention these services and their potential uses.

The standard database table represents a flat matrix; SQL Server 2000 Analysis Services use the notion of *cubes*. The data and corresponding objects are multidimensional, having more dimensions than our four-dimensional space-time continuum; the number of dimensions is limited only by your imagination and hardware capabilities.

You must install SQL Server Analytical Services. You do this in much the same way that you install English Query. Make sure you go through Books Online for the Analytical Services and work through the samples it includes, because using them isn't simple.

## Running the Web Assistant Wizard

I briefly introduced the Web Assistant Wizard in Session 4. This wizard provides you with an easy way to publish your information on the Internet. Follow these steps to use it:

1.  Launch the Web Assistant Wizard from the Enterprise Management Console (Tools ➪ Wizards ➪ Management ➪ Web Assistant Wizard). Click Next on the Welcome screen.

    The next screen, Select Database, will prompt you to select the database you wish to publish. Select Pubs and click Next.

2.  On the next screen, Start a New Web Assistant Job, specify a job name and the data you want to be published. The choices are as follows:

    - Data from the tables and columns you specify
    - Result set of a stored procedure you specify
    - Data from a T-SQL query you specify

    Name your Web assistant job and select Data from the Tables and Columns you specify. Click Next.

3. On this screen, Select a Table and Columns, select Authors and all its columns except the Contract column.

4. The next screen, Select Rows, enables you to limit the number of rows displayed on the page, and to format them into several pages. Select the option All of the Rows to publish all the rows in the authors table. Click Next.

5. On the next screen, Schedule the Web Assistant Job, determine a schedule. Do you want this page to be a one-time creation, or should it be created only when requested, or should it be created at regular intervals?

   I've chosen to update my page every time data are changed in the underlying table (say, when an author moves to a different location). Click Next.

6. This screen, Monitor a Table and Columns, prompts you to specify the exact column(s) in which the change of data would trigger an update. Click Next.

7. The next screen, Publish the Web Page, prompts you for a physical location for the HTML file you're going to produce. The best place is in the directory of your Web server. Click Next.

   If you wish, you can specify a template for your Web page, or format one with the help of SQL Server. If you choose to accept SQL Server's help, the next several pages will guide you through formatting issues such as selecting captions and choosing fonts. Click Next on each of these screens when you are through.

Figure 30-1 shows the final result of the example you've just completed as it appears in your Web browser. Of course, you may enhance your Web page by adding a colorful background, a texture, sound, and so forth, but the idea remains the same. Because I scheduled the information on this page to be refreshed every time the author's information is changed, the update will be triggered as soon as at least one value in the Authors table is updated or deleted. The authors.htm file will then be overwritten, and whoever requests this page afterward will get an updated version of it.

**In order to publish information on the Internet you will need a Web server such as Microsoft Internet Information Server or Apache Server.**

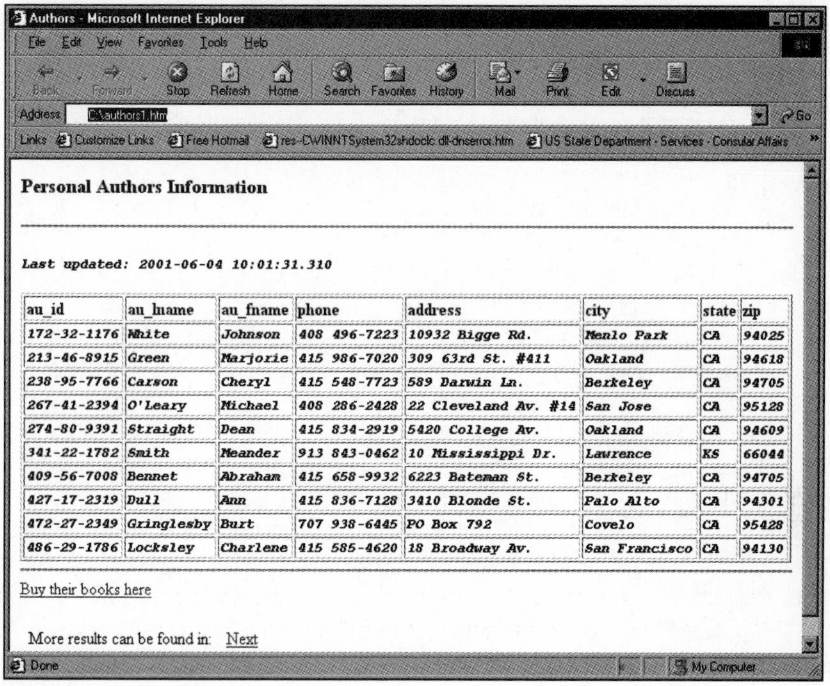

**Figure 30-1**
*Displaying information in Internet Explorer*

## Getting SQL Server XML Support

**10 Min.
To Go**

If you have ever opened a trade magazine, browsed the Web, or watched the news, you must have heard about eXtensible Markup Language (XML). It is touted as the best thing since sliced bread, or even the best thing ever — period. Marketing hype aside, I do believe that XML is useful. It represents a superset of HTML. Both HTML and XML use tags, special markers that tell a browser how to interpret a document.

XML is all about data, never about its visual representation. Unlike HTML, which you have to learn, and which has only a finite number of tags, XML enables you to define your own language and a practically unlimited number of tags. What's the catch? You will be the only one who understands this language, though its structure will be transparent to everybody.

The following HTML tag will instruct the browser to display the text in size H3.

```
<H3>Personal Authors Information</H3>
```

And this sample represents XML notation of a single author record:

```
<author>
    <name>Johnson White</name>
    <address>10932 Bigge Rd.</address>
    <city>Menlo Park</city>
    <state>CA</state>
    <zip>94025</zip>
</author>
```

As you can see, XML logically orders data in a hierarchy and uses pairs of tags to define the data. Note that XML says nothing about how to represent the data — nothing about font type, size, or anything similar.

Displaying the preceding XML document in your browser will — in the best case — present the information in exactly the structure you see here. To format these data into a visually pleasing page with color, different fonts, and such, you use XSL (eXtensible Stylesheet Language) or CSS (Cascading Stylesheets). A discussion of either of these languages is well beyond the scope of this book.

SQL Server 2000 adds XML support. This means that you can query a SQL Server instance by using a URL (a Web address) via HTTP (HyperText Transfer protocol, which is the Internet standard), and the SQL Server will return results as XML documents. To do this you have to use the special clause FOR XML:

```
SELECT authors.au_fname,au_lname,address,city,state,zip
FROM authors WHERE au_fname = 'Johnson'
FOR XML AUTO
```

You can submit this query over HTTP and receive a result set formatted as XML to be parsed later by an application or displayed in a browser accompanied by a Cascading Stylesheet link.

**The new OPENXML function enables you to convert an XML document into a rowset, and then use it to insert, update, or delete data in the database. You also can use the results of OPENXML as a table in a standard T-SQL query.**

**Done!**

## REVIEW

- You learned about some advanced features of SQL Server 2000, such as English Query, full-text search, Analysis Services, and Internet-related capabilities.

- English Query provides a framework and support services for creating and distributing SQL applications that enable users to query relational data in English instead of in Transact-SQL.

- Full-text searches enable you to query unstructured data in SQL Server tables and outside documents.

- You can publish data from your database on the Internet using the Web Assistant Wizard (you need a Web server to actually publish the data on the Internet).

- SQL Server 2000 provides internal support for XML, including the ability for the user to submit a query over the Internet and get the results as an XML document.

## QUIZ YOURSELF

1. How do you install Microsoft English Query?
2. What programming language would you use to create an English Query application?
3. What does OLAP stand for?
4. Under what circumstances would you use a full-text search?
5. Where are full-text indexes physically stored?
6. What is XML and can you use it to retrieve data from SQL Server?

# PART

# VI

## *Sunday Afternoon*

1. What are the three major components of a database system?
2. How does preparing a disaster scenario help in the recovery process?
3. What is a standby server?
4. How do you rebuild the Registry for SQL Server 2000?
5. How do you rebuild the Master database in SQL Server 2000?
6. What are the two Authentication modes for SQL Server 2000?
7. What are the two groups of roles in SQL Server 2000?
8. What is a fixed role?
9. To which groups does an application role belong?
10. What makes a SQL Server view suitable for security purposes?
11. What are the most commonly used connection interfaces for SQL Server 2000?
12. How do you configure an ODBC data source?
13. What are ADO, RDO, and DAO in the context of SQL Server 2000?
14. What Microsoft application is required to provide access to SQL Server via the Internet?
15. How do you install the English Query? What would you use it for?
16. What data sources can you search once you've installed the full-text search capabilities?

**17.** Where is a full-text index physically stored?

**18.** What is the primary use of SQL Server Analytical Services?

**19.** How can you automatically update a Web page created with the Web Publishing Wizard for SQL Server 2000?

**20.** What is XML and how does SQL Server 2000 support it?

# Answers to Part Reviews

Following are the answers to the part review questions at the end of each part in this book. Think of these reviews as mini-tests that are designed to help you prepare for the final – the Skills Assessment Test on the CD.

## Friday Evening Review Answers

1.  SQL Server 2000 is a relational database management system (RDBMS) from Microsoft.

2.  You can install SQL Server 2000 on Windows NT 4.0, Windows 2000 Server, Windows 98 and Windows CE.

3.  Enterprise, Standard, Professional, Developer Edition and Windows CE Edition.

    The differences between these versions lie in the maximum size of the supported database, the number of CPUs, and support for enterprise-level features such as replication, scheduling, and so forth.

4.  *Collation order* refers to the way the data in a database are sorted and compared. Collation order for the server is set during installation; you can change it later, though it requires reinstalling the SQL Server.

    Collation order for a custom database can be set during creation of the database - it could be different from the default collation order of the server.

5. Starting from SQL Server version 7.0 you can run several instances of SQL Server on the same machine. The first installed instance is designated the default and given the name of the machine on which it is installed; every named instance must have a unique name.

6. Windows authentication mode and mixed mode.

7. The SQL Server Enterprise Server Manager.

8. *Services* are a specific type of Windows programs that run as background process and usually do not require(or allow) direct user interaction. SQL Server depends on the following services to run: SQL Server Service, SQL Server Agent Service and MSDTC Service; you manage services through the SQL Server Service Manager or from Control Panel's Services option.

9. Through the Register SQL Server Wizard in the Enterprise Manager Console.

10. Depending on the installation version, you will have anywhere from five to seven top-level objects with each registered server.

11. Yes. Doing so usually requires re-running install and selecting different options; sometimes it might be necessary to reinstall SQL Server altogether.

12. By re-running installation and selecting the components you wish to add.

13. Rerun the installation program and select the uninstall option, or use the Add/Remove Programs utility in the Control Panel.

14. They are the most comprehensive source of information on SQL Server, and they are installed with every version of SQL Server.

15. A program that guides you step by step through the process of completing a specific task.

16. A *relational database management system* (*RDBMS*) is a means of storing and managing data in a system of related entities/tables; SQL Server is one of many implementations of the RDBMS concept.

17. It assists in speedily transferring large amount of data into or out of a database.

18. Both are command-line utilities for performing ad-hoc SQL queries. ISQL is a command-line utility based on the DB Library interface; it is provided for compatibility with previous versions of SQL Server and does not support all SQL Server 2000 features. OSQL is ODBC-based and supports all the features of SQL Server 2000; it can also run UNICODE stored scripts.

19. SQL Server Agent assists with automating some of your database-management chores. A SQL Server Agent job is a sequence of database tasks scheduled for execution, either periodically or as the result of some predetermined condition. SQL Server alerts enable you to take action in response to some event that occurs on the system by notifying an operator - either via e-mail or pager.

20. The *Web Assistant Wizard* is a tool for generating (HyperText Markup Language (HTML) documents based on the data extracted from SQL Server databases.

## Saturday Morning Review Answers

1. A *relational database* is a collection of database objects: tables maintaining relationships based on the primary/foreign key principle, various means of manipulating these tables, and the rules that enforce the relationships and their integrity. Unlike spreadsheet tables or flat files, RDBMS tables are related in a parent/child-like relationship.

2. *Referential integrity* is a relational database concept referring to a state of data meaning that there are no "orphaned" records; each record in the child table must be linked to an existing record in the parent table.

3. Data integrity is enforced on four levels through indices, constraints, rules, and triggers.

4. A *key* is a column or combination of columns within the table; each table can have one primary key and several foreign keys. An *index* is a separate database structure created to facilitate faster data access.

5. System databases (Master, MSDB, Model, Temp) and sample databases (Pubs, Northwind).

6. The Master database contains information about the entire SQL Server instance: settings, startup information, a description of every database created on the system, and system stored procedures.

7. The Model database serves as a template for every custom database created on the system.

8. You resolve a many-to-many relationship with an intermediate table, which usually consists of primary-key columns of the tables it relates.

9. *Data normalization* is a process of breaking large tables into smaller ones to prevent redundancy and data duplication.

10. The first normal form eliminates repeating groups.

11. In order to create a database you must define the data component and the transaction log component.

12. Execute the statement CREATE DATABASE *<database name>* with all the appropriate optional parameters.

13. DROP DATABASE *<database name>*. You can specify more than one database in a single statement.

14. You cannot delete any system databases.

15. A database created within SQL Server 2000 is physically maintained as two or more system files.

16. Transact SQL (Structured Query Language).

17. You can pass Transact SQL statements to SQL Server to be executed through a number of interfaces: Query Analyzer, ISQL command line, OSQL, or any client application programmed to connect to the SQL Server.

18. A *variable* is a data holder; declaring a variable reserves space where eventually value would put when it assigned to the variable. You declare a variable in Transact-SQL with the DECLARE keyword, followed by the variable name and type. (For example, DECLARE @MyVariable VARCHAR(10)).

19. Any text data (character string) up to a length specified in that variable declaration. It cannot be a number, or date or binary.

20. SELECT, INSERT, UPDATE, and DELETE.

21. IF, IF...ELSE, WHILE, GOTO *<label>*, BREAK, and CONTINUE.

22a. INNER JOIN — Selects the matching records from both joined tables: for each record from one table there must be a corresponding record in the second table.

22b. LEFT JOIN or LEFT OUTER JOIN — Selects additional records from the left joined table; even if no matching rows exist these returned fields will contain NULLs.

22c. RIGHT JOIN or RIGHT OUTER JOIN — Works like a LEFT JOIN or LEFT OUTER JOIN, except that it applies to the right table.

22d. CROSS JOIN — Returns a result set containing every possible combination of the rows in both tables.

# Saturday Afternoon Review Answers

1. A *stored procedure* is a database object compiled and stored under a unique name and is stored in SQL Server; it can have input and output parameters as well as a return value. A T-SQL batch is stored as a file and must be executed through one of the SQL Server interfaces; it does not have input or output parameters and it is always interpreted.

2. It is stored in the Stored Procedures collection of a particular database on SQL Server. Stored procedures global in their scope reside in the Master database.

3. The scope of the stored procedure is usually within the database in which it is created; stored procedures prefixed with sp_ and stored in the Master database are global for the SQL Server instance.

4. It always has a global scope.

5. Calling a stored procedure from within another stored procedure makes it a nested stored procedure.

6. Stored procedures usually execute faster than T-SQL batches and consume fewer resources; they are maintained by SQL Server; they enable you to create reusable libraries; also they give you benefits of structured programming.

   However, they shift control to SQL Server from the client application and are usually more difficult to modify than batches.

7. Unlike a stored procedure, a trigger is tied to a specific table and is executed only in response to certain actions performed on this table; you cannot call a trigger directly; and a trigger is compiled.

8. Any events that modify data: A trigger can be set to respond to an INSERT, UPDATE, or DELETE event.

9. DELETED and INSERTED.

10. An INSTEAD OF trigger is executed instead of the T-SQL statement that triggered the action.

11. A programming object (structure) established on the result-set base. It enables you to manipulate records in the set row by row.

12. Static, dynamic, forward-only, and keyset-driven.

13. *Concurrency* refers to the visibility of the data set, which may be accessible by several users at the same time; you set the cursor's concurrency in the cursor declaration or client application.

14. An *index* speeds up search operations by creating a system of pointers to the actual data. It is maintained separately from the table it indexes.

15. A *clustered index* physically re-organizes data in the table; a non-clustered index just maintains pointers to the actual locations of the records.

16. You can define only one clustered index and up to 249 non-clustered indices.

17. No. For a small amount of data, a table scan is more efficient than an index.

18. Columns used in JOIN queries, aggregate functions, GROUP BY, or ORDER BY clauses.

19. Entity, domain, referential and user-defined.

20. Domain integrity (range of values) and referential integrity (preserves relationship among tables).

21. You can define the CHECK constraint during the creation of the table, or later with the ALTER TABLE statement.

22. You need to bind it to a column or user-defined type.

23. NULL indicates an absence of data; unless your server is set to compare NULLs, one NULL is never equal to another. Zero is an actual value represented by a number.

24. A SQL Server transaction is a collection of T-SQL statements that either executes as a whole or fails and leaves data unchanged.

25. Atomicity, consistency, isolation and durability.

26. Any transaction that you explicitly start (BEGIN TRANSACTION), end (END TRANSACTION), or commit (COMMIT TRANSACTION) is an explicit transaction. Implicit transactions are those that SQL Server automatically starts when it encounters one of the following T-SQL statements:

```
SELECT, INSERT, UPDATE, DELETE
ALTER TABLE
TRUNCATE TABLE
OPEN, FETCH
GRANT, REVOKE
```

27. Optimistic and pessimistic.

28. Read uncommitted, read committed, repeatable read, and serializable.

29. *Lock escalation* converts fine-grained locks into coarser-grained locks (for example, row-level locking to table-level locking) when SQL Server figures out that another lock will use less system resources.

30. A *deadlock* refers to a situation wherein a process (transaction) has obtained a lock on a resource and tries to get a lock on a second resource while another process tries to simultaneously obtain a lock on that same resource and keep a lock on some third resource; neither of the processes can get the lock on the resource, nor can they commit or abort.

    To avoid deadlocks applications should access database objects in a specific order, user interaction during transactions should be eliminated, transactions should be kept as short as possible, and you should use the lowest isolation level possible.

## Saturday Evening Review Answers

1. DTS imports and exports data from a SQL Server database.

2. Any data source for which there is a valid OLE DB provider.

3. Either by attaching a VBScript module or T-SQL conversions to the DTS package.

4. DTS Export/Import wizards.

5. *BCP* is the Bulk Copy command-line utility program; it uses the DB Library interface to import and export large amounts of data into or out of SQL Server.

6. BCP has only limited support for transferring data between heterogeneous data sources, virtually no support for data transformation, and no visual interface for administration.

7. The system databases, especially the Master database, must be backed up periodically, and before and after any major change to server properties, so that you will be able to recover from a disaster. User databases should be backed up periodically to minimize potential data loss.

8. Tape backup devices, files, and logical backup devices.

9. A *backup device* is a structured storage file. You can organize it in such a way that it becomes storage for logical devices.

10. With the Database Backup Wizard or with Transact-SQL statements.

11. It is a sequential record of all transactions since the last differential or database backup. You can use it to recover a database up to the point of failure.

12. Unfinished transactions.

13. A differential backup backs up all data that have changed since the last complete backup. It is much faster than a complete backup but can only be used in conjunction with a full backup, and is not allowed on the Master database.

14. No, transaction log can be backed up only all at once. Transaction log keeps track of the changes made to the database and is used to determine what part is supposed to be backed up during a differential backup of the database.

15. First restore the last full backup; then apply all transaction-log backups, starting from the oldest.

16. You can only perform a full backup of the Master database, not a differential or transaction-log backup; when restoring the Master database you should use only the Recovery Complete option.

17. Distribution of identical data across several data sources.

18. Publisher — A source server for the distributed data. It maintains all the information about the data specified for publishing.

    Distributor — An intermediary between the Publisher and the Subscriber, which can also be both Publisher and Subscriber. Its role varies depending on the type of replication you select.

    Subscriber — The final destination of the distributed data.

19. PUSH subscriptions and PULL subscriptions.

20. Replication agents are utilities that assist in the replication process.

## Sunday Morning Review Answers

1. A *Database Maintenance Plan* is a job scheduled under SQL Server Agent. It consists of one or more steps such as backup, reclaiming unused space, updating statistics, checking database integrity, and so on.

2. To document the database structure and possibly restore it in case of a disaster.

3. By using the appropriate options from the right-click menu of the Databases node or by using the system stored procedures sp_attach_db and sp_detach_db.

4. System databases cannot be attached, detached, or copied.

5. *Remote servers* allow a client application connected to one SQL Server to run a stored procedure on another without having to connect to it explicitly. Linked servers extend this functionality to heterogeneous data sources, and also support Distributed transactions.

6. Any data source that has an OLE DB provider or ODBC driver for it.

7. Explicitly, by using the BEGIN DISTRIBUTED TRANSACTION keyword, or implicitly, by using a distributed query or calling a remote stored procedure within the local transaction.

8. The way to ensure the integrity of a distributed transaction process across multiple servers.

9. By using the system catalog stored procedures or the INFORMATION_SCHEMA tables.

10. An INFORMATION_SCHEMA is a view created for each user database that provides access to the metadata for the database objects.

11. System stored procedures have global scope. To execute a system stored procedure on a local server you do not need to specify the fully qualified path or be in the context of any particular database.

12. System stored procedures that provide information about SQL Server database objects.

13. A compiled dynamic link library that SQL Server can call to perform tasks that are difficult or impossible to implement in Transact-SQL.

14. To define, schedule for execution, and execute various database tasks.

15. MSDB contains all the information about scheduled tasks.

16. An *operator* is a contact to which an alert will send notification via e-mail or pager.

17. Configuring SQL Server to send events to a central server in a multi-server environment to be processed there.

18. Most of the mail servers are MAPI compliant. The samples would be: Microsoft Exchange, Sun Internet Mail Server, Mdaemon Mail Server and dozens more.

19. You use SQL Server Mail to execute stored procedures remotely and return results by e-mail; you use SQL Server Agent Mail to send e-mail and pager notifications.

20. SQL Server Mail runs in the security context of MSSQLService.

21. Using extended stored procedures.

22. SQL Server Profiler is a graphical tool you can use to trace the performance of SQL Server in your server and to help analyze the results to find potential bottlenecks and problems.

23. From the Query Analyzer toolbar menu Query, select Display Estimated Execution Plan.

24. Statistics information is created automatically whenever an index is created for a table, but you can also create statistics using the CREATE STATISTICS statement. Statistics are used by SQL Server Query Optimizer to determine the best path of execution for a particular query.

25. Workload data created with SQL Server Profiler.

26. By setting a large initial size and big increments, so resources are not wasted when you expand the log.

27. *DBCC* is a set of SQL Server commands for performing consistency checks and various database-management tasks pertaining to the integrity of the database.

## Sunday Afternoon Review Answers

1. Every SQL Server RDBMS system consists of at least three components: an operating system, SQL Server, and the client applications that connect to SQL Server.

2. It enables you to identify potential problems and practice steps for recovery in order to minimize downtime and data loss.

3. A *standby server* is an identical copy of a production SQL Server that is usually installed on a different machine. It mirrors the production server very closely so you can use it as a substitute production server in case of a server disaster.

4. By running the SQL Server installation program again and choosing Advanced options.

5. Using the command-line utility Rebuildm.exe.

6. Windows Authentication and Mixed Authentication modes.

7. *Server roles*, which are applied and administered at the SQL Server level, and *database roles*, which are applied and administered at the database level.

8. A predefined role in SQL Server that cannot be changed. There are eight fixed server roles.

9. It is a database role.

10. Normally, a SQL Server view does not allow updates and inserts into underlying tables; you can limit a view to several columns in the table while hiding the rest.

11. OLE DB and ODBC.

12. Through the ODBC component in the Control Panel (Windows NT) or Data Sources from the Administrative Tools menu.

13. ADO, RDO, and DAO are ActiveX components for accessing data sources through ODBC or OLEDB provider interfaces.

14. Microsoft Internet Information Server.

15. By choosing English Query during the SQL Server 2000 installation process. This helps to create custom solutions that enable you to query SQL Server in plain English rather than with Transact-SQL.

16. Any data in SQL Server database as well as any text contained in system files.

17. It is stored as a system file, separate from SQL Server.

18. Analyzing large amount of data in a process called data mining in order to discover hidden trends.

19. Using the SQL Server Web Publishing Wizard you may specify that the data in the published set be updated periodically or upon changes to the data in a particular column(s).

20. *XML* stands for eXtensible Markup Language. It is an emerging standard for data-interchange formats for the distributed systems. SQL Server 2000 supports XML by providing special keywords, FOR XML and OPENXML.

# What's on the CD-ROM

There are two CD-ROMs included with this book to help you to make the most of it. One CD-ROM contains the 120-day evaluation version of SQL Server 2000. It is a fully functional version provided by Microsoft that is yours to use and explore for three months.

On the other CD-ROM, you get an electronic form of this book in PDF format (which is great for searching and sharing); you may or may not have software for reading this file so I also included Adobe Acrobat Reader 5.0 as well as some other general-purpose utilities.

Several products on this CD-ROM may make your life easier. While Microsoft tries very hard to provide everything you need, in certain areas third-party tools such as the ones in the following list might be better or easier to use:

- *ER/Studio* — A data-modeling tool from Embarcadero Technologies that enables you to create (or reverse-engineer) your logical and database design. It is a rather advanced tool for data architects, database administrators, and developers.

- *DBArtisan* — An advanced database-administration tool from Embarcadero Technologies. It helps you with routine database tasks in order to achieve and maintain high availability, optimize performance, and enhance security. It also enables you to manage heterogeneous databases like SQL Server, Oracle, and DB2 from one place. It fits nicely into the database-administrator toolbox, though it is no substitute for Enterprise Manager for SQL Server.

- *Rapid SQL* — A development tool from Embarcadero Technologies for creating and deploying server-side objects residing in SQL Server databases. It supports HTML and Java Web development as well as plain vanilla Transact-SQL.

- *Sylvain SQL Programmer 2001* — A development tool from BMC Software with an extensive support for debugging, documenting, and scripting. It works with every major database (MS SQL server, DB2, Oracle).

- *Microsoft Internet Explorer* — Yes, it is still free to download. It looks as if Microsoft has won the battle of the browsers — this version of its popular browser is faster and has more support for the latest technologies (like XML) than its rivals.

- *WinZip* — By far the most popular archiving utility on the Web, this utility from Nico Mak Computing supports most of the popular archiving formats like ARC, ZIP, TAR, GZIP, and ARJ; it also compresses your files by up to 90 percent. Great for reclaiming hard-drive space, storing e-mails, and much more.

- *SnagIt* — A very popular screen-capture utility from TechSmith. If you can see it you can save it — onto the clipboard or into a variety of file formats (BMP, JPEG, GIF, TIF, and so on). Works on any Windows platform.

Each of these programs resides in its own folder on the CD-ROM and comes with its own installation program. Try them out!

## Links on the Internet

Sooner or later you are going to have a question that this book won't be able to answer. Unless you have a seasoned database administrator to coach you, the only place to find up-to-date information is going to be the Internet.

Here are sites for all your SQL Server questions. You'll also find tons of articles, downloadable scripts, programs, and newsletter groups.

### General-interest SQL Server sites

```
http://www.sqlservercentral.com/
http://www.sswug.org
http://www.swynk.com
http://www.mssqlserver.com/
http://www.sql-server-performance.com/
http://www.sqlwire.com/
```

### Publishers of SQL Server magazines

```
http://www.sqlmag.com
http://www.pinnaclepublishing.com/sq
```

### Windows NT/2K sites with some SQL Server–related stuff

```
http://www.ntfaq.com/Articles/
http://www.windows2000faq.com/
```

### SQL Security issues

```
http://www.sqlsecurity.com/
```

### Ask all your questions here — you might get an answer

```
http://www.devx.com/gethelp/
http://www.experts-exchange.com/jsp/qList.jsp?ta=mssql
```

### Microsoft sites

```
http://www.msdn.microsoft.com/sqlserver/
http://www.microsoft.com/sql/evaluation/compare/tpc.asp
http://www.microsoft.com/sql/
http://www.microsoft.com/technet/
http://www.microsoft.com/sql/support/
```

### *The most comprehensive site for any technical questions you may have about MSFT products*

```
http://msdn.microsoft.com/library/default.asp
```

### *Independent organizations conducting comparative benchmark testing*

Here you'll find information on the latest performance benchmarks across all database vendors.

```
http://www.tpc.org
```

# *Index*

## Numerics

*1033 file, 23*

## A

*access*
  logins, 226–230, 232
  multiuser environments,
    233–234
  permissions, 230–234
  restrictions, 78
  roles, 226
  *See also* connections
*accessing*
  external data sources, 258
  SQL Books Online, 35
  SQL Server Agent, 45
  system information, 263–264
  wizards, 37–39
*accounts*
  mail accounts, 284–286
  SQL Server Agent, 275
  startup account, 275
  user accounts, 225–234
*ACID, 178*
*Active Data Objects (ADO),*
  *337–338*
*Active Server Pages (ASP), 342*
*ActiveX, 342*
*adding*
  components, 25
  servers, 31
*administration, multi-server,*
  *281*
*ADO (Active Data Objects),*
  *337–338*
*advanced options, 10*
*AFTER keyword, 138*
*AFTER triggers, 138–141*
*Agent*
  accessing, 45
  accounts, 275

alerts, 45, 275, 278–280
  capabilities, 21, 45, 273–274
  configuration screen, 274
  configuring, 274–275
  connections, 275
  event forwarding, 281
  jobs, 45, 275–278
  MSDB database, 63
  operators, 45
  properties, 274–275
  starting, 274
  stored procedures, 269
*aggregate functions, 118*
*alerts*
  creating, 278–279
  definition, 45
  deleting, 280
  jobs, 277, 279
  messages, 279
  modifying, 280
  options, 275
  performance counters, 280
  removing, 280
  viewing, 280
*altering*
  databases, 99–100
  tables, 101
  triggers, 144
*Analytical Services, 345–347*
*analyzing queries with Query*
  *Analyzer*
  capabilities, 40
  connections, 98
  display options for results, 97
  e-mail, 288
  execution mode, 97
  execution plan, 98, 296–298
  starting, 40, 96
  templates, 103
  testing, 96
  Transact-SQL, 95–102
  triggers, 139
  uses, 95
  using, 96

*answer key to review*
  *questions, 355–365*
*App Viewer (CAST), 367*
*application roles, 326–327*
*arguments (command-line*
  *utilities), 43*
*ASP (Active Server Pages), 342*
*assigning permissions, 232*
*attributes, 66*
*audit logs, 328*
*authentication modes, 14,*
  *320–321*
*automating tasks, 273*

## B

*Backup Wizard, 203–206*
*backups*
  backup header, 211
  complete database backups,
    202–207
  databases, 312
  differential backups, 202–203,
    207
  file backups, 203
  file group backups, 203
  importance, 312
  managing, 211
  Master database, 62
  media header, 211
  operating systems, 311
  planning, 201–202
  recovery modes, 207–208
  restoring, 208–210
  storing, 211
  strategies, 202
  transaction-log backups,
    203, 207
  verifying, 211
*bcp utility, 42–43, 198, 200*
*BEGIN TRANSACTION*
  *statement, 178–179*
*benchmarks for RDBMSs, 57*

## Hungry Minds, Inc.
## End-User License Agreement

**READ THIS.** You should carefully read these terms and conditions before opening the software packet(s) included with this book ("Book"). This is a license agreement ("Agreement") between you and Hungry Minds, Inc. ("HMI"). By opening the accompanying software packet(s), you acknowledge that you have read and accept the following terms and conditions. If you do not agree and do not want to be bound by such terms and conditions, promptly return the Book and the unopened software packet(s) to the place you obtained them for a full refund.

1. **License Grant.** HMI grants to you (either an individual or entity) a nonexclusive license to use one copy of the enclosed software program(s) (collectively, the "Software") solely for your own personal or business purposes on a single computer (whether a standard computer or a workstation component of a multi-user network). The Software is in use on a computer when it is loaded into temporary memory (RAM) or installed into permanent memory (hard disk, CD-ROM, or other storage device). HMI reserves all rights not expressly granted herein.

2. **Ownership.** HMI is the owner of all right, title, and interest, including copyright, in and to the compilation of the Software recorded on the disk(s) or CD-ROM ("Software Media"). Copyright to the individual programs recorded on the Software Media is owned by the author or other authorized copyright owner of each program. Ownership of the Software and all proprietary rights relating thereto remain with HMI and its licensers.

3. **Restrictions On Use and Transfer.**

    **(a)** You may only (i) make one copy of the Software for backup or archival purposes, or (ii) transfer the Software to a single hard disk, provided that you keep the original for backup or archival purposes. You may not (i) rent or lease the Software, (ii) copy or reproduce the Software through a LAN or other network system or through any computer subscriber system or bulletin-board system, or (iii) modify, adapt, or create derivative works based on the Software.

    **(b)** You may not reverse engineer, decompile, or disassemble the Software. You may transfer the Software and user documentation on a permanent basis, provided that the transferee agrees to accept the terms and conditions of this Agreement and you retain no copies. If the Software is an update or has been updated, any transfer must include the most recent update and all prior versions.

4. **Restrictions on Use of Individual Programs.** You must follow the individual requirements and restrictions detailed for each individual program in the About the CD appendix of this Book. These limitations are also contained in the individual license agreements recorded on the Software Media. These limitations may include a requirement that after using the program for a specified period of time, the user must pay a registration fee or discontinue use. By opening the Software packet(s), you will be agreeing to abide by the licenses and restrictions for these individual programs that are detailed in the About the CD appendix and on the Software

Media. None of the material on this Software Media or listed in this Book may ever be redistributed, in original or modified form, for commercial purposes.

5. **Limited Warranty.**

   **(a)** HMI warrants that the Software and Software Media are free from defects in materials and workmanship under normal use for a period of sixty (60) days from the date of purchase of this Book. If HMI receives notification within the warranty period of defects in materials or workmanship, HMI will replace the defective Software Media.

   **(b)** **HMI AND THE AUTHOR OF THE BOOK DISCLAIM ALL OTHER WARRANTIES, EXPRESS OR IMPLIED, INCLUDING WITHOUT LIMITATION IMPLIED WARRANTIES OF MERCHANTABILITY AND FITNESS FOR A PARTICULAR PURPOSE, WITH RESPECT TO THE SOFTWARE, THE PROGRAMS, THE SOURCE CODE CONTAINED THEREIN, AND/OR THE TECHNIQUES DESCRIBED IN THIS BOOK. HMI DOES NOT WARRANT THAT THE FUNCTIONS CONTAINED IN THE SOFTWARE WILL MEET YOUR REQUIREMENTS OR THAT THE OPERATION OF THE SOFTWARE WILL BE ERROR FREE.**

   **(c)** This limited warranty gives you specific legal rights, and you may have other rights that vary from jurisdiction to jurisdiction.

6. **Remedies.**

   **(a)** HMI's entire liability and your exclusive remedy for defects in materials and workmanship shall be limited to replacement of the Software Media, which may be returned to HMI with a copy of your receipt at the following address: Software Media Fulfillment Department, Attn.: *Microsoft SQL Server 2000 Crash Course*, Hungry Minds, Inc., 10475 Crosspoint Blvd., Indianapolis, IN 46256, or call 1-800-762-2974. Please allow four to six weeks for delivery. This Limited Warranty is void if failure of the Software Media has resulted from accident, abuse, or misapplication. Any replacement Software Media will be warranted for the remainder of the original warranty period or thirty (30) days, whichever is longer.

   **(b)** In no event shall HMI or the author be liable for any damages whatsoever (including without limitation damages for loss of business profits, business interruption, loss of business information, or any other pecuniary loss) arising from the use of or inability to use the Book or the Software, even if HMI has been advised of the possibility of such damages.

   **(c)** Because some jurisdictions do not allow the exclusion or limitation of liability for consequential or incidental damages, the above limitation or exclusion may not apply to you.

7. **U.S. Government Restricted Rights.** Use, duplication, or disclosure of the Software for or on behalf of the United States of America, its agencies and/or instrumentalities (the "U.S. Government") is subject to restrictions as stated in paragraph (c)(1)(ii) of the Rights in Technical Data and Computer Software clause of DFARS 252.227-7013, or subparagraphs (c) (1) and (2) of the Commercial Computer Software - Restricted Rights clause at FAR 52.227-19, and in similar clauses in the NASA FAR supplement, as applicable.

8.  **General.** This Agreement constitutes the entire understanding of the parties and revokes and supersedes all prior agreements, oral or written, between them and may not be modified or amended except in a writing signed by both parties hereto that specifically refers to this Agreement. This Agreement shall take precedence over any other documents that may be in conflict herewith. If any one or more provisions contained in this Agreement are held by any court or tribunal to be invalid, illegal, or otherwise unenforceable, each and every other provision shall remain in full force and effect.

## CD-ROM Installation Instructions

The CD that comes with this product features an Autorun program. Install the disc (face-up) into your CD-ROM drive and wait for the program to begin. You will see an interface with five buttons, as follows:

- **Install Test:** This button starts the process that installs the special Weekend Crash Course assessment test onto your computer.
- **View eBook:** This button allows you to view the book in a searchable, electronic format.
- **Browse CD:** Look through the contents of this CD, and install the preview materials included on the CD.
- **Links:** This button provides you with a compendium of the URLs in this book presented as live Internet links.
- **Exit:** Quits the autorun program.

For more information about the CD, see the "What's on the CD-ROM" appendix.